Despatch Note

Order Number 701-6289024-8101819   **Supplied by** More4U Books & Music

ogue Number   **Title and Artist**   **Qty**

3190960908082   The First Bourbon: Henry IV of France & Navarre [P   1

SOME ITEMS MAY BE SHIPPED SEPARATELY

Order Processed: 13/06/2016 08:52:

Payment has been received from: Rose Marie Jaco

RETURNS: Return the item with this despatch note to the following address: Paperbackshop.co.uk Ltd, Unit 22
Horcott Industrial Estate, Horcott Road, FAIRFORD, Gloucestershire GL7 4BX, UK. Please tick one reason for
return: 1. | | Damaged   2. | | Faulty   3. | | Wrong Item   4. | | Other
Would you like: a refund | | a replacement | |

Henri IV, by Pourbus

THE FIRST BOURBON

HENRI IV, KING OF FRANCE AND NAVARRE

DESMOND SEWARD

ISBN-10: 1-909609-08-0
ISBN-13: 978-1-909609-08-2

PATRI MATRIQUE LIBRUM DICAVI

CONTENTS

$\mathcal{I}$LLUSTRATIONS

ACKNOWLEDGEMENTS

I should like to thank the Duc de Gramont for permission to reproduce the portrait of Corisande d'Andoins, Comtesse de Guiche, with her daughter, Catherine de Gramont, later Comtesse de Lauzun, by an unknown artist, and the following publishers for permission to quote from recent books: Jonathan Cape Ltd., the publishers of *The Age of Catherine de Medici*, by Sir John Neale; Cambridge University Press, the publishers of *The Cambridge Economic History of Europe* ('*Trade, Society and the State*', by C. H. Wilson in Vol. IV); Weidenfeld & Nicolson Ltd., the publishers of *The Age of Courts and Kings*, ed. by Philippe Erlanger; Albin Michel, the publishers of *Henri IV Lui Même; l'Homme*, by Raymond Ritter; Harvard University Press, the publishers of *The Paris of Henry of Navarre*, translated by N. L. Roelker.

I would also like to thank Mr Richard Bancroft, Superintendent of the British Museum Reading Room, and the members of his staff for much courteous and patient assistance.

THE FIRST BOURBON

'*Le père des Bourbons, du sein des immortels...*'
VOLTAIRE

$\mathcal{I}$NTRODUCTION

'*Vive Henri Quatre*
Vive ce roi vaillant
Ce diable-à-quatre
Qui eut le triple talent
De boire et de battre
Et d'être vert galant.'
song of the French Royalists[1]

Each nation has a hero king from whose legend a good deal can be learnt about his fellow countrymen. Spaniards admire Philip II, and the Germans Frederick Barbarossa, while England's favourite sovereign is undoubtedly Elizabeth I, with her insular blend of courage and compromise, grandeur and double dealing. Most foreigners regard Louis XIV as France's archetypal monarch but the French themselves prefer Henri IV; Louis epitomizes France, Henri Frenchmen. For no ruler in history can rival his achievement in embodying his people's virtues and vices in the way they themselves wish to see them. The Bourbons are frequently credited with bigotry, arrogance and lack of imagination, yet the first King produced by their branch of the Capetian house had none of these failings. He was nevertheless a hero to his own dynasty and until the final decline of French royalism remained its ideal of the perfect ruler. It is only justice that a family whose name has been made synonymous with obscurantism should be given credit for a founder remarkable above all else for humanity.

The two great hero myths of modern French history are those of Henri de Bourbon and Napoleon Bonaparte. In England the latter's cult is considerable, but that of Henri IV is little appreciated, though acquaintance with him and his legend is no less vital for an understanding of modern France: during an election address in 1969 President Pompidou named Henri IV as his favourite monarch and many Frenchmen would agree with him. The King and the Emperor were both soldiers, even if most of Henri's battles were fought at home in civil wars, while Napoleon's victories were won abroad. Each saved and rebuilt a ruined country torn to pieces by rival ideologies, leaving a reconstruction which long outlived them, Henri's by a hundred and eighty years and Napoleon's until the present day. Finally, each was a superb leader in both peace and war, idolized by the French people as well as by their troops. However, this book is not a comparison of two great men or of two great legends. Its purpose is first to show that the old France which was destroyed in 1789, and yet which remains a part of the national heritage, had a hero no less inspiring than the one who built the new France after the Revolution, and to give some account of the reality behind the legend.

Henri IV was not only the grandfather of Louis XIV, creator of the splendours of Versailles but also of one of history's greatest ironies, of a King who was in spirit a typical Frenchman with typically French vices and virtues but who sat on the English throne and encouraged his subjects to emerge from a particularly sanctimonious phase. Charles II cannot be understood without some knowledge of this grandfather whom he so much resembled. As young men both faced the gloomiest adversity. Prisoners of a hostile court, Henri at the Louvre, Charles at Holyrood, each dissembled with sublime hypocrisy while as youthful leaders of broken, hunted oppositions they endured crushing reverses with unshakeable optimism. They shared the same insatiable appetite for women and the same charm of manner. It is curious that so few historians have commented on the striking affinities between the English wit and the French hero.

In France biographies and romances of Henri IV proliferate but there are few English studies. Yet almost every year a new life of Louis XIV is published in London and meets an avid reception; his far more attractive grandfather, a King who over the centuries has won the admiration of such demanding critics as Montaigne, Voltaire and Mme de Stael, is only known from passing references in general histories. Luckily Henri lived in an articulate age which left an abundance of memoirs of campaign and court life, by Brantôme, d'Aubigné, L'Estoile, Sully, Bassompierre and many others including Henri's mother and his wife. Most valuable of all, a great mass of his correspondence survives. There are also several contemporary or near contemporary histories, like the biography by Bishop Péréfixe. So it is possible to see Henri through the eyes of his own world.

In addition there are English contemporary sources which have not received sufficient attention. French biographers of Henri IV turn to Italy or Spain when consulting foreign authorities while almost all the modern English studies have been based on secondary material. As this book is intended for English or American readers I have employed English primary sources as much as possible because they possess the very real merit of seeing Henri and his kingdom as Anglo-Saxons of the time saw them. For similar reasons I have also made use of seventeenth- and eighteenth-century English translations of primary French works, such as Montaigne, Péréfixe and Sully, after checking them against the original French text.

Lastly, the ecumenical climate of recent years has now made it possible even for Catholics to understand something of the attraction of French Calvinism in the sixteenth century. Writing as a Catholic brought up in England and therefore to admire the diehard Papists of the Elizabethan era, one feels a natural sympathy with the Huguenots who so strongly resembled them in stubborn loyalty to an outlawed creed. Further, this new spirit makes it easier to realize that 'Politiques' were not necessarily cynical opportunists ready to betray their co-religionists.

All modern historians of Henri IV try to disentangle the man from his legend. He was named 'Henri le Grand' even in his own lifetime, a soubriquet which persisted into the eighteenth century when his cult achieved epic status with Voltaire's *Henriade*. In so far as the Ancien Régime had an anthem to drown the *Marseillaise* it was the old song of *Vive Henri Quatre*, popular among French monarchists until the 1914 War. But the legend did not stem merely from the Bourbons' need of a dynastic beau ideal. During his campaigns soldiers had come to give this laughing, swaggering leader in tattered clothes who joked with them and who shared their hardships, the same doglike devotion which the Grande Armée gave Napoleon. And there were other roots far deeper; in the eighteenth century it was noted that Henri IV was the one King whose memory was kept green by the common people of France, that they believed he had genuinely cared for them, telling tales of how he had wished for each peasant to have *'une poule au pot tous les dimanches'*. In consequence *'le bon roi Henri'* became a folk hero; this King was a rough mountaineer who chewed cloves of garlic like fruit so that his breath felled an ox at twenty paces, who killed bears with a knife, who ate and drank enough for ten, who fought like a lion and whose virility was, of course, superhuman. Even now it is *le Vert Galant's* countless love affairs which ensure the cult's survival in a modern industrial France. Obviously no human being could have been quite like this and Henri was certainly neither so great, nor so paternal, nor so charming. Yet one must beware of being over sceptical, of demolishing truth as well as fiction. Properly used, his legend can be of vital assistance in understanding Henri for it reflects his personality to a remarkable extent besides preserving much of the impression which he left on his contemporaries.

It may be thought that certain chapters in this book consider too fully the almost perennial Wars of Religion, the ever shifting power groupings and the incessant intrigues which filled the first half of his life. But a knowledge of these, even during the early years when he was too young to take part, is indispensable for an understanding of his motives and his methods, and for a just assessment of his development as a statesman. However, as a seventeenth-century biographer admitted:

'It would be a Task mighty painful and without end, to him who aims to express everything that's Brave in the Life of Henry the Great.'[2]

Finally, it would be pleasant to think that acquaintance with Henri's character might increase English understanding of the French. Charles II, that supremely Gallic figure, now rivals Queen Elizabeth in popular affection and if the English can like him they can like his grandfather, whom Mme de Stael once called 'the most French of French Kings'. After the débâcle of the Second World War Marshal Pétain's aide and lifelong friend who had been with him since Verdun told the tragic old man why he had betrayed France and himself— *'mon maréchal, vous avez trop aimé les français, pas assez la France.'* Other French rulers, Kings and Presidents, have gone to the opposite extreme, loving France as a glorious abstraction yet ignoring her people. Henri IV was the only one who really loved both and herein lies his importance—he was France and he was all Frenchmen too.

1. *T*HE WARS OF RELIGION

'O France désolée! O terre sanguinaire …'
                                            Agrippa d'Aubigné[1]

'C'est la Réligion dont le zèle inhumain
Met à tous les François les armes à la main …'
                                            Voltaire[2]

Few modern scientists attain to that awesome prestige and influence which belonged to astrologers in the sixteenth century. Of these the greatest was Nostradamus. In October 1564 the French court on a royal progress through southern France came to Salon-de-Crau where the sage lived and, as often before, the Queen Mother, Catherine de Medici, sought his advice; he had prophesied the death of her husband Henri II and would err only once in foretelling her children's fate. With the court was a boy of eleven, Henri de Bourbon, Prince of Navarre and Béarn and premier peer of France, a Prince of the Blood Royal but without any hope of the throne for his Valois cousin King Charles IX had good health and two lively brothers. The master of Henri's household was therefore amazed when Nostradamus visited him secretly, begging to see the young Prince. Afterwards the old seer told him: 'If you live, you will have for master a King of France and Navarre.'[3]

From his birth at Pau Henri's life has a quality of legend. When his mother was with child, her father, King Henri d'Albret, made her promise that while in labour she would sing him a song 'so that', he told her, 'you will not bear a puling, sulky infant.' Jeanne d'Albret sang in her own language the song of all Béarnais mothers,

> *Nouste Dame deu cap deu pount*
> *Adyudatz-me ad aqueste hore*
> *Pregatz au Diu deu ceu …*[4]

imploring the Virgin, whose chapel stood on the bridge over the river at Pau, to pray God for a speedy delivery and the gift of a son. Lying beneath the Pyrenees Jeanne herself prayed *'tout denq au haut deus mountz'*—from the very tops of the mountains. Henri was born in the early morning of 13 December 1553, neither weeping nor crying. His delighted grandfather wrapped the baby in a fold of his cloak and gave a gold box containing his will to the exhausted mother, saying 'that's for you but this is for me'. Then he rubbed the child's lips with a clove of garlic and made it sip some wine from his gold cup, to ensure 'that his temperament would be manly and vigorous'; the wine was eagerly swallowed—'You will be a real Béarnais' pronounced Henri d'Albret.[5] Then this hopeful heir to a lost kingdom was enshrined in his cradle, a turtle's carapace.[6] By some instinct the exiled, disappointed King of Navarre was confident that the little boy was going to avenge all his wrongs.

The christening was regal enough. In March 1554 the infant Henri was baptized in a silver gilt font, specially constructed for the occasion. The godfathers were two kings, both Henris, his grandfather, who was Henri II of Navarre, with Henri II of France, his godmother being that Madame Claude de France, who later became Duchesse de Guise. A local poet wrote how his faithful people would help him *'far vasals toutz autres en batalha'*,[7] a polite compliment which became a prophecy.

However, when the Baron de Dourcoedipe spoke of making vassals he meant in Navarre, not France. Until the advent of Ferdinand and Isabella that ancient and once great kingdom had been one of the Five Spains, a small, mountainous land stretching from the northern slopes of the Pyrenees to the Ebro, inhabited by Latinized Basques, fierce hillmen who were noted for their attachment to old customs. Then in

1512, southern Navarre, the greater part of the realm, was overrun, and henceforward a tiny strip of territory north of the mountains constituted the entire Kingdom. Yet this minute border state retained considerable influence. Its ruling family, the d'Albrets, had for centuries been rich and powerful lords in the area between Dax and Bayonne and the little kingdom was buttressed by the Counties of Béarn, Grailly, Albret, Foix, Armagnac and Bigorre, so that Henri d'Albret could style himself 'Henric Second, Rey de Navarra et Senhor Souviran de Béarn'.[8] Nor was it impossible that his subjects north of the Pyrenees might one day be reunited to their southern brothers; as late as 1559 Spanish grandees advised Philip II to restore southern Navarre to the King at Pau. But King Henri had died in 1555, stipulating that he must be buried at Pamplona when his parents' capital had been recovered. To his descendants he bequeathed his hatred of the Habsburg usurpers.

The new King and Queen of Navarre had made a love match in 1548 when Jeanne's first marriage to the Duke of Cleves was annulled, for non-consummation. Her husband was Antoine de Bourbon, eldest son of the Duc de Vendôme, a descendant of Robert de Clermont, sixth son of St Louis, and claimant to the French throne should the Valois fail. He was a man of enormous charm, generous, enthusiastic, witty, sympathetic as much to inferiors as to equals, and very brave. Unfortunately he was also wildly unstable and just as he adored women he loved a lost cause; his father-in-law made him determined to recover Navarre. A charming blue stocking, in her youth the exquisite Jeanne had been called 'la mignonne des rois' because both her father and her uncle, François I, were excessively fond of her. Gay yet melancholy, in her later years stern Protestant dévote, she was always an enigma, perhaps even to her dutiful son. This was a poetess who could reply to a tribute from Joachim du Bellay in no less graceful lines. She and Antoine were devoted to their Prince de Viana, whose title had been born by all heirs of Navarre since 1423 even if the Béarnais knew him as Duc de Beaumont.[9] It is odd that this supreme man of action should have inherited such a world of dreams.

He had forbears no less colourful than his parents. Among them was a paladin of the Hundred Years War, Gaston III of Foix, that host of Froissart who refused to pay homage to the Black Prince and was surnamed Phoebus for his beauty and magnificence. Henri's grandmother, Marguerite d'Angoulême, wife of Henri d'Albret and sister to François I, was perhaps the most gifted of all. This half-Lutheran mystic who had protected Calvin and been reverenced by Clément Marot belonged as much to the Renaissance as to the Reformation; her *Heptameron* was another Decameron, but less bawdy. These mingled strains of Valois, Bourbon, Albret and Foix were a potent, indeed an explosive heritage.

Yet Henri's earliest years were spent in a world neither courtly nor intellectual. He was a difficult child to wean, requiring eight wet nurses, before his governess, Suzanne d'Albret, took him to her husband's castle of Coarraze in the Pyrenees. Here, by command of his grandfather, Henri was not treated as a prince or given toys but brought up *à la Béarnoise* with the local peasant children, running barefoot among the mountains and eating the same food of coarse bread, beef, cheese and garlic.[10] His time at the *castel* was the foundation of an unfailing common touch, and of iron health. His first language was *Bernes*, a form of Provençal which was still a written as well as a spoken tongue. Later, like his mother, Henri learnt to speak French, in which his correspondence was always conducted. The people of the Midi continued to refer to France as distinct from their own country while the northern French regarded them as foreigners. It cannot be too much emphasized that Henri was essentially a man of the south.

At the end of 1556 he visited 'France'. Paris, the largest city of northern Europe, must have been a bewildering experience for a small boy from rustic Béarn. Despite the new Louvre it still belonged to the Middle Ages, not the Renaissance. Behind crenellated ramparts a maze of narrow streets, dark alleys, turreted bridges and embattled watergates traversed a vast Gothic warren of tall, steep roofed wooden houses surrounding innumerable stone churches, convents and halls, gabled, buttressed, crocketed and pinnacled, each with its own spire or bell tower, a spectacle so beautiful as to be almost magical, yet also menacing. The dirt and the noise were overpowering. If its palaces and hôtels housed the greatest lords and prelates in the land and if its stalls sold the richest wares, Villon's underworld remained untamed while the mob could show staggering ferocity. Henceforward, this gorgeous, sinister city would always be in Henri's mind even when he was absent from it. One day Paris would deny him a throne.

In February 1557 he was presented to Henri II who took a great fancy to him, asking if he would like to become his son.[11] *'Quet es lo senhor pay'*—that's my father, replied the small Béarnais, pointing to Antoine. 'My son-in-law, then?' laughed the King. *'O bé'*—Oh yes, came the reply and thus Henri of Navarre was affianced to Marguerite de Valois. Next year he returned to Pau where, as Regent and Lieutenant-General of the King and Queen of Navarre, he remained for three eventful years until 1561.

On 2 April 1559 France and Spain signed the Treaty of Câteau-Cambresis. For Spain it meant political and military dominance for almost a century. For France it was disaster; though in the previous year she had regained Calais from England, Spain's Catholic ally, she had not recovered from her terrible defeat at St Quentin in 1557. Further, she was bankrupt; in an era of chronic and bewildering inflation the French Crown had staked its entire resources and lost them. The Lyons money market collapsed, the whole machinery of government was imperilled, and vast numbers of Frenchmen were ruined. The nobility, which in France included the gentry, suffered most, many of its members being forced to sell their lands while peace closed the only profession open to them, military service. The country swarmed with discharged soldiery, officers and men, all without hope of employment.

Antoine de Bourbon was outraged that France should conveniently forget his claims to southern Navarre. Taking matters into his own maladroit hands he summoned the muster of Guyenne, of which he was Governor, and marched on Fonterrabia, the key to the Navarrese frontier, deaf to anguished pleas from Paris which saw the peace in jeopardy. But the autumn of 1559 was unusually wet and mountain roads became torrents of impassable mud, fortunately as it turned out, for the army's guide was a Spanish agent leading them into a trap.[12] Antoine turned back, his great expedition ending in farce. A new scheme was still more harebrained; he negotiated with the Sherif of Fez for a north African base from whence he could conquer territory to offer Spain in exchange for Navarre—but the response of Philip II was not encouraging. However, Henri II had died in July 1559, mortally wounded in a tournament by a lance thrust, so Antoine's fanciful ambition saw glittering opportunities in France itself.

François II was a sickly fifteen year old and, although he was legally of age and as no one yet understood 'that Florentine shopkeeper' the Queen Mother, Catherine de Medici, three factions had high hopes of winning control of the King and France. The first group was that of the stern old Constable, Anne, Duc de Montmorency, and his three Chatillon nephews: Gaspard, Admiral de Coligny, a notable hero of the recent wars, Odon, Cardinal de Chatillon, and François, Sieur d' Andelot. However, they could hardly match the might of the house of Guise whose estates spread over all northern France and which as a cadet line of the Dukes of Lorraine enjoyed immense respect. Its six gifted brothers were led by the two eldest: François, Duc de Guise, named *le Balafré* or Scarface after a lance-thrust in the face and France's most redoubtable soldier, and Charles, the Cardinal of Lorraine, renowned for avarice and intrigue, who as Archbishop of Rheims had the right of crowning the King. These mighty feudatories were uncles to King François' young consort, Mary, Queen of Scots. None of the three Bourbon brothers could command such power. Antoine received scant respect, the Cardinal de Bourbon was a timid, retiring nonentity, while the youngest, Louis, Prince de Condé, was a hunchback with insufficient means to support his rank. Nonetheless Condé with his feverish ambition was a born leader whose drive and latent panache were reinforced by personal magnetism. And the Bourbons let no one forget that they were Princes of the Blood Royal, that the throne must be theirs should the Valois line fail.

France was threatened by a return of its Wars of the Roses, that struggle between Armagnac and Burgundy which made the Kingdom incapable of resisting Henry V. Feudal appanages were still very much of a reality, their lords wielding life and death, levying taxes, tolls and customs; frequently the Crown gave them the governorship of a province. France had never curbed the private armies of these magnates who, from the later Middle Ages, had been accustomed to hire troops with the rents their tenants gave instead of military service; veterans of the Spanish war now looked to such patrons for rich pickings. Bastard feudalism was in full noxious flower.

Another source of strife menaced the Kingdom, heresy, more dangerous than any feudal revival. Hitherto the Reformation had made scant headway in France, its converts being mainly academics. But the doctrines of Geneva with their terrible logic and simplicity had inherent appeal for cerebral Frenchmen and towards the close of the late King's reign had begun to spread through the universities, then down the rivers, the period's railways, to the provincial towns. Noblemen and bourgeois were converted but comparatively few peasants; the latter clung to their Catholicism, especially to those semi-pagan rites which tied it so closely to the soil. Henri II took fright, reacting in the same tragic fashion as Mary Tudor; one reason for ending the lost war with Spain was the need to extirpate heresy at home. Under François II the Guises, convinced, uncomplicated Catholics, rigorously implemented Henri's ferocious Edict of Ecouen against heretics; the Cardinal wished to bring back the Inquisition. Fewer were burnt than in England, and at the stake were often shown mercy of strangling, but France was horrified. The Reform found a whole host of ardent converts.

Even so they were not so numerous as the Cardinal feared; he believed that two-thirds of the Kingdom had turned heretic. In 1559 the Calvinist divine, Theodore Beza, thought that 'the Religion' numbered four hundred thousand, though this may well have been too modest a figure. Probably there were never more than a million Huguenots in the period of their greatest success. They were therefore a comparatively small proportion of the total French population, variously estimated at between sixteen and twenty million, a ratio less than that of Recusant Catholics to Anglicans in the England of the Armada. But these Huguenots included many of the most able and influential elements in the country while political and social circumstances gave them a strength out of all proportion to their numbers. If they were few they nonetheless hoped to establish the Reform as the state church, even though their immediate object was freedom of worship. Calvinism was no more tolerant than Romanism.

In the sixteenth century most educated men—and many who were illiterate—had a Byzantine familiarity with theology. Every Protestant knew how to analyse and refute such Romish errors as Transubstantiation or the Sacrificial Priesthood while Catholics could skilfully demolish the heresies of predestination or justification by faith alone. For issues of this sort men fought and died with sublime courage. Nowadays their fanaticism is incomprehensible but it becomes understandable when related to the psychology of the age. Protestantism's strength lay in its annihilation of the guilt complex. The century preceding the Reformation had, in northern Europe, been one of morbid gloom, until Luther wrote *'Pecca fortiter, crede fortius';* a modern disciple has re-written this doctrine of justification by faith as 'Man cannot accept himself, therefore God accepts him'.[13] To this the Calvinist added the conviction that from all eternity he had been predestined to be saved. The Catholic's inspiration was the embattled barque of Peter, launched by Christ Himself, which would ride out the storm raised by Satan and carry the Faithful safely through this world's sorrows and temptations. Those who took part in the Wars of Religion did not fight for metaphysical abstractions but for the meaning of life itself, for their very sanity.

War did not come in François II's reign. During this time the Guises were all powerful; the Duke commanded the royal armies and the Cardinal Archbishop directed the actual machinery of government. Their position seemed impregnable. Condé, poor, proud and resentful was too hotheaded to suffer this insulting dominance; Princes of the Blood could not take second place. He would overthrow the *Balafré* and that priest. In any case Condé and his brother had been converted to the reformed faith.

So early as 1558 Antoine had been involved with Calvinists and in 1559 he accepted the Reform, giving Henri a Protestant tutor, the Sieur de la Gaucherie, who was told to instruct the child in the faith of

Geneva. From his correspondence it is clear that Antoine was genuinely religious and there is no need to doubt the sincerity of his conversion even if he afterwards reneged. But there were compelling secular reasons why he should turn Huguenot. First, the Reform was making ground in his own domains; there is to this day a strong element of puritanism in the southern French and it is significant that Albigensians had once flourished in this area. Secondly, he would establish a bond with many of those opposed to the Guises; the Chatillon brothers were in process of conversion. Thirdly, and most promisingly, the Huguenots constituted a political party with an ideology and structure no less dynamic than those of Fascists or Communists in the 1930s; a cell system of consistories (the governing bodies of the local churches), colloquies, provincial synods and a national synod, was organized with formidable efficiency. Each consistory had not only a minister but also a captain, each colloquy its colonel, experienced soldiers who were responsible for their protection, while there was an invaluable intelligence network. With the Huguenots the Bourbons might well capture France. No doubt Antoine still hoped for a policy which might regain southern Navarre, Condé for a no less substantial reward.

Condé's first bid for power ended in disaster. With English money he hired troops to seize the King. On 20 March 1560 the little force was discovered near Amboise by royal troops and quickly routed, a skirmish named the 'tumult of Amboise' for it was hardly more than an armed brawl. Nothing could be proved against Condé but he was tried for his life while bloody reprisals followed among the less mighty. Catholics and Huguenots began to murder each other.

Now the Queen Mother began to assert herself. Protestant hagiographers and Alexandre Dumas portray Catherine de Medici as an amoral virago while Jean Heritier has discerned a tolerant bourgeoise mother whose sole ambition was to preserve her children's heritage. In his later years Henri himself inclined to this latter view, in a mood of particularly extravagant tolerance: 'I ask you, what could she have done, the poor woman, left at her husband's death with five small children and two families in France—ours and the Guises—who hoped to get the

Crown for themselves? Wasn't it necessary for her to play some strange roles, to deceive each and everybody to defend her sons [as she did] who reigned in turn by the wise guidance of that wily woman? You are going to say that she did harm to France. The marvel is that she didn't do worse.'[14] In many ways *'cette rusée femme'*, though not so fortunate and certainly more human, resembled Elizabeth of England; neither Queen lacked religion nor scruple while sharing a genius for politics and a taste for Machiavelli, and if she never had the Tudor majesty, as a matriarch with ineffectual sons Catherine acquired all the Tudor lust for power. Sometimes too clever but always resourceful the Florentine did in fact employ the famous *escadron volant* of court beauties to ensnare susceptible opponents, though she was never a poisoner. This plump little woman with her white face and black clothes, her passion for good food, astrology and horsemanship, and her careful charm, would one day be Henri's greatest and most dangerous opponent.

In the spring of 1560, though the Cardinal was still in full control, she obtained the appointment of a like-minded Chancellor of France, Michel de L'Hôpital, the first of the 'Politiques', those Catholics who preferred peace to religious war. Desperately he and Catherine worked for an understanding between Huguenot and Papist. The glacier left by the Reformation and Counter-Reformation has only just begun to recede so it is seldom realized that the sixteenth century had its own ecumenists. Among Catholics Cardinal Contarini was the most positive while Pope Adrian VI could admit that his Church bore much guilt. The Emperor Charles V did not despair of rapprochement and there were such concessions as that of the cup to Bohemian laity. Most optimistic of all was the Flemish theologian, Georges Cassander. It was inevitable that Reformers and Papists would part company yet many contemporaries thought co-existence was possible. L'Hôpital, a devout Catholic and an ambassador for France at the Council of Trent, believed that whatever their differences Christians ought to be able to live together in peace: 'Let us get rid of these devilish words, these names of party, of faction, of sedition—Lutheran, Huguenot, Papist—let us keep unadulterated the name of Christian.'[15] Politiques were not yielding to expediency when they wished to recognize Protestant Baptism, a proposal which outraged Tridentine hardliners: today the Roman Church accepts the common Baptism of all Christians. Even if it did not prevail and was disowned by the majority of theologians an ecumenical solution undoubtedly existed. The ultimate heir of Michel de L'Hôpital would be Henri IV.

It was tragic and timely that François II should die in 1560, struck down by mastoiditis. His young widow returned to Scotland and a destiny which ended on the block at Fotheringay. The Guise rule was over: there had to be a Regent, as Charles IX was not of age. This might have been Antoine de Bourbon in his capacity as First Prince of the Blood but he let Catherine have the Regency, taking for himself the second greatest position in the Kingdom, that of Lieutenant-General. A policy of compromise succeeded one of extermination.

King Antoine has rarely been given credit for commonsense yet he recognized Catherine's ability and avoided a head-on clash with the Guises. His next step, in 1561, is usually regarded as one of shallow inconstancy, his return to Catholicism. No doubt he detested the Papacy which had obliged Spain by excommunicating King Jean d'Albret in 1512 when she invaded Navarre; and like many Frenchmen in the 1550s, Antoine, who was probably nearer Lutheranism than Calvinism, had regarded the Reform as a reform of Gallicanism, not as a rival church, preferring to retain the bulk of Catholic doctrine; in England he would have been an Anglican. But the prospect of *jacqueries*—there was trouble with his own southwestern peasants—and a growing realization that most Frenchmen opted for Catholicism had made him believe that the Church must be reformed from within and that Protestantism meant war. Further, Spain now dangled the bait of Navarre before this resilient optimist's credulous eyes.[16] Alas, his statesmanlike attitude was not well received by his wife who, the previous year, had herself been received into the Reform; in her memoirs she wrote that her husband's apostasy was *'une dure espine, je ne diray pas au pied, mais au coeur ...'*.[17] Poor Jeanne's sorrow was hardly assuaged by Antoine's many and notorious adulteries, for which he was rebuked by Calvin himself. The love match had foundered in noisy recrimination.

Young Henri had good cause to ponder on his father's spiritual *volte face*. He was brought to Paris and entrusted to a new tutor, who would instruct him in the Catholic faith. But Henri, at eight, was a staunch Protestant for La Gaucherie had been a preceptor of genius. His methods were far removed from the period's brutal pedagogy; instead the boy was taught by 'discourses and entertainments'. Some of the aphorisms learnt from La Gaucherie remained with Henri all his life, e.g. *'Ou vaincre avec justice ou mourir avec gloire'*[18] It was some months before the little Huguenot would go to Mass, a long time for a child, and then only after Jeanne d'Albret had been ordered from the Court in March 1562.

The first of the French Wars of Religion had begun at the end of the same month despite frantic efforts by Catherine and L'Hôpital which had even included debate; the Colloquy of Poissy in September 1561 was a brave attempt to find a compromise, but Protestant and Catholic theologians, the latter led by the Cardinal de Lorraine, wrangled implacably. The Colloquy proved a disaster; stated differences hardened into insurmountable barriers, making conflict inevitable. On Sunday, 1 March 1562, a Congregation of Reformers were holding their service at Wassy, outside the town walls in accordance with the law. The Duc de Guise, who was staying near by, arrived with his retinue, ordering them to disperse. They refused whereupon over seventy unarmed men and women were massacred. Though the Huguenots had themselves perpetrated worse slaughters during recent months Condé called upon the Religion to be ready for war; he wanted a Rubicon. Ordered to leave Paris he was soon at Orléans with Coligny, d'Andelot and an army of Reformers. Meanwhile the Queen turned to the Catholic *Triumvirat*: the Duc de Guise, the Constable de Montmorency and the Marshal de St André. Throughout France members of the rival creeds attacked each other, killing, burning, raping, torturing, and looting. As Pascal said, a hundred years later, 'Men never do evil so completely and cheerfully as when they do it from religious conviction.'

The atrocities were as outrageous as they were cruel. In a frenzy of Protestant iconoclasm churches were desecrated and their clergy hunted down like vermin; one Huguenot captain wore a necklace of priests' ears while the infamous Baron des Adrets made Catholic prisoners leap to their death from a high tower. Even the dead were attacked; at Orléans a Reformist mob burnt the heart of poor François II and threw Joan of Arc's statue into the river. The Counter-Reformation was not yet in evidence so Papist fanatics were rare but nonetheless Catholics were goaded into fury. At Tours two hundred Huguenots were drowned in the Loire while the bodies of those slaughtered at Sens came floating down to Paris. That grim old soldier Blaise de Montluc made Protestant captives jump from the battlements[19] and remarked with satisfaction that all knew where he had passed by the trees which bore his livery—a hanged Huguenot;[20] on one occasion he strangled a pastor with his own hands.

The *Triumvirs* petitioned Spain for help. Philip II was neither the brooding demon of the Escorial conjured up by English Protestantism and Verdi's *Don Carlos*, nor the hero King of Spanish tradition, but an arch-bureaucrat trying to play an impossible world role. His own domains included Spain and the Americas, with from 1580, Portugal and her empire in America, Africa and Asia, besides the Two Sicilies, Milan, Franche Comté, the Netherlands and many lesser territories, while his cousin held the Habsburg lands in Austria together with Hungary, Bohemia and the Imperial Crown. Protestantism within these vast possessions meant political as well as spiritual disruption, so it was inevitable that Habsburg hegemony should become the secular axis of the Counter-Reformation with Philip as Catholic champion, even if he sometimes put Spain before Rome. His attitude towards France was complex; while he welcomed her weakness and growing division he also dreaded not only a Protestant France but a France whose King, swayed by Huguenots, might aid dissident Netherlanders. Ceaselessly he urged Catherine to crush her heretics without mercy, advice which held a tacit threat of invasion. Spanish pikemen remained the most important external factor throughout the French Wars of Religion. However, fear of uniting France by a national war would deter Philip for many years yet.

Condé took a desperate step. The English ambassador, that zealous Reformer Sir Nicholas Throckmorton,[21] was a loud advocate of a Protestant Front. On his advice Elizabeth graciously accepted Le Havre from the Huguenot leaders at the secret treaty of Richmond in September; it was to be exchanged for Calais. An English garrison occupied the port, waiting to be reinforced by a detachment of German Protestants under d'Andelot, but even Huguenots regarded this International Brigade with mixed feelings.

Rouen, held by the Religion and the most important city of Normandy, was besieged by the *Triumvirs*. In October the Lieutenant-General of the Kingdom, *'pissant aux trenchée'*[22] as Agrippa d'Aubigné puts it, was shot and mortally wounded, expiring a month later in the arms of his most recent mistress and dying not a Catholic or a Calvinist but a Lutheran. This amiable weathercock, who till the very end was deluded by the *ignis fatuus* of a Navarrese restoration, has seldom been taken seriously, yet Antoine had a good deal in common with his son who must have mourned him.

In December the Reformers were defeated at Dreux and Condé was captured. The Guises had triumphed. But in February 1563 the Sieur Poltrot de Méré pistolled *le Balafré* as he was attacking Orléans; under torture he confessed, falsely, that he had been commissioned by Coligny. Next month the Peace of Amboise ended the war, Condé settling for freedom of worship for noblemen of the Religion. Le Havre was taken from the English in July; despite plague it was bravely defended but Huguenots joined with Catholics to expel the ancient enemy and as the Constable said, *'d'ici à Bayonne tout crie "Vive France"'.*[23]

The peace was an uneasy one. Persecution and counter-persecution continued, especially in Béarn where Jeanne d'Albret had been establishing the Reform since 1562; 'the Catholics there were very badly treated, pillaged and massacred, Churches and Monasteries reduced to ashes, and Priests cruelly martyred and hunted down by the new reformers.'[24] In September 1563 Pius IV excommunicated her, but, thanks to the Queen Regent's protection, Jeanne was unscathed though she promised Catherine to treat her Catholics more kindly. Nonetheless some Basque gentry rose, unsuccessfully, to defend their clergy. Meanwhile Henri remained at the French court where he was allowed to rejoin the Reform and La Gaucherie became his tutor once more.

During the first War of Religion and for most of the years which followed the young Prince of Navarre was in Paris away from his mother. If the Valois looked for a political settlement between the rival creeds they nonetheless practised Catholicism and were surrounded by Catholics while the capital itself was Papist. Henri had to grow up in an atmosphere which was covertly hostile and this must have induced a feeling of isolation in an enthusiastic boy, at his age naturally partisan, as well as developing aggressive instincts; no doubt he welcomed eagerly every victory of his uncle Condé, praying for the Religion's ultimate triumph which with the innate optimism of childhood he probably assumed to be inevitable, while Huguenot reverses would have bewildered him. From an early age the little Béarnais had a sharp nose for politics; at eleven he attended the Bayonne conference, unregarded, and afterwards warned Queen Jeanne of Spanish pressure on Catherine to crush the heretics. His adolescence was passed in an atmosphere of intrigue and sectarian hatred. Yet somehow he learnt how to compromise and how not to give way to bitterness. To mature in such a hostile and fearful world into a balanced, tolerant human being was a considerable achievement.

The young Prince attended classes at the Collège de Navarre, together with the new Duc de Guise and the future Henri III. This college on the hill of St Geneviève had been founded by Philippe le Bel and was a notable ornament of the Paris University. Henri learnt to speak, read and write Latin and Greek with some fluency, obtaining a thorough knowledge of the Classics, including Plutarch's *Lives* in the much admired translation by Catherine's chaplain, Jacques Amyot; in these troubled times the statesmen and soldiers of antiquity were excellent models for apprentice princes. It must never be forgotten that despite its optimism the Renaissance looked to the past, to the Golden Age of Antiquity; Bernini and Palladio believed that they built in the purest Graeco-Roman style, while Machiavelli could advocate arming soldiers as Roman legionaries or equipping the Venetian navy with triremes. The Prince of Navarre was also well grounded in theology, both devotional and polemic; in the early summer of 1566 he wrote to his mother about a parcel of Protestant books, 'fine artillery to frighten Romans'. He was beginning to write letters of real literary merit, so much so that he has been called a writer without knowing it. In March 1567 Henri returned to Béarn to complete his education.

In 1567 he visited Bordeaux from where a magistrate wrote to the Duc de Nevers that 'it must be confessed he is a pretty youth'.[25] At thirteen Henri seemed more like a boy of nineteen and 'enters into conversation like a polished gentleman'. And it was all too prophetic that 'though his hair be a little red the ladies do not think him the less agreeable for that. His face is finely shaped, his nose neither too large nor too small, his eyes full of sweetness, his skin brown but very clear and his whole mien animated with an uncommon vivacity so that if he is not well with the ladies he is very unfortunate.'[26]

At Pau he had found a new tutor, Florent Chrestian, *'homme de très agréable conversation et fort versé aux belles lettres, mais tout-à-fait Huguenot'*.[27] Though no record survives one may surmise what other instruction he received besides letters. Naturally war came first. He was taught to be a skilled swordsman in the fashionable Italian manner, his lengthy rapier balanced by a poignard, and also to handle pole-axe, halberd or spontoon, or even the great infantry spear, eighteen foot long, in an age when gentlemen did not disdain 'to trail the puissant pike'. For shooting he had only the arquebus with its clumsy firing rest and spluttering match. On active service 'three quarters armour' was worn, his reins' hand holding a dag or wheel-lock pistol while the rapier was discarded for a heavy broadsword. To carry this weight Renaissance warriors still rode the mediaeval *destrier*, more like a cart horse than a cavalry charger, and spent long hours at battle drill; understandably tilting remained a useful exercise.

Fighting instincts and powers of endurance were developed by hunting to which Henri like all Bourbons was passionately addicted.[28] Thirty-mile points after buck or stag inured him to hard riding, while the *valet de limier* or harbourer taught him to pit his wits against elusive quarry. This was especially true of otter hunting; wading through perilous mountain streams, great skill and patience were required before a dim shape could be speared beneath the water. Courage was needed when killing boar or wolf; the animal had to be dispatched with a short sword—which meant seizing one of its legs and stabbing upwards—or in the case of boar with a spear, one's back against a tree, butt on one's foot, point aimed at the charging brute's forehead. To face half a ton of grey bristled wrath wielding blood-stained tusks, unshaken by disembowelled hounds, was dangerous sport yet not so perilous as bear hunting, in which Pyrennean mountaineers traditionally dispatched the beast with a knife. No doubt stalking birds with a crossbow or a primitive fowling piece improved Henri's marksmanship, but hawking took the place of modern shooting, Iceland falcons or peregrines being the equivalent to a pair of Purdeys. This sport brought out other qualities; patience while training, persistence in retrieving lost hawks and a knack of judging wind and rain. French forests were a trackless waste infested with outlaws and savage animals, as were the mountains. It was easy to lose one's way and lonely sportsmen faced many hazards; in rainy autumns streams became unfordable and marshes turned into evil quagmires while sport in the winter snow was more hazardous still—huntsmen often died from cold or in avalanches.

Besides arms and venery a young magnate's education included heraldry and genealogy, a most practical study; in an age without directories an encyclopaedic knowledge of the influential families of each province and their relationships was indispensable. Henri would also have learnt manners and dancing, singing, and such parlour games as chess, dice and backgammon. He played skittles and became very fond of royal tennis, for which there was a court in the château at Pau.

These pleasant pursuits were interrupted by the Second and Third Wars of Religion. In September 1567 the Huguenots who had become increasingly suspicious of the Queen Mother, tried to seize her and Charles IX at Meaux, a plot which miscarried lamentably though François de la Noue—*Bras-de-Fer*—and fifteen horsemen seized Orléans.[29] The Religion desecrated more churches and slaughtered more Papists; in Nîmes, at Michaelmas, the Huguenot mob threw eighty-eight of them down wells, monks, priests and laymen, then heaped earth on top, a horror commemorated as the *Michelade*. Catholics retaliated in like fashion. A pitched battle was fought at St Denis, outside Paris, in November, where the old Constable de Montmorency, last of the Papist Triumvirs, was killed. In March 1568 peace was made at Longjumeau, an unreal peace, for the Queen was still determined to discipline these insolent heretics. The Third War broke out in the autumn, Catherine's plot to seize Condé and Coligny having failed in its turn, and the Prince and the Admiral fled to La Rochelle, now the citadel of French Protestantism and soon in a state of siege. Hither came Jeanne d'Albret and her son, Jeanne writing to that other Protestant Queen, Elizabeth of England, to beg for advice and munitions, and sending her jewels and tapestry as a pledge of repayment.[30] Charles IX announced his intention of invading Béarn, and though the invasion never took place this was going to be a more serious war than the previous two whose desultory raids and skirmishes were replaced by full-scale campaigns conducted by large and well equipped armies. Bloodshed flared all over France, worse than before, while Michel de l'Hôpital was forced to leave court for ever; on 28 September 1568 the Religion was forbidden all public worship and, shortly afterwards, its members were excluded from any public office.

The Counter-Reformation did not begin to make itself felt in northern Europe until the late 1560s; hence the failure of the Marian reaction in England and the early success of the French Reform. However, when at length it came, the balance of religious power changed dramatically. Long before, an implacable Jesuit General had denounced Beza and his friends as '*loupi, volpi, serpenti, assassini*'.[31] Now at a time when Protestantism was losing its initial momentum Catholic theologians, who had hitherto been hopelessly inadequate, became the equals and often the masters of their Calvinist adversaries, while Jesuits, together with revitalized friars, roused mobs no less efficiently than Protestant ministers. In France's first two Wars of Religion Rome was on the defensive; by the Third she had gone over to the attack so that the Huguenots would be hard put to hold their ground despite a brave spirit and an iron party system. For Catholics compromise had become a sin.[32]

King Charles was growing up into a violent, nervous youth and had conceived a peculiar hatred for Condé; it seems that the previous year the Prince had a medal struck bearing his own effigy with the legend 'Louis XIII, first Christian King of the French'. After this year's mutual plots neither Royal family nor Princes of the Blood dared trust each other. Now the army was given a Royal commander, the King's seventeen-year-old brother Henri, Duc d'Anjou, known as Monsieur. With the aid of experienced advisers he engaged and smashed the Protestant rearguard at Jarnac on 13 March 1569. Condé, unhorsed and helpless after leading a charge with the splintered bones of a shattered leg sticking through his boot, was taken prisoner, but an officer of Anjou's Guards blew his brains out; the body was paraded on a donkey through the Catholic camp by the Duke's order. The Huguenot Prince Rupert left much to his nephew, panache, ambition and an inability to admit defeat. Also he bequeathed the leadership of the Religion. Queen Jeanne presented her fifteen-year-old son to the Huguenot army who acclaimed him, but the real leader was that grim zealot, the Admiral de Coligny. Henri accompanied the army throughout, showing fine spirit, though one must discount tales of precocious military talent.

The war continued. Both sides were aided by co-religionists from Germany, Italy and Spain. The Reform's troops numbered 25,000, mainly cavalry, German *schwarz-reiters* or *diables noirs*—'armoured pistoleers'—and Huguenot squires. The Catholics had 30,000, including Spanish infantry, the most formidable soldiers of their day. The wretched conflict raged throughout France, not merely in sieges or on the battlefield but in countless bestial riots and man-hunts. In September the Admiral was tortured and beheaded in effigy at Paris, his coat-of-arms debruised and a rich price laid on his body, while the same month the Duc d'Anjou caught him at Montcontour; 10,000 Protestants were killed or wounded, the Catholics losing only 200, though that strange young man, Monsieur, was as merciful as he had been pitiless at Jarnac, ordering that the wounded Huguenots be given medical care. Coligny and the Prince of Navarre limped away but they were still able to fight at Arnay-le-Duc in June 1570. Catherine and King Charles now sought a compromise, as both sides were bled white. On 8 August the Peace of St Germain restored the Religion's right of public worship, guaranteeing the settlement with four *places de sûreté*, Huguenot strongholds manned by Huguenot garrisons—La Rochelle, Montauban, La Charité and Cognac.[33] The Reiters were sent home, while Catholic Béarnais were given freedom of worship. The Reformers, though still hopeful of ultimate triumph, were exhausted and ready to try co-existence until they regained their strength.

Much of the Reform's ardour came from the nearness of Calvin's Geneva; Huguenot ministers were trained in this French-speaking city where God's Kingdom had been set up. However, no minister had more burning zeal than Gaspard de Coligny. Middle-aged, but a patriarch before his time, the Admiral with this thick grey beard, sober clothes and quiet, reflective eyes was no cavalier like Condé, but a Calvinist missionary who thought only of converting France. Over cautious as a soldier, Coligny was a bold and imaginative politician. In view of the Huguenots' relatively small numbers—perhaps one in every fifteen Frenchmen—it may be supposed that their leader would have been content with freedom of worship, yet he hoped for nothing less than the evangelization of the entire Kingdom and the extirpation of 'idolatry'. This pious hope did not depend on purely supernatural factors. The triumph of the Reformation in England had been won by the personal faith of the Sovereign; Coligny believed that even if Charles IX were not converted the ambitions of the Guise party might force Catherine to give him control of the government, that he could then ensure the Huguenots' success by declaring war on Spain—Le Havre had shown how national sentiment could conquer religious division. But the sense of divine mission impaired the Admiral's judgement and he could not see that Catherine would never entrust herself and her children to a minority, let alone go to war with Spain.

Henri returned to Pau. His residence befitted the Prince of a proud minority for it was the château where he had been born, a Renaissance palace from the Loire valley built by his grandparents which had once sheltered such reformers as Clément Marot. In this splendid setting Queen

Jeanne held her sober court, far removed from *Love's Labour Lost*,[34] her time was given up to the Religion—even carnivals were frowned upon. Henri's two brothers had died in infancy so, apart from his eleven-year-old sister Catherine de Bourbon, he enjoyed his mother's undivided attention and there must have been clashes between the gay young sensualist and the stern *dévote* who worried about his salvation. In view of his name for wenching the pious Queen had good cause for concern. Anxious that he should find healthy outlet for his youthful energy she had the tennis court at Pau rebuilt in 1571. When she died Henri was deeply upset, writing of his *'deuil et angoisse'*,[35] of his unbearable grief.

He was now a short slender youth with dark hair, no longer reddish, brushed up *en brosse* from a long brown face with a long nose, a full mouth and amused eyes; already he gave an impression of strength and amiability.[36]

Queen Jeanne died in June 1572 as her son was on his way to his marriage, probably of tuberculosis though rumour claimed she had been murdered by Catherine's perfumer—with poisoned gloves whose noxious scent penetrated the brain.[37] Even Henri seems to have suspected poison. When he rode into Paris that same month, in mourning with eight hundred horsemen in black,[38] he came as a King, occupier of the lost throne of the d'Albrets; for Huguenots he was a Gideon, to Catholics a King out of Moab. He had grown up amid hatreds which would continue to rend France for another quarter of a century and he must now start on the long road to her salvation through the same enemies who had overcome his father and his uncle. Few men have inherited so daunting a destiny. To survive, let alone succeed, this son of a weathercock trimmer and nephew of a bitter hunchback adventurer would have to be a veritable David. It was lucky that he could not foresee what lay immediately in store, for seldom has a bridegroom hasted to a wedding which would end in such infamy and horror.

2. THE PRISONER

'*Le chemin de la mort et de la honte, c'est Paris ...*'

Agrippa d'Aubigné[1]

'*La Cour est la plus estrange que vous l'ayez
jamais veue. Nous sommes presque tousjours prestz
à nous couper la gorge les uns aux aul tres ...*'

Henri of Navarre in 1575[2]

Paris overflowed with gaiety and optimism in the summer of 1572. The marriage about to be celebrated between the new King of Navarre and the Princess Marguerite, Charles IX's only surviving sister, was acclaimed with real joy because it showed the resolve of Papists and Huguenots to live side by side in harmony and to end the killing and sacrilege which still convulsed the entire Kingdom. It did indeed seem that the policy of the Queen Mother and her Politiques was going to prevail. Even fanatics grew conciliatory. Alas, this outburst of euphoria coincided with Catherine's terrible realization that Gaspard de Coligny could never be a Politique, that he would accept nothing short of the Reform's total victory, that for him the idea of coexistence with 'idolaters' was a blasphemy; the Admiral's quiet manner and subtle diplomacy hid inflexible purpose. Worse, not only did she now see that the King himself was incapable of ruling as a Politique but that he was moving away from the Catholic camp into that of the Religion. Worst of all it was likely he would soon throw off her own maternal guidance. For

Catherine this meant the destruction of the monarchy and her children's inheritance.

Though she directed policy she nonetheless depended on controlling the King, the most tragic of all her diseased brood. At twenty-two Charles IX looked ten years older, to judge from Clouet's portrait, but he was aged by ill health, not maturity. His frail constitution, undermined by tuberculosis, had now been strained beyond endurance by his wild passion for hunting where the thrill of hard riding and the joy of killing helped satisfy his pathological need for violence; knowing himself to be weak, Charles over-compensated. Besides his mother's dominance he resented the success of Monsieur at Jarnac and Moncontour which had driven this *'violent ennemi et inesgal ami'*[3] into a frenzy of jealousy. Feverishly unstable and easily swayed he might well turn against his own family, while dreams of being a great King might lead him into a ruinous war with Spain. His mistress, Marie Touchet, was a Protestant and Charles, who was not without imagination and possessed a real love of poetry, had learnt to admire the Huguenots' idealism and fervour. He began to listen to Coligny.

For two years Catherine had tried to enlist the Admiral's support in building a true peace so he had become a member of the Royal Council, living in Paris. This warrior patriarch with his iron charm made a deep impression on Charles and by the autumn of 1572 the King had all but transferred his trust from the Queen Mother to Coligny who was a perfect father figure—indeed Charles actually addressed him as *'mon père'*. During this year the Dutch Sea Beggars had risen while, at the Treaty of Blois, France and England had concluded a mutual pact against Spain. In addition a powerful and growing group of Politiques, moderate Catholic nobles led by the new Duc de Montmorency, had come to believe religious differences would be forgotten in war with Spain. The King was intoxicated at the prospect of invading the Netherlands.

Catherine's closest ally was her favourite son, Monsieur. At this date Henri, Duc d'Anjou, was an epicene youth of twenty-two, admired not only for his good looks and brilliant intelligence but also for his gallantry during the Third War of Religion. His homosexuality was not yet apparent for he enjoyed a charming mistress nor had he given way to those strange impulses of frivolity and superstition which later ruined him. Indeed it must have seemed that should Henri of Anjou succeed to the throne France might have her greatest King since Louis XII. It was not surprising that his half crazy brother should distrust him. Monsieur had everything to gain from Catherine retaining her supremacy, much to lose were she supplanted. He had driven Coligny from the field and would do so again—this time from the Louvre.

Marguerite de Valois, the future bride of Henri of Navarre and the sole remaining daughter of Henri II, was nineteen, only seven months older than her future husband but already a byword for beauty, learning and promiscuity. Her portraits show a brunette (though she frequently wore a blonde wig) with a round, pudding face and sly eyes, yet all contemporaries agree on her extraordinary good looks. Brantôme, who adored her, wrote 'for if in the world there has ever been one more perfect in beauty it is the Queen of Navarre … and I think that all women who are, who shall be and who ever were are ugly near her'.[4] He describes her faultless dressing and her exquisite grace in dancing the Spanish pavane, the Italian *passamezzo* and the *branle* with lights and torches. A gifted linguist who spoke Greek with a fluency unusual even among savants, she enjoyed theology no less than the classics. She had already taken lovers, though not from the age of twelve as the violently hostile *Divorce Satyrique* claims;[5] later her *impudiques baisers* became legendary.[6]

It was partly because of her that the Guises and the Catholic extremists were in a temporary eclipse. At seventeen Marguerite had taken a wild fancy to the young and handsome Henri de Guise, *'fort caressé des dames'*. The Cardinal of Lorraine was eager for such a match which would bring his house still nearer the throne. Pierre de L'Estoile's outrageous belief that the Queen Mother slept with the Cardinal was peculiarly ill-founded, for she abominated that domineering hierarch with whom she had a long score to settle. This latest intrigue angered Catherine and infuriated Charles, and together with his party's opposition to the 'Shameful Peace' of St Germain, made it necessary for the Cardinal-Archbishop to leave court in 1570 while Duc Henri was safely married in the autumn of that year to a strong-minded widow, the Princesse de Croy.

The Queen Mother was anxious to demonstrate her genuine desire for peace between Papists and Huguenots. As titular head of the Protestants of France Henri of Navarre was the obvious bridegroom for Marguerite de Valois. The English ambassador, Francis Walsingham, believed that such a marriage might strengthen the French Crown to an unwelcome degree and tried to block it by offering, with questionable sincerity, the hand of his Queen *'bien que l'aage feust fort inégal'*,[7] Henri being eighteen and Elizabeth thirty-six. Eventually Queen Jeanne decided against the bizarre union; such a marriage makes fascinating speculation—a partnership between the Virgin Queen and the *Vert Galant*.[8] But Jeanne was no less opposed to her son's marriage with Marguerite—she knew the Valois court and trembled for his virtue were he allied to such a wanton. There was the obstacle of the Religion and she wrote to him of his intended bride that *'sy elle demeure opiniastre en sa religion il ne peult estre ... que ce marriage ne fust la ruyne premierement de nos amis et de nos pays'*.[9] At last she decided that the marriage would benefit the Reform; possibly Coligny told her it would strengthen his position. On the other hand the Papacy was loath to grant a dispensation, but the Cardinal de Bourbon who was to officiate at the marriage was told, falsely, that Papal permission was on its way.

The great nobles of the Kingdom, Protestant and Catholic, flocked to Paris, with a few notable exceptions, the Duc de Montmorency who smelt some sort of evil in the wind and Sully's father who foresaw that 'the bridal favours would be very red'.[10] All the leading Huguenots were there, including the Comte de la Rochefoucauld and the Vidâme de Chartres, though one future paladin of the religion, Agrippa d'Aubigné, had to leave hurriedly after killing a royal archer in a duel. They had good reason to feel safe for not even the wily Admiral smelt treachery while the King showed them special favour.

On 18 August the noticeably unenthusiastic couple were married on a scaffold draped in cloth of gold, outside Notre Dame. Years later Marguerite remembered how she was dressed; *'moy habillé à la royale'*,[11] with a crown, an ermine cape studded with jewels, and a great blue cloak four ells long born by three princesses. The festivities lasted for nearly a week with balls, suppers and *divertissements;* one tableau at the Louvre, in which the King and his two brothers took part, seemed to imply that Huguenots generally went to hell, an imputation which caused much amusement.

In the meantime Catherine, though by nature averse to bloodshed, had reluctantly decided that there was no way of eliminating Gaspard de Coligny other than assassination. Every day he established himself more firmly in the King's graces. His demise would leave the Huguenots leaderless while the obvious scapegoats were the Guises who had never ceased to mutter threats of vengeance against the Admiral for his alleged complicity in the murder of Duke François. Only one man would die, in the interests of peace, and his death would ensure the continuity of the Politique policy. Monsieur, always his mother's boy, supported her in this tempting but dangerous resolution. Unfortunately for them no amount of careful planning could eliminate the human element.

On the morning of 22 August that skilled *bravo* and killer, the Sieur de Maurevert, fired his arquebus from a window, twice. The Queen Mother had given the Guises *carte blanche* to take their revenge. Coligny staggered; his finger was smashed and there was a bullet in his elbow but he remained standing. His attendants rushed into the house from where the shots had come but found only a smoking arquebus and heard a galloping horse. No one looked further than the Guises—for the time being.

Catherine was appalled; an enquiry would disgrace her, leaving a triumphant Coligny, to whom Charles must surely turn, free at last to lead France into a suicidal struggle with Spain during which the country's Catholic majority would certainly rise in rebellion. In the meantime her own life was in danger; worse, so was Monsieur's. There was only one way out of this terrible impasse, a bloody way, but if as a woman faced with ruin Catherine knew fear she also possessed such a woman's lack of scruple; the Guises must be quickly and quietly unleashed to kill the Huguenot leaders and the Admiral with them, for '*tous les oiseaux estoient en cage*'.[12] Bereft of their great lords the Protestant commons would soon come to heel. Monsieur, that hardly less feminine son, again agreed with the Queen Mother in her grim resolve.

All that day the Huguenots raged, vowing that they would have satisfaction for the wounds of their beloved patriarch. In her memoirs Queen Marguerite recorded that when she went to her husband's bed on the night of 22 August she found it surrounded by thirty or forty Huguenots, who she did not yet know as she had only been married for a few days, and how they did nothing but talk of the misfortune which had befallen *Monsieur l'Admiral*, resolving that as soon as it was day they would demand justice of the King against Monsieur de Guise. '*Le temps se passa de cette façon sans fermer l'oeil.*'[13]

The King still favoured Coligny, whom he continued to call '*mon père*', but on the evening of Saturday the 23rd his mother bullied him into submission at a council meeting with stories of plots by the Religion. Her maternal instinct did not fail; Charles IX, unbalanced and bewildered as ever, and made even more feverish than usual by this barrage of accusation, broke down screaming 'Kill them all'. He had given his assent to the massacre of St Bartholomew whose eve it was. Besides the bravos and bully-boys of the Guise household many others were eagerly waiting to begin the good work, not only the King's guards and those of Monsieur but also the great bourgeois and the mob of Paris, at one in their hatred of heretics.

All save a few Catholics saw the horror which they were about to perpetrate as an act of self defence and the Huguenots as the real aggressors. For years this small minority had kept the Kingdom in anarchy and misery, terrorizing their 'idolatrous' neighbours; few days passed without reports of some fresh sacrilege in which Protestants profaned the House of God, throwing down its crucifix, smashing its statues and blowing up its altar with gunpowder, outraging the very Sacrament itself, and hunting down its priests. Each villager dreaded the descent of bandit partisans, every townsman lived in fear of rabble roused to frenzy by sectarian bigots. But now the Counter-Reformation had begun to teach its flock that, far from being a sin, it was a mercy to kill heretics so that they might sin no more.[14] From a purely secular point of view the Catholic Parisians were about to rescue the Kingdom from a divisive poison unknown to their forefathers. It must be remembered that most, though not all, sixteenth-century Christians, whether Catholic or Protestant, thought tolerance a sin. This attitude was now to be given terrible expression in 'the Matins of Paris'.

At four o'clock in the morning of Sunday 24 August the door of Coligny's bedroom in his lodging was broken down by Guise's swordsmen and Monsieur's Swiss. The Admiral was skewered with a pike, then flung out of the window into the street below where the Duke and a bastard brother kicked the dead man's face; after further mutilation the battered corpse was hanged by its heels from the public gibbet. At the Louvre Charles personally gave the orders to kill the Huguenot nobles. Condé and the King of Navarre were summoned to the King's chamber but their attendants were barred from entering; 'Goodbye, my friends,' said Henri, 'God knows if we will ever see each other again.' He and Condé were spared because they were Princes of the Blood and there is no foundation for Brantôme's claim that Marguerite saved her husband's life, nor for the legend that she hid him under the skirts of her farthingale.

However, she saved other lives. The Queen of Navarre was asleep when the Vicomte de Leran, wounded by a sword cut in the neck and a halberd thrust in the arm, burst into her room pursued by a band of enraged archers and flung himself on to her bed; the Queen and the Vicomte rolled on to the floor—'*nous crions tous deux et estions aussy effrayés l'un que l'autre*'.[15] Fortunately the Captain of the Guard came in and, shaking with laughter, ordered his men out. When Marguerite went into the corridor a Huguenot courtier was killed with a halberd only three paces from her, while in Mme de Lorraine's room she found two of her husband's gentlemen who begged her to save them; to do so she had to beseech the Queen Mother and the King on her knees.

The Louvre's staircases, chambers, withdrawing rooms and antechambers all dripped with blood and were littered with dead or dying Protestant lords, though many had been assembled in a courtyard to be cut down by the royal soldiery. Henri and his cousin Condé spent a terrifying night listening to their friends' screams, some of whom were 'murdered disrespectfully before their eyes',[16] and fearing that the demented Charles might turn on them. However, he was too busy, firing happily at his Protestant subjects with an arquebus from the palace windows.

The mob, organized by the municipality of Paris, was taking care of the Huguenot commons with the same gusto which its descendants would one day give to hunting enemies of the Revolution. The tocsin which summoned the Faithful, to kill, also warned the Religion so that a few of its nobles who had slept outside the Louvre were able to escape, pursued by Guise at full gallop, but most of the Protestant bourgeois were hounded to their deaths in a *totentanz* of lynching and plunder. The troops of the King and Monsieur assisted the loyal Parisians in countless man-hunts; some heretics were chased over the rooftops or into cellars before being cut down, many were flung into the 'Seine's empurpled flood' including a basketful of babies, for neither children nor pregnant women were spared and whole families had their throats slit. Even great Catholic nobles joined in the killing; old Marshal de Tavannes tottered through the streets brandishing his sword and shouting 'bleed them, bleed them—doctors say that bleeding is as good in August as in May'. Paris became a slaughterhouse. The rabble got out of hand and over five hundred houses were sacked, many rich Papists dying too, falsely accused of heresy by those who coveted their wealth. The killing went on throughout Sunday and Monday until most of the Faithful were exhausted, though for several days survivors continued to be flushed out and butchered. Estimates of just how many died vary, but it cannot have been less than four thousand.

This figure was more than doubled in the provinces where local fanatics were roused by the thrilling tales from Paris. Within the octave of St Bartholomew seven hundred Protestants were despatched in the prison at Lyons to which they had gone for their own safety, while the mobs went hunting in a score of towns, frequently joined by the royal garrisons. At Rouen zealots were heartened in their pious work by the bodies which came floating down the river from Paris. Perhaps ten thousand provincial Huguenots died in September.

At the time it was generally believed that at least a hundred thousand had been slain. Europe reacted predictably, Protestant rulers like Elizabeth being horrified while sovereigns such as the Emperor or the King of Poland who had both Protestant and Catholic subjects were disapproving. Philip II laughed heartily, a rare and notable occurrence, and Pope Gregory XIII said that the news was better than that of fifty Lepantos, he and the College of Cardinals attending a *Te Deum* after which the cannon of St Angelo fired salutes and Rome was illuminated for three nights. It is indicative of the mind of the time that many Huguenots instead of crying out for vengeance believed that the massacre was a visitation of God brought upon them by too much ambition. Some French Protestants even abjured the Religion and it is undoubtedly true that these bloody events were the beginning of the Catholic triumph.

However, the immediate result within France was the Fourth War of Religion. Though one of the Huguenots' *places de sûreté* was taken three remained. Fighting men of the Reform rose throughout France, riding to rallying points in the South and West, above all to La Rochelle. Their great lords were dead and many of their rich bourgeois had fled abroad but new leaders came forward, country squires and poor gentlemen who lived by soldiering, while preachers whipped up morale like the chaplains of Cromwell's army whose troopers the soldiers of Protestant France anticipated in so many ways. The war was one of sieges, in particular the siege of La Rochelle, 'bastion of the Gospel'. This western sea-port, well fortified now for many years and manned by vigorous merchants and tough sailors, easily revictualled from England, was a hard nut to crack, too hard for the Royal army under Monsieur which besieged it from February 1573. Four assaults were beaten back with ferocious resolution. Then in May Monsieur was elected King of Poland so peace was proclaimed in July at the Treaty of La Rochelle whereby the Religion was given freedom of worship in those towns which were *places de sûreté* and freedom of conscience elsewhere.

Henri had had to be present during the siege of his former brethren. After the St Bartholomew he and Condé had been given a choice of '*La mort ou la Messe*'[17] by a raging Charles IX; on St Michael's Day, 29

September 1572, the new Papist received Communion at Mass with his brother Knights of St Michael wearing the Order's white habit and red hood—the Queen Mother was seen to smile. On 3 October the King of Navarre was made to beg the Pope's pardon and on 16 October to publish an ineffectual edict which re-established Catholicism in Béarn. During the La Rochelle expedition he surprised people by '*faisant bonne mine*' and bearing no apparent resentment. Indeed he had played tennis with the Duc de Guise only a few weeks after the Paris Matins. However, he remained a virtual prisoner at the Royal court.

For more than three years he would be under close surveillance, sometimes under arrest. 'He was subjected to a thousand caprices and a thousand insults from the court; at times free, oftener closely confined, and treated as a criminal.'[18] Throughout this time he did his best to disarm suspicion so that he could escape. He assumed a role which Dumas shrewdly interpreted as '*Nul désir, nulle ambition, nulle capacité; je suis un bon gentilhomme de campagne, pauvre, sensuel et timide …*'.[19] Ironically, this triumph of hypocrisy would one day be rivalled by his grandson Charles II's heroic 'conversion' to the Kirk during that brief and awful sojourn at Holyrood as a guest of the distrustful Covenanters. Despite the demands on his self control and the awareness of very real danger, for he was surrounded by enemies as well as exposed to Charles IX's mad rages, Henri became noted for his astonishing amiability and his capacity for enjoyment; '*il aimoit la frequentation des gens qui estoient d'humour gaie et joviale*',[20] hunting, playing tennis, gambling and whoring with unflagging zest. If he maintained a decorous Catholicism—receiving Communion and taking part in flagellant processions—he seemed to wish only for a life of pleasure. Though he was an eighteen-year-old boy when he began his captivity, untried and without experience, and retained a youthful look throughout by remaining unfashionably clean shaven, he did not altogether deceive Catherine who never underestimated her opponents. But in these early days it was impossible to know that here was an adversary far more wily than Coligny. The real reason for the Béarnais' detention was simply that he was a Prince of the Blood who might be used as a figurehead by the Religion.

Henri's life at the court of Charles IX was rendered still more uneasy by his odd relationship with his wife. From the start the marriage was a failure. Marguerite's lack of enthusiasm had been remarked on at the wedding when the King all but forced her to make the responses yet even if she remained in love with Guise this does not explain Henri's lack of attraction for her—nor hers for him. Physical incompatibility is unlikely as both were notorious for sexual voracity, and infidelity would have played small part even if d'Aubigné, who loathed her, asserts that Henri was upset by his Queen's gallantries.[21] Some historians have depicted the natural aversion of an exquisite, Italianate blue-stocking for a wild mountaineer from the provinces but this is doubtful; Henri was a great Prince of high education with sophisticated tastes who had been brought up in close proximity to his bride until the age of thirteen and who only acquired rough habits after years of campaigning. Brantôme believed that the fundamental reason was religious difference, for Marguerite, despite her promiscuity, was a devout Catholic.[22] However, the most probable explanation is the simplest—temperamental incompatibility. Henri was too human and too well balanced to enjoy a wife so complicated and eccentric as the last Princess of the perverse Valois. Nevertheless they were excellent friends, tolerating each other's love affairs with perfect equanimity, and forwarding each other's interests.

François, Duc d'Alençon, the youngest of Catherine's children, was also the most repellent, physically as well as morally. Dwarfish and dark skinned, all contemporaries agree on his ugliness, some alleging that smallpox had given him a double nose. Writing of a projected marriage with Queen Elizabeth, Walsingham stated that the 'great impediment that I find in the same is the contentment of the eye. The Gentleman sure is void of any good favour, besides the blemish of the small pocks';[23] when the English Queen finally set eyes on François she named him 'the frog'. His nature was even less pleasant than his person, false, greedy and cowardly. His brothers loathed him while his mother had small liking for this untrustworthy son. Marguerite was his only friend, a relationship which even modern historians suggest was incestuous. Brother and sister formed an alliance with Henri which was regarded with deep disfavour by his mother-in-law. Later Henri credited his brother-in-law with 'a double heart, a soul as maligned and deformed as his body', but for the moment he seemed to hold him in deep affection.

His mother-in-law's unblinking scrutiny, suave but baleful, was perhaps the most terrifying circumstance. Well informed courtiers said she was a poisoner and Henri, who possibly suspected her of murdering his mother, must have feared that any illness or malaise meant poison, that each mouthful of food or drink might be his last. In 1575 a scurrilous pamphlet insinuated that 'this Florentine Brunhilda'[24] would have seen he died by strange pains had not Condé managed to escape.[25] As yet Catherine had not identified Henri of Navarre with 'le grand Chyren' of Nostradamus' verse:

> *Au chef du monde le grand Chyren sera*
> *Plus outre après aymé, criant, redouté:*
> *Son bruit et los les cieux surpassera,*
> *Et du seul titre victeur fort contenté.*

Nostradamus is always almost impossible to translate, since he deliberately used vague grammar and obscure vocabulary in order to be as enigmatic as possible. However, *'le grand Chyren'* is an anagram for Henri, and the general sense of these lines is that Henri's deeds will astound the heavens, while nothing less than the title of conqueror will satisfy him. Had Catherine understood this prophecy her son-in-law would have had real cause for terror. As it was his life was a nightmare even if his courage never failed him.

A new political alignment had now emerged, far more complex than the old, simple division into Papist and Huguenot, producing a situation which might easily end in the Kingdom's collapse and disintegration. 'Malcontents' was the name given to d'Alençon's party of discontented courtiers, adventurers very like those who would later follow Elizabeth of England's foolish favourite, the Earl of Essex; men so unprincipled were quite ready to side with heretics. As yet fewer but much more formidable were the Politiques, Catholics who preferred peace to religious war and were therefore also prepared to ally with Protestants. St Bartholomew had made the latter stronger than before, if no more numerous; hostilities had never ceased in the South, whose Huguenots were linked to those of the 'pacified' North and West by the Protestant Union. While in *places de sûreté* like La Rochelle there was a contempt for Royal authority and a desire for self-rule which approached republicanism, a government tantamount to a republic had already been set up in Languedoc.

Sir John Neale has given a powerful and succinct description:

> Languedoc was divided into two governments, centred at Nîmes and Montauban, each with a Count at the head controlled by an elected council or estates, which in important matters consulted the estates of each diocese. The two supreme councils were given control of finance, and money was obtained by levying taxes on towns and villages, whether they were Huguenot or Catholic.... All France south of the Loire was in due course proclaimed to be under Damville as governor and general chief, while he in turn acknowledged the supremacy of the Prince of Condé, who had escaped from Court and was safe in Germany. A veritable republican government was elaborated, with a Council of State to advise Damville, an Assembly of Deputies, Provincial Councils, offices of Justice and Finance, four Law Courts, and a financial division of the whole area. Customs duties and taxes were levied, and this revolutionary organisation ran its own police, schools and hospitals. Condé and Damville were assigned specified salaries, and money and authority were provided to levy troops abroad.[26]

Significantly Damville, a younger brother of the Duc de Montmorency, was a Catholic. No longer were Papists necessarily Royalists. Any further advance by the threefold alliance of Huguenots, Malcontents and Politiques meant the emergence of other republics like Languedoc and the possible dissolution of the Kingdom. This terrible new opposition would be still more dangerous if led by a Prince of the Blood. It was therefore understandable that Catherine should dread the escape of either Henri or François d'Alençon.

Close watch was kept on the King of Navarre who complained of Royal guards searching his apartments and even looking under his bed. In any case the court always swarmed with spies.[27] However, the glittering prospect of the Huguenot leadership was always in his mind. His first attempt to escape, together with d'Alençon, while hunting at St Germain in February 1574 was betrayed and the two Princes were arrested. François behaved despicably, begging the King's forgiveness on his knees and confessing that the Huguenots were about to rise, but Henri kept his nerve and coolly explained that he simply wanted to return to Navarre. In April they had another try, attempting as before to escape from St Germain and join the rebels who had now risen. Again the plot was betrayed. This time the two Princes were incarcerated in the strong castle of Vincennes. Once more d'Alençon broke down while Henri stayed cool, claiming that he went in fear of the Guises.

Their two chief abettors, the Vicomte de la Molle and Count Annibale de Coconato, were tortured and beheaded by the specific orders of an infuriated Charles IX.[28] After their deaths these somewhat unsavoury gentlemen achieved a certain distinction. La Molle, an ingratiating adventurer who was renowned at court for his sexual prowess, had been Queen Marguerite's current lover while Coconato, a ferocious bravo who was the Captain of d'Alençon's bodyguard, had been that of the Duchesse de Nevers. Popular rumour believed that these great ladies bought their lovers' remains from the executioner and buried them secretly by night; as they had been quartered as well as beheaded this must have been a messy business. An even more dramatic version of the tale claims that Marguerite embalmed La Molle's head, had it set with jewels and placed in a lead casket, and then interred it with her own hands.[29]

Because his illness grew worse at exactly the same time that Henri and d'Alençon began their plotting, King Charles, 'his eyes ghastly and his countenance fierce',[30] suspected poison or witchcraft, screaming out that he was being *'horriblement et cruellement tourmenté'*.[31] Hence the execution of La Molle and Coconato and the arrest of two Italian astrologers.

In fact the King was dying of pulmonary tuberculosis which induced 'a bloody sweat' of ecchymoses or effusions of blood all over his body. Understandably Huguenots claimed that, like Richard III, the last hallucinated days of this *'grand blasphémateur'*[32] were further tormented by the memory of evil deeds, one Protestant courtier alleging that since the St Bartholomew the King had had no rest undisturbed by starts and groans.[33] Charles IX died an agonized death on 30 May 1574. Before the end he summoned Henri and, saying goodbye with surprising affection, commended his wife and daughter to him.[34]

Monsieur, the King of Poland, who now succeeded as Henri III was far away, sulking in his palace at Cracow where he had taken refuge from his unloved and demanding subjects—*'cete nation plus seuere et serieuse que la nostre'*.[35] Unable to speak Polish he had given way to melancholy and idleness while his barbarous and perpetually drunken nobles, who shaved their heads like Tartars, loudly insisted that the fastidious young Valois must marry the forty-year-old *Królewna* Anna, the last Princess of their native Jagiellon dynasty. If unruly they were infuriatingly loyal and would not let *'Król Henryk'* leave for France, shrewdly suspecting he would never return. He therefore gave a banquet for their leaders and after his guests had drunk themselves into a stupor fled in diguise[36] to Vienna, hotly pursued by tearful Poles during an epic flight in which he rode his horse into the ground. Reaction from this terrible interlude set in at Venice where, after a solemn entrance up the Grand Canal when he was received by the Doge and Senate, he gave himself up to fêtes and entertainments and the purchase of jewels, glass, rich clothes and scents.

Henri III returned to France in the autumn of 1574, freeing d'Alençon and his cousin of Navarre on his arrival; it had been necessary to confine them during his absence because the Fifth War of Religion which had broken out in February was still raging with no prospect of abatement and they were therefore likely to make determined efforts to join the rebels. After the usual protestations of loyalty Navarre made another unsuccessful attempt to escape in July.

The new King's court was certainly very different from the *wilde-jagd* of Charles IX but perhaps even more nerve-racking. Though sufficiently normal to have several mistresses and marry for love Henri III gave way increasingly to homosexual tendencies so that the Louvre became a byword for unnatural vice, where *'l'amour philosophique et sacré'* was openly, and shrilly, proclaimed. On occasion this Renaissance Heliogabulus dressed as a woman, while he was invariably surrounded by *mignons*, more rouged, curled and bedecked than any woman, young men of obscure origin who vied for the King's favour and whose noisy quarrels frequently ended in lethal duels. There were other *'deportemens mols et effemés'*[37] which hardly endeared their King to a virile and warlike nobility; he hid in the cellars when it thundered and, worst of all, at his Coronation in 1575 he shrieked that the Crown had hurt him when it was placed on his head.[38] These eccentricities took time to emerge in full bloom but as early as Christmas 1574 France was startled to learn that His Most Christian Majesty, always devout, had taken part in a procession of flagellant penitents where barefoot courtiers had whipped each other with enthusiasm, the King wearing a necklace of little skulls. Yet this strange, Proustian figure could in his rare moments of energy show bravery and wisdom and prove that he was no less of a statesman than his mother, a true King who inspired genuine affection as well as fear. Indeed he would one day destroy himself by his determination to rule. And his rage could be terrible—he was the only one of her children of whom Catherine was ever frightened even if she loved him the best.

Henri III seems to have liked rather than disliked his Béarnais cousin; when the King fell ill in 1575, suspecting that Monsieur had poisoned him, he told Henri to seize the throne in the event of his death. But the Béarnais' position grew daily more uncomfortable. He was closely watched by the King's beloved bully-boys, such as the arrogant Colonel of the Royal guard, Louis de Guast, while Catherine decided that the friendship with d'Alençon, now known as Monsieur, must be broken. To do so she employed an even more Machiavellian method than usual—

she would set Henri of Navarre himself against Queen Marguerite who would complain to Monsieur.

Charlotte de Beaune, Baronne de Sauve, the Queen Mother's lady-in-waiting and a member of the *escadron volant* was an ideal instrument. This beautiful and accomplished blonde, twenty-five years old and the first of Henri's great loves, was a collector of conquests who had added not only Henri but also Monsieur to her list of triumphs and the two Princes were competing for her with some jealousy. Relations between them deteriorated to such an extent that in 1575 Henri wrote to Jean d'Albret (at Coarraze)—the son of his old governess—that

> We [i.e. the court] are nearly always ready to cut each other's throats. We carry daggers and wear mail shirts, even breast-plates, under our cloaks.... You have no idea how hardy I am for I have everyone against me. The faction of which you know all want me dead for Monsieur's sake and, for the third time, have forbidden my mistress to speak to me, keeping so close to her that she doesn't even dare look at me. I'm only waiting for the moment when I shall have to fight a pitched battle as they all say they're going to kill me and I'd like to forestall them. ...[39]

Marguerite, in her memoirs, recorded her astonishment on hearing that Mme de Sauve was trying to turn Henri against her. Despite her own notorious affairs with François de Balsac d'Entragues and a famous swordsman, 'the brave Bussy', the attempt failed, for Marguerite and her husband were too shrewd to be deceived and too little in love with each other to be jealous. Nonetheless Henri remained enamoured of Charlotte de Sauve for some time to come, maintaining amiable relations for many years. The story conjures up the labyrinthine intrigue and venomous rumour, which together with fear of poison or the dagger, infected the air of the last Valois court, where amidst the stately dances and gorgeous *divertissements* at the Louvre and the Tuileries or during the splendid ritual of hunting at St Germain, ruin or violent death lay in wait for so many great noblemen.

The Crown, once again near bankruptcy, proved incapable of dispersing the Huguenot forces, who were secretly subsidised by Elizabeth of England, while Languedoc and the other all but independent régimes continued to flourish. If Henri could reach Béarn he would indeed be a sovereign in this feudal anarchy which was becoming separatism. His discontent reached a peak even when Monsieur succeeded in escaping, alone, in September 1575. But the captive King of Navarre had to go on playing the man of pleasure, pretending to have quarrelled with d'Alençon,[40] affecting complete indifference towards the Huguenot party, and cultivating the friendship of the Duc de Guise. It was an astonishing excercise of self control by a young man who was near to despair.

In 1575 the Venetian ambassador, Giovanni Michel, sent the Serene Republic a detailed description of the young King of Navarre who was 'of medium height but very well built, with no beard as yet, brown skinned, and *"ardito e molto vivo come era la madre";* he is pleasant, in every way affable and very friendly in manner, and generous too, so people say. He is devoted to hunting in which he spends all his time'.[41] Messer Giovanni also noted that Henri still dreamt of Navarre and that he spoke a little too freely—*'parlando forse troppo più liberamente'*—about recovering his lost provinces.[42] Sully had already observed these hopes which were encouraged by secret contacts with the *Moriscos*. It is scarcely to be wondered at that the captive King should take refuge in such fantasies.

However, by January 1576 he had finally given way to hopeless misery which perhaps induced the fever that made him take to his bed. It also inclined his mind to thoughts of religion. This debaucher of maidens and cheerful maker of cuckolds may seem an unlikely Calvinist. But Puritans are tempted no less than Papists, nor need they be gloomy; assurance of salvation is an excellent reason for gaiety—British historians tend to forget that so joyous a cavalier as Montrose was a devout Presbyterian. In the sixteenth century French Protestantism was an aristocratic and seductive creed, distinguished by the freshness and purity of its religious experience and by a lyrical awareness of the reality of God's love; it is significant that many of the period's poets were Huguenots. Certainly no man so typical of his age as Henri, however much a sinner and a sceptic, would have fallen into atheism which could then be plumbed only by a few execrated misfits. In 1574 L'Estoile noted with approval that 'a wretched atheist and madman (one is never one without being the other) ... was hanged and strangled at Paris, his body burnt with his book ...';[43] no doubt Henri approved too. Perhaps he had small sense of the spiritual and gave little thought to his salvation, like those who respect art without appreciating it, but, despite Montaigne's suspicions at a later date, he nonetheless accepted his religion, that of a Protestant Christian, *croyant* though hardly *pratiquant*. Even when he professed Catholicism, in his heart he remained a Calvinist, until the final conversion at St Denis.

So, lying on his bed. Henri turned to the comfort of the Psalms, reciting one which expressed perfectly his frustration and despair:

> O Lord God of my salvation, I have cried day and
> night before thee: O let my prayer enter into thy
> presence, incline thine ear unto my calling.
> For my soul is full of trouble: and my life draweth
> nigh unto hell....
> Thou hast put away mine acquaintance far from
> me: and made me to be abhorred of them.
> I am so fast in prison: that I cannot get forth....
> I am in misery, and like unto him that is at the
> point to die: even from my youth up thy terrors
> have
> I suffered with a troubled mind....

By chance two gentlemen of his household waiting in the antechamber heard him. Zealous Huguenots, they rushed in and one, d'Aubigné, asked the King of Navarre whether God still lived within him, promising that if He did anything was possible, even escape.[44]

Agrippa d'Aubigné was an heroic figure, poet, swordsman and mystic. Of noble but obscure origin, he was definitely not a natural child of Jeanne d'Albret as has been claimed, though he would certainly have been a son far more to her taste than Henri. Still only twenty-four in 1576 he had been a soldier since he was fifteen; at the age of eight his father had made him swear on the gory heads of the executed conspirators of Amboise that he would fight for the Religion. Despite his burning Calvinist faith Agrippa, like Henri, had fallen into sin; not only was he a popular ladies' man at court who had taken a mistress but he had actually fought against his brethren, under the Duc de Guise. He became the King of Navarre's gentleman-in-waiting in 1573 but had spent much time away from his master. Now he believed that he was an instrument of God, sent to free Henri from a Babylonian captivity. That a follower of such fine and tempered steel should be at Henri's side at this moment was to have incalculable consequences. Agrippa would become his King's 'right arm and on some days his conscience too'.

To Henri his gentleman's startling irruption must have seemed miraculous; there is something of Bruce and the spider in the story so carefully recorded by Agrippa years later, of St Joan and the Dauphin at Bourges. It was the beginning of the salvation not only of Henri but of France. His fever left him and with renewed energy he started to plan one more attempt at escape.

He gave a last brilliant performance as the man of pleasure without ambition. Having hidden himself in Paris he then spread the rumour that the King of Navarre had fled while hunting; he could be found nowhere and in the ensuing panic it was assumed that he had been successful. Next day, 1 February, when the disconsolate Henri III and his mother were at Mass in the Sainte Chapelle, he came to them, booted and spurred as though returning from hunting and laughed that as they wanted to see him, here he was.[45] After this he went on to the Duc de Guise to whom he showed deep affection and expressed a ludicrous belief that soon he would be made Lieutenant-General of the Kingdom.[46]

Henri spent 3 February 1576 hunting near St Germain with every intention of returning to Paris but that evening when he was about to leave Senlis for home, after a hard day in the saddle, a breathless d'Aubigné suddenly appeared with news that their plans had been betrayed. Henri was aghast but the fiery Agrippa rallied his master—'le *chemin de la mort et de la honte, c'est Paris; ceux de la vie et de la gloire sont par tout d'ailleurs ...'.*[47] Overpowering the few King's men present Henri and his friends galloped into the darkness towards Frontenac, finding their way through the trackless forest with great difficulty in *'une nuict très obscure et fort glacieuse'.*[48] Next morning they met a gentleman who offered to guide them. Not recognizing the King of Navarre he jokingly asked for news of the court, especially of the Princesses' love affairs in which Queen Marguerite was so prominent. Henri laughed but when *'nôtre pauvre Croniqueur des amours des Princesses'*[49] learnt his identity he was so panic-stricken that he dared not go home for three days. Henri did not pause in his flight southwards until they reached Samur three weeks later.

Even if the odds were less, that first desperate gallop from Senlis was as much a turning point in the Béarnais' life as the flight from Worcester was for his grandson seventy-five years later. One of the noblemen who rode with him remembered afterwards that Henri did not speak until they crossed the Loire, whereupon he heaved a long sigh and said, 'God be praised Who has delivered me; at Paris they killed the Queen my mother, they murdered the Admiral and all our best servants, and would have treated me no better had not God protected me. I will never return there unless they drag me.' Then, grinning, he added that he only regretted leaving two things behind; the Mass and his wife. 'I will try to manage without Mass but I can't do without my wife and I mean to have her.'[50] The mask which had almost slipped was now in place again.

3. THE LORD OF GASCONY

'... *Nérac on nostre Cour estoit si belle que nous
n'envions point celle de France.*'

Marguerite de Valois[1]

'*Ceulx qui suivent tout droict leur conscience
sont de ma religion; et moy je suis de celle
de tous ceulx-là qui sont braves et bons.*'

Henri of Navarre in 1577[2]

Henri joined forces with Monsieur and Condé. Together they commanded an army of thirty thousand men but Monsieur could not muster the courage to march on Paris though his brother had neither the troops nor the money to withstand them. In May 1576 France returned to the Middle Ages with 'the Peace of Monsieur' when the King bought off the three princes with feudal appendages; as Michelet says 'Henri III's first regal act was to re-create Charles the Bold'.[3] Monsieur obtained Anjou, Touraine and Berry with his brother's old title of Duc d'Anjou, while Henri had the governorship of Guyenne and Condé that of Picardy. For the first time the Béarnais was a great prince in truth as well as name; now he could set up his own court and learn to rule. However, he must also learn to be a soldier, to become '*un prudent et hasardeux capitaine*'.[4]

The Huguenots had not only kept their *places de sûreté* but had also secured hitherto unheard of concessions; freedom of worship everywhere save Paris, and *chambres mi-parties* in all *parlements* which meant that in

every important law court in the Kingdom any Protestant could demand
a tribunal which was half Huguenot. This last privilege aroused the fury
of Catholic townsmen throughout France and the Peace of Monsieur
welded Papist zealots into a force far stronger than the Huguenots. The
Catholic League was born at Péronne in Picardy, a staunchly Papist
town which refused to be handed over to the Religion as a *place de sûreté*,
and quickly spread over the entire Kingdom. Appropriating the para-
military organization of the Protestant League, the Catholic Faithful
were mobilized by parishes just as the Religion was by presbyteries, each
one with its own armoury and magazine, while supporters swore, on
pain of 'anathematization and eternal damnation', to uphold it 'till the
last drop of my blood'.[5] This 'Holy Union' was a genuine outburst of
popular religious feeling which, if supported by many nobles and bourgeois, was strongest in the towns and among the mob. They demanded
the revocation of all concessions made to the heretics.

A leader was waiting. At twenty-five Henri, Duc de Guise, was accomplished, ambitious and unscrupulous, but though he had seen plenty of
fighting and was *balafré* like his father he lacked the brutal drive of that
harsh, proud warrior. Duc Henri, very much a ladies' man, was an erratic
politician and mediocre in the field. Even so he was formidable enough,
being both bloodthirsty and treacherous, and with his gracious manner
and tall, handsome presence, admirably equipped to be a popular idol.
Papist France began to rally to him, grandees as well as rabble.

The Crown was in no position to curb this new challenge. Now
that Henri of Navarre and Politique lords like Damville had left Paris,
apart from the universally mistrusted Monsieur only the Guise faction
remained at court and there was no other power grouping with which
the King could oppose it. Admittedly Henri III had his own party,
more effective than might be expected; if his *mignons* were effeminate
they were nonetheless brave and pugnacious, frequently able, and above
all, as young men of obscure family who owed everything to him, they
were loyal—Henri's special bodyguard of such favourites, called the
Quarante-Cinq, was notorious for blind and bloody obedience. But an
almost bankrupt King, too frivolous for sustained effort, could hardly

hope to resist a combination of the Guises and popular fanaticism. Suddenly Henri III saw that were he to wrest the League's leadership from Guise he would have a King's party with which he might bring France to heel; moderation had failed the Valois, now they would try extremism. The States General was summoned at Blois to provide a convenient rostrum for the King to proclaim himself the Catholic Joshua. He hoped that the estates, delighted by his conversion, would hail him as head of the League and vote subsidies for a final war. The plan was feasible, for Henri III could look every inch a King, with an air of real if disdainful majesty, and was also an impressive orator. But he had not reckoned with the Politiques. Jean Bodin, *avocat de Laon*,[6] a firm believer in peace, persuaded his fellow bourgeois to refuse the subsidies. The King revoked his concessions to the Religion on 1 January 1577 but without money he could do nothing. More hopeless and disordered than ever, France embarked upon its Sixth War of Religion.

As Governor of Guyenne Henri of Navarre ruled all Gascony. The south-west, ethnically Gallo-Roman and Basque instead of Frankish, still thought of itself almost as a separate nation, distinct from the French of the north, and spoke its own Gascon tongue, while the regional temperament was noted for exuberance and pugnacity expressed in its taste for bullfighting and bragging. Henri was a typical Gascon, of the same mould as Dumas' d'Artagnan and Rostand's Cyrano de Bergerac, and his countrymen instinctively understood and loved him. If Bordeaux, the greatest city of Guyenne, would not open its gates for fear he might outlaw Catholicism, when he arrived at Pau in the autumn of 1576 he was received with wild enthusiasm. Ostensibly he had come to see his sister Catherine who welcomed him with joyous balls and *divertissements;* a very young but very serious M. de Rosny—the future Sully—was made to dance, most unwillingly, in a ballet which lasted for eight days. Henri's real motive in visiting Béarn was to pursue his new mistress, '*la jeune Tignonville*', daughter of Jeanne d'Albret's maître d'hôtel. D'Aubigné, his First Gentleman of the Bedchamber, declined to intercede with her despite his master's frantic appeals and the coldness which ensued was not assuaged by this unfeeling young woman's continued refusals to grace the royal bed. But Henri was soon on the move again, and he quickly came to know Gascony from one end to the other, not just his own southern mountains but the wild hills of the Dordogne and the marshy wastes of the Landes, riding through innumerable little towns with yellow walls and red roofs. Though he never stayed long in one place, Nérac in Armagnac was his favourite residence.

The Béarnais' position was not altogether enviable as he was short of both money and men while among his officers the Huguenots squabbled continually with the Catholics. Naturally the latter felt insecure in the Religion's territory, so Henri reassured them by saying that he owed them the most, for prejudicing their own faith. Indeed he delayed his reconciliation with the Reform as long as possible; d'Aubigné observed grimly that for three months after his escape his court was without religion and that only two of its gentlemen took the Communion. Now that the crisis of his captivity had passed Henri's Politique sentiments reasserted themselves; in early 1577 he wrote to a friend that 'those who genuinely follow their conscience are of my religion—as for me, my religion is that of everyone who is brave and true.' Protestant zealots could hardly be expected to relish such opinions: '*Henri de Navarre, attaché par raison à la paix, n'était le maître ni de son parti ni de son entourage, ni même de ses sentiments.*'[7]

The year 1577 was occupied by the Sixth War of Religion, in which the Huguenots were on the defensive; the Queen Mother's relentless diplomacy had succeeded in detaching Monsieur, Damville and many of the Malcontent allies. Henri fought countless little campaigns and skirmishes with growing skill and panache. When the town of Eauze in Armagnac turned against him Henri rode in with a small troop disguised as a hunting party. The garrison dropped the portcullis, trapping him inside with only fifteen men, and leaving the main body outside. Cries of 'Kill! Kill!' rang out as fifty mutineers rushed to attack them, someone shouting, 'Fire at the scarlet jacket and white plume—it's the King of Navarre.' Henri kept his head, saying, 'Now my friends, my comrades, show your courage and your steadiness—our safety depends on them.' He ordered his men to close with the enemy before firing as their pistols had too short a range. This tactic was successful but the little band was soon besieged in a gate tower by two hundred angry troops and townsmen. Fortunately Henri's followers outside managed to force the gate and the town was quickly taken. He was merciful, hanging only four prisoners who had deliberately shot at him.

Just how bestial this warfare could be is evident from Sully's account of some soldiers who were executed for 'a most villainous debauch' in which they had raped six local girls, filled them up with gunpowder and set light to it.[8] The peasants suffered terribly; some begged the Duc de Montpensier for peace on their knees. Languedoc suffered the worst, from bands of Huguenot and Papist partisans who preyed on travellers, raided villages and plundered châteaux, torturing and killing. Nor was Gascony immune from such scourges.

The royal troops had some successes, mainly in Languedoc under Monsieur, but outright victory was an impossibility. The Crown's finances were collapsing despite such desperate expedients as a prodigal sale of offices and titles, defaulting on loans and devaluing the currency, so that it could no more afford a long war than the Religion. In 1582 Francis Bacon wrote that the French King was 'very poor through exacting inordinately by all devices of his subjects.... The division in his country for matters of religion and state, through miscontentment of the nobility to see strangers advanced to the greatest charges of the realm, the offices of justice sold, the treasury wasted, the people polled, the country destroyed, hath bred great trouble and like to see more'.[9] Henri III was hardly the man to effect a cure.

When, in February 1577, that monarch received news that the Swedish and Danish Kings, together with the Queen of England and the Protestant Princes of Germany, had allied against him with the Huguenots, His Most Christian Majesty was diverting himself at balls and tournaments *en femme*, his doublet thrown open to reveal the Royal throat on which lay a pearl necklace. Clothes and jewellery were more important than any matter of state. When the only woman he ever really loved, the young Princesse de Condé, had died in 1574 he had appeared in black embroidered with white skulls instead of in the violet which French Kings traditionally wore for mourning. To hide his baldness his head was invariably covered by a little velvet cap with an aigrette and he was festooned with rings and bangles. His *mignons* could be distinguished by similar hats, on top of curled and frizzed ringlets, and by enormous ruffs which made their heads look like that of 'St John the Baptist in a charger'. The King's passion for monkeys and parrots was supplemented by one for poodles, a menagerie accompanying him everywhere so that a Royal progress had the appearance of a travelling circus while pious frenzies of remorse, expressed in spectacular flagellant processions, made his antics seem all the more bizarre. Indeed this 'androgyne passing from Sodom to Gomorrah' was by now wholly given up to '*les délices de la France*', yielding to every frivolous impulse.

Henri III only kept his throne because of his mother who was always ready to take the reins; the régime of the last Valois has been described as a diarchy with occasional interludes of monarchy. Peace came for a time in September 1577, when all Leagues, whether Protestant or Catholic, were proscribed. But war could easily flare up again, so in the autumn of 1578 the Queen Mother went on a pacificatory progress through the south-west, bringing inducements for her son-in-law in the forms of Mme de Sauve, 'his Circe',[10] Mlle d'Ayelle, a Cypriot refugee who had also been his mistress, and Queen Marguerite herself. Henri had quite enough amusing feminine company but wanted his wife back if only for the sake of prestige. Marguerite took pains to look her best; on one occasion, says Brantôme, people would have thought her to be a 'goddess from heaven rather than a queen on earth'.[11] She was reunited to her unappreciative spouse in October 1578. Next month the two courts joined in gay festivities at Auch where, wrote Sully, making a ponderous *jeu de mots*, one heard no more '*d'armes mais seulement de Dames*'.[12] The Queen Mother was busy sowing 'divisions and dissensions' and one of her ladies brought off a spectacular coup; old M. d'Ussac, the governor of La Réole and a battle scarred pillar of the Religion, fell violently in love with her, turned Papist and handed his town over to Catherine. The news was brought to Henri in the middle of a ball at which the Queen

Mother was also present. Betraying no emotion he gave orders for his men to assemble within the hour and that same night captured the Catholic town of Fleurance. Catherine laughed when she was told—she always respected a really able opponent.

The negotiations and the entertainments continued. However, nothing would persuade the ladies of either court to go up into the mountains when a bear hunt was arranged. 'There were two bears which disembowelled some fair sized horses, others which slew ten Swiss pikemen and ten musketeers, and one—the biggest ever seen—which, riddled by several volleys and with half a dozen broken pikes and halberds sticking in it, grasped seven or eight men it caught on a high peak and threw itself down to the ground where they were all crushed and broken in pieces.' The European bear, which still survives in the Pyrenees today, is hardly so formidable and one may suspect that the solemn young M. de Rosny, to whom we owe this horrific account, had stayed behind with the ladies and was victim of Henri's Gascon wit.[13]

The Peace of Nérac, which it was hoped would prevent further hostilities, was signed in February 1579 and enabled the King and Queen of Navarre to organize their life on a more permanent basis. After a brief, triumphant visit to Pau they returned to Nérac where the Court remained for several years. Though small it was sufficiently gay and splendid to inspire the setting of *Love's Labour Lost*[14]—'a park with a palace in it'. One one side of a pleasant river was the mediaeval *château fort* with its courtyard and flanking towers; Jeanne d'Albret had added a more graceful wing built with stone from plundered monasteries. Tapestries, plate and rich furnishings were brought from Pau including, perhaps, those black taffeta sheets between which *la reine Margot* loved to disport herself.[15] There was a charming formal garden with rows of laurels and cypress trees and a park with a *Pavillon d'Amour* and long wooded alleys ran beside the river where the Queen would stroll with her ladies while their lords played at tennis and quoits. In the evenings there were balls and Italian 'enterludes and commedies'. Indeed Nérac was *'florissante en brave Noblesse, en Dames excellentes'* though most of them had to live in somewhat cramped quarters across the river, in the sleepy little town's stone houses. Long afterwards Marguerite wrote that, at Nérac, 'our Court was so fine we did not envy that of France.'

According to Agrippa d'Aubigné 'ease hatched vice as heat does serpents'[16] and the entire court gave itself up to the pleasures of love. The Queen, who told her husband that 'a cavalier without a mistress is without a soul',[17] took the Vicomte de Turenne for her lover, while even young M. de Rosny acquired a mistress and Agrippa himself was hopelessly in love with the girl he later married. But no one outdid Henri's too abundant virility; he resembled the Duke of Mantua in *Rigoletto*. Mlle d'Ayelle was succeeded by the delicate Mlle de Rebours who in turn gave place. Legends tell of one girl who, because of Henri's desertion, starved herself and her baby to death, of another who threw herself out of a window from shame, and of Fleurette, a baker's daughter, who drowned herself in the river for similar reasons, while there seems to be some truth in the story of the charcoal-burner's wife whose husband was ennobled when the Béarnais became King.[18] There was also Xainte, one of the Queen's women of the bedchamber.

However, Henri's chief passion at this period was Françoise de Montmorency-Fosseuse, *'jeune fille de quatorze ans'*,[19] for whom Henri had abandoned Rebours when the latter fell ill at Pau in 1579. Scandalized biographers have suggested she was older but there is no reason to doubt d'Aubigné. The Béarnais, a patriarch of twenty-five, is known to have called her 'my daughter' and plied her with marzipan and other childish sweets; probably Fosseuse was well developed for her age as Henri was no pervert. It was certainly a strange court for the Puritan champion.

News of the goings-on at Nérac caused considerable amusement in Paris and some of Henri III's jokes so infuriated Marguerite that, through the still biddable Fosseuse *'craintive pour son age'*[20] and abetted by Xainte, *'cette femme artificieuse'* is supposed to have incensed her husband against his brother-in-law; 'the peace and war of France lay between their arms'.[21] Such, claims Agrippa, was the origin of 'the Lovers' War' which only concerned a small section of the Huguenots. However, 'the only proper and essentiall forme of our nobility in France is military vocation'[22] and it is far more likely that the soldier gentlemen of Gascony, greedy for profitable employment, persuaded Henri who had himself developed a taste for war to re-open hostilities in the spring of 1580.

In June Henri decided to capture the wealthy town of Cahors which was staunchly anti-Huguenot. He attacked at midnight; the heat was oppressive, there was thunder but no rain. However, though he managed to storm his way in, the garrison and armed townsmen, twelve hundred all told, took to the rooftops from where they hurled down stones, wooden beams and tiles. Henri and his troops, slightly more in number and mostly musketeers, fought from street to street. The battle lasted for five days and nights, the combatants snatching mouthfuls of food and drink whenever they could and sleeping on their feet, leaning against the shop shutters. Always in front, Henri's armour was scratched and dented by bullets and by sword and pike thrusts and he himself broke two halberds, but despite the pleas of his officers he refused to retreat, saying he would enjoy dying with his men better than giving way. At last reinforcements arrived and the town surrendered, yielding rich plunder. The conqueror wrote cheerfully to a friend's wife that he was *'tout sang et poudre'*.[23] Marguerite commented that her husband had 'shown his judgement and valour, not like a Prince of high rank but like a shrewd and daring Captain'.[24] The affair gained him a well deserved reputation of being a bonny fighter. Though he had to go over to the defensive the *status quo* was restored in November by the Peace of Fleix. As d'Aubigné wrote, this war had been no more than *'un feu de paille'*.[25]

Brutish anarchy was now France's habitual condition in this time of 'blood and ruin'. Society had simply collapsed. Squires turned robber barons preyed on their tenantry; peasants, fighting by communes, attacked each other in their *jacqueries* while the raiders who sacked abbeys or conventicles were no less merciless to co-religionists. Taxes were not collected or else levied twice over at the point of the sword. Nor were those enclaves ruled by *appanagistes* immune; despite their private armies even such great lords as the King of Navarre were attacked. Henri III's frivolity and the excesses of a catamite court were bad enough but it was *'le malaise économique qui a rendu les peuples sensibles aux vices de Henri III'*;[26]

the Crown was bankrupt, morally and financially. However, though Huguenots were on the defensive—even at La Rochelle rich bourgeois were for peace when the mob was for war—Catholics could only find energy for a concerted onslaught if Holy Church was in real danger.

Freedom and power affected Henri to an extent which cannot be exaggerated. The Béarnais, maturing, experienced an extraordinary access of energy. He acquired his fabled air of virility, and grew his famous fan-shaped beard. Yet after setting what little of his domains he really controlled in order, there was not enough to do, and, understandably, he had recourse to the same outlets he had employed when a captive; hunting and women. His affections were usually centred on one particular mistress. After several years little Fosseuse grew conceited and even hoped to displace Marguerite as Queen of Navarre. The latter's failure to give Henri an heir made the wretched slut lose all sense of reality on finding herself with child in 1581 and she became unpleasantly arrogant; it was hardly tactful of Henri to ask his wife to nurse Fosseuse during the delivery and Marguerite was thankful when her would-be rival bore a blind girl who lived only a few hours.[27] After this Fosseuse began to lose her hold and next year Henri was to meet one of the most famous of his concubines.

His marriage had so far survived the absence of physical ties and when in the summer of 1580 he had been dangerously ill with a high fever Marguerite had nursed him devotedly, day and night, not even changing her clothes. However, the business of Fosseuse's delivery finally dissipated any remnants of affection and the Queen tired of Nérac, pined for the splendours of a Valois court. In 1583 she deserted Gascony for Paris in pursuit of her latest lover. Oddly enough she took Fosseuse, who had now been discarded by Henri, with her as a companion.

Henri III had always disliked his sister, if only because of her strange affection for Monsieur, and was far from pleased by her return. A few months after, in early August, when, in the absence of the Queen, Marguerite was presiding over a ball he fell into one of his hysterical rages and publicly upbraided her, screaming that she was an adulteress and ordering her to leave court at once; on the way to her place of banishment the guards treated her with studied discourtesy by the King's explicit instructions. It was the worst humiliation of Marguerite's sad and misspent life.

Her husband was infuriated when he heard the story, not for the injury done to Marguerite as his wife but for the insult to her as Queen of Navarre. Henri III wrote explanatory and apologetic letters to his cousin and for months messengers travelled to and fro between the two courts; the King had no wish to antagonize Henri, who like a wily Gascon exploited the situation with relish to obtain control of various royal strongholds in Guyenne, laughing that in one letter he had been called cuckold, in another the son of a whore. With diabolical irony, he sent d'Aubigné to defend Marguerite's honour; when Henri III shouted that he would take a stick to his master for trying to play the Grand Seigneur, the pugnacious poet replied with such insolence that the enraged Valois clutched his dagger. Eventually Marguerite was allowed to return to Gascony in 1584, but her reputation was now so bad that Henri had small use for her and in 1585 she installed herself in her dowry town of Agen which she tried to rule as an independent fief. She claimed that her husband's new mistress had been plotting to murder her.

Henri, surfeited with youthful femininity and easy women, was ready for something more mature and stable. In January 1583 he met the twenty-six-year old Diane de Gramont, Comtesse de Guiche, known to history as 'la grande Corisande' after the heroine in Amadis of Gaul. Her husband, a formidable Papist warrior to whom she had been married at thirteen, had been killed in battle some years before. It is clear that this young widow, a brunette with black eyes, a pink complexion and a high forehead, had learnt how to manage men. During a relationship which would last for the remainder of the decade Corisande was to exercise remarkable power over Henri, due as much to her intelligence as to her beauty. Hitherto his relations with his mistresses had been purely physical but now, for the first and perhaps the only time, he enjoyed complete companionship with a woman, a companionship which was no less intellectual and spiritual than it was physical. That she was a devout Catholic was no barrier though he could sometimes say harsh things about her co-religionists, claiming on one occasion that all poisoners were Papists; indeed Corisande's influence may well have made possible his ultimate conversion to Catholicism.

Henri's delightful letters with their natural grace and infectious enthusiasm, redolent of 'country warmth and Gascon poetry'[28] give him some title to be considered as a writer in his own right. Indeed, even Proust admired his prose.[29] Henri wrote often to Corisande, on every conceivable subject. Thus, in June 1586:

> This place is more to your taste than any I've ever seen. For that reason alone I'm trying to obtain possession of it. It is an island wholly surrounded by marshes and trees in which every hundred paces there are canals so that one can pass through the woods by boat. The water is clear and seldom still, the canals wide and the boats large. In this wild place there are a thousand gardens which one can only reach by boat…. It [the river Sèvre] is a canal, not a river. Up it go great ships as far as Niort which is twelve leagues away. There are all kinds of birds which sing and every kind of seabird. I'm sending you some of their feathers. As for fish, they are extraordinary both for size and price; a large carp costs three sous, a pike five.[30]

He sent her other presents besides feathers: 'I have captured two little wild boars and two doe fawns. Command me if you want them.'[31] He wanted to share every experience. Corisande must have read with somewhat mixed feelings of his sorrow in November 1588 at the death of Gédéon, his son by Esther Imbert: 'I am deeply upset at losing my little fellow who died yesterday. He was just beginning to talk. Think what it would have been like had he been legitimate!'[32] Physical faithfulness was an impossibility for Henri even if he might assure Corisande 'believe me, my fidelity is pure and stainless—there was never its like'[33] or 'my heart, do you still remember your Petiot (her pet name for him)? Certes, his fidelity is a miracle'.[34] Nonetheless his letters always ended on a note of passion: 'loving nothing in the world so much as you … my soul, I kiss a million times those beautiful eyes which all my life I shall hold dearer than anything else in the world …';[35] 'Until the grave, to which I am perhaps nearer than I know, I will live as your faithful slave. Goodnight, my soul';[36] 'Your slave adores you violently. My heart, I kiss your hands a million times'.[37] In the end he would want to marry her.

Among her friends was the Sieur de Montaigne who dedicated 'Nine and twentie sonnets of Steven de la Boetie, to the Lady of Grammont, Countesse of Guissen', telling her that 'I have deemed this present fit for your Ladiship, forsomuch as there are few Ladies in France, that either can better judge of Poesie, or fitter apply the use of it, than your worthy selfe: and since in these her drooping daies, none can give it more life, or vigorous spirit, than you, by those rich and high-tuned accords, wherewith amongst a million of other rare beauties, nature hath richly graced you'.[38] He also counselled 'this glorious Corisanda of Andoins' on how to help Henri: 'I had advised her not to engage the interest and fortune of this prince in her passions but, since she had so much power over him, to look more to his advantage than to her personal inclinations.'[39] The essayist was a keen supporter of Henri who returned his respect and almost certainly read his works. In 1577 Montaigne was made a Gentleman of the King of Navarre's Bedchamber and in 1580 Henri used his influence, successfully, to procure his fellow Gascon's election as Mayor of Bordeaux. Henri visited Montaigne in his château at least twice and met him on many other occasions.[40] The legend of the Béarnais' lack of religious faith rests largely upon this shrewd, perhaps too shrewd, observer's impressions of Henri and Guise:

> That religion, which is alleged by both, is used speciously as a pretext by those who follow them; for the rest, neither one regards it. For Navarre, if he did not fear to be deserted by his followers, would be ready to return of his own accord to the religion of his forefathers; and Guise, if there were no danger, would not be averse to the Augsburg Confession [i.e. Lutheranism], of which he had once had a certain taste under his paternal uncle Charles,

the cardinal. These were the feelings that he had observed in them both when he was conferring between them.[41]

Even so, for both Henri and Corisande it was something of an honour to be claimed as a kindred spirit by the keenest mind in France.

The First Gentleman of the Bedchamber ascribed Henri's passion for an idolatress to witchcraft. Though Agrippa d'Aubigné was now happily married he remained incapable of half-measures and publicly stated his considered opinion that this new mistress was a witch, even asking the court doctor for philtres to cure Henri of her spells. He jeered at her attending Mass accompanied by only 'an errand boy, a fool, a blacka-moor, a lackey, a monkey and a spaniel'.[42] It is hardly surprising that Mme de Guiche soon conceived a deadly loathing for her waspish foe, who having left court learnt that she had made *son Amoureux* promise to have his First Gentleman put to death. Returning by a secret staircase he caught them *tête-à-tête* and rebuked Henri for his ingratitude, after which he was forgiven. Even Agrippa's admirers have to admit that he must have been an infuriating servant.

Since 1578 Monsieur had been pursuing the hand of Elizabeth of England and also a throne in the Low Countries where William the Silent had invited him to become Duke of Brabant. Henri had always been sceptical about his unattractive cousin's prospects. In 1583 rioting French troops were driven out of Antwerp by angry burghers, a débâcle which finally ruined the 'thousand agreeable hopes' of Monsieur who soon had to return to France *'furieux, mélancolique et malade'*.[43] Within a few months he had fallen ill of the same terrible consumption as his brother Charles IX, blood streaming through every pore in his body as though all his veins had burst. The Valois Catiline died in agony on 10 June 1584. Some believed that a lady with whom he had recently slept had murdered him with a poisoned nosegay which she made him smell,[44] but even Agrippa d'Aubigné subscribed to the generally accepted view that Monsieur died of sorrow at the failure of all his great hopes.[45] Shortly afterwards William the Silent was assassinated. Henri of Navarre had become both heir to the Crown of France and 'the most prominent champion of Protestantism on the Continent'.

By the mid-1580s Henri was fully mature, a stocky, jaunty little man with a black beard and a tanned face, in stained, shabby clothes who looked more like a common cavalry captain than a great prince. He joked unceasingly in his broad Gascon accent—he used to say he would have been hanged as a thief had he not been born a King[46]— and swore horribly, his mildest oath being the fabled *Ventre Saint-Gris* ('Grey Friar's Belly'). He relied on familiar charm rather than majesty and gave orders as one asking favours rather than as a sovereign who commanded: 'My old ruffian. Put wings on your best horse; I've already told Montespan to founder his. Why? You will learn from me at Nérac so run, hasten, fly—it's your master's command and your friend's plea.'[47] Vows of affection, compliments and promises overwhelmed his follow-ers who found it hard to refuse anything to this delightful companion who had such infectious zest and gaiety. Yet his good comradeship and amiability were deceptive for, like his grandson Charles II, Henri of Navarre was without either gratitude or bitterness to friend or mistress; he could forget a service no less easily than a grudge. A true Gascon, if he flattered he was niggardly in his praise though prone to brag himself. Yet even his critics agreed 'that no one ever saw a prince more human or who loved his people more'. His faults may all be ascribed to an over-riding sense of kingship. As Bacon puts it: 'The referring of all to a man's self is more tolerable in a sovereign prince because themselves are not only themselves, but their good and evil is at the peril of the public fortune.'[48]

Ebullient and mercurial, crying as easily as he laughed, his forehead, over the big hooked nose and sparkling eyes with their charming smile, was deeply lined and the daunting prospect of the road he must follow could plunge him into desperate sadness. Sometimes he wrote to Corisande in this mood: 'until the tomb which is nearer than perhaps I realize';[49] 'all the Gehennas where a spirit can go are busy with mine';[50] or 'Those who trust in God and serve Him will never be confounded.'[51] While he campaigned with ferocious energy, going for twenty-four hours without

sleep or sleeping on the ground for a fortnight at a stretch, his health
was surprisingly poor; highly strung, he was often prostrated by fever,
catarrh, gravel, stomach pains, gout—the penalty of an exclusively meat
diet—or sheer nervous exhaustion. Cynical despite his humanity, secre-
tive despite his candour, and sceptical despite his enthusiasm, all these
vices and virtues were employed in the service of a freshly discovered
and consuming passion, France. He had found his destiny.

He was sure of the succession; though the last Valois still prayed
that the long-suffering Queen Louise might yet give him an heir, popular
opinion discountenanced any such likelihood in view of an illness the
King was supposed to have contracted during that abandoned sojourn
in Venice.[52] Understandably the reaction was violent, both at home and
abroad. The Holy League which had been flagging derived new vigour
from this threat of a heretic sovereign, while Philip II saw the Low
Countries and the entire Counter-Reformation in jeopardy. The Duc de
Guise, who had never ceased to cherish a vast ambition in secret realized that here was his great opportunity and his propagandists feverishly
circulated the tale, quite without foundation, of his descent in the direct
male line from Charlemagne; were it true his right to the French throne
was better than that of Henri III himself. Nonetheless Guise, wholly in
the pay of Spain, had sufficient subtlety to propose as interim candidate
Henri's uncle, Cardinal Charles de Bourbon, who was weak, stupid and
prematurely aged. Yet despite his extraordinary faults Henri III loved
his country, venerated his dynasty and genuinely sought peace. Shortly
before Monsieur's death he begged his cousin to be reconciled to Rome
and to come to Paris where he would be recognised as heir presumptive.
Henri of Navarre declined. Had he accepted he would have alienated
both Huguenots and Politiques and probably failed to gain the League's
support.

The Papist reaction gained furious momentum. Throughout Catholic
France the League sprang up again to begin a reign of savage terror and
in December 1584 at the Treaty of Joinville with Philip II became far
more of a state within a state than ever the Religion had been; Guise
and the Leaguers swore that the vain old Cardinal de Bourbon should

be heir to the throne of France while Philip gave them money to hire troops. The crusade escalated, overwhelming Henri III. In July 1585, by the Treaty of Nemours the League obtained his word that the entire north-east of France was to remain in Guise hands while all Huguenots must go to Mass or leave the Kingdom within six months. Henri of Navarre declared that the side of his moustache which he twirled turned white when he heard the news. In the autumn of the same year the Pope debarred him from the succession by a special edict which Henri in his public reply dismissed as 'an idiotic thunderbolt' (*fulmen brutum*). Thus began 'the War of the Three Henries'.

A seventeenth-century panegyrist admits that until the League's resurrection his hero had been '*endormi en voluptez*', meaning dalliance with Corisande. But Henri of Navarre woke with a vengeance. Before war broke out he had challenged Guise to a trial by battle in which the two of them were to settle France's future by personal combat. This bloodthirsty solution did not appeal to Duc Henri. It must be admitted that scanty resources rather than archaic romanticism prompted Henri of Navarre to make his challenge, for he was crippled by lack of troops. He spent the winter of 1585–86 cutting enemy supply lines, mopping up their stragglers and relieving his own beleaguered garrisons.

In January 1586 he issued a moving appeal in which he took his stand upon the fundamental laws of the Kingdom. 'We believe in one God, we recognize one Jesus Christ, we accept the same Gospel,' he told the clergy, 'I believe that the war you prosecute so keenly is unworthy of Christians, unworthy between Christians, above all of those who claim to be teachers of the Gospel. If war pleases you so much, if a battle pleases you more than a disputation, a bloodthirsty plot more than a Council, I wash my hands. The blood which flows will be upon your heads.' Likewise the nobility were told that 'the blood would be on those responsible for these miseries'.[53]

His position became desperate when three Catholic armies marched into Gascony; some courtiers advised him to seek refuge in England. However, the storm passed and the same year his mother-in-law made another of her peace-making progresses, to begin again '*la batterie assiduelle de cette puissante femme*'.[54] Henri met her in Cognac where, among other things, it was agreed that he might divorce Marguerite, now an enthusiastic Leaguer. Desperately Catherine begged him to turn Catholic but 'the most crafty and cunning prince in the world' refused, repeating that he and he alone was heir to France, consciously identifying himself with peace and the old laws. Many Catholics, sick of war and bloodshed, were beginning to listen to him, among them the Maréchal de Montmorency, 'King of Languedoc'. In 1587 he went over to the offensive, invading Poitou where town after town succumbed; his aim was to join forces with a German Protestant army advancing from the north as he had less than two thousand horse and four thousand foot.

Henri III intervened, sending half the royal army to catch Henri of Navarre and destroy him. The King hoped that the Germans would defeat Guise who had gone to meet them; with the elimination of both his cousin and Duc Henri he would have little to fear. He appointed a *mignon* as commander, Anne, Duc de Joyeuse, not without ability but over-confident. Joyeuse outnumbered the Huguenots and his two thousand five hundred cavalry and five thousand infantry were better armed. The Béarnais retreated until on 27 October 1587 at Coutras, a town on the borders of Périgord, he was forced to give battle. The river Dronne cut off any hope of retreat.

The Catholics seemed 'as though clad in gold'[55] with showy, damascened weapons, gilt armour, nodding plumes, richly embroidered sashes and the velvet tunics in which each magnate dressed his followers. The Huguenots made a drab contrast in their buff jerkins and plain steel; as usual Henri wore a white cockade so his men could recognize him. As he drew his troops up to receive the enemy onslaught he shouted to his cousins, Condé and the Comte de Soissons, 'I have only one thing to say to you which is that you are of Bourbon blood and, *Vive Dieu*, I will show you who is your senior.' Condé shouted back, 'And we will show you that there is a good younger branch.'[56] Like Cromwell's Roundheads the Religion and its champion fell to prayer, singing their Battle Psalm—verses 24 and 25 of Psalm 118: 'This is the day which the Lord hath made: we will rejoice and be glad in it. Help me now, O Lord: O Lord send us now your prosperity.' Joyeuse, who was 'a Papist of the fiercer and more violent sort', thought that these *razats* were making ready to die, but an older campaigner knew better.

At first Joyeuse's headlong frontal attack looked as though it would carry all before it. Turenne's men broke and ran; the entire Huguenot army began to falter. Then, at point blank range, the arquebusiers Henri had mixed with his cavalry together with his artillery—three cannon but perfectly sited and loaded with grape and chain shot—opened up crimson swathes in the enemy ranks which were only two deep. Men and horses fell by the dozen at each fusillade, while three squadrons, six deep, led by Condé, Soissons and Henri himself, after smashing the enemy formation all along the line, charged again and again. Little quarter was given, though the exultant Henri, fighting recklessly as always at the head of his troops, his sword red with blood, took several prisoners; disarming one of these he shouted, 'Yield ye, Philistine,' like a true Protestant David. Five thousand Catholics died, including Joyeuse who was shot as he surrendered, and five hundred were captured. In little more than an hour Henri of Navarre had annihilated the royal army, losing only forty men himself. Yet his joy was not unmixed with sadness. Four days before he had written, 'it angers me much that blood should flow and that only I can staunch it, though all know I am innocent of it'.[57] The League had made the painful discovery that its opponents were led by a prince who was not only a wily politician but also a most formidable general. So had the Politiques.

To the bewilderment, and afterwards the amusement, of all France Henri instead of advancing '*donna toutes ces paroles au vent et sa victoire à l'amour*'[58] and galloped off to present Corisande with the standards captured at Coutras. After a triumphant idyll he rejoined his anxious followers. Strolling with Turenne and d'Aubigné he confided 'the anguish and perplexity in which he found himself over his intention of marrying the Comtesse de Guiche to whom he had already given a firm promise of marriage; he asked us to spend all night on the advice for which he was going to ask next day on this thorny problem'. The following morning

Agrippa, always ready to give good advice however unwelcome, lectured his master on the theme *aut Caesar aut nihil*.[59] 'In a word Sire if in these present circumstances you marry your mistress you will bar for ever the road that could one day lead to the throne of the French monarchy.' Henri agreed not to see Corisande again for at least two years and stuck to his resolve with surprising firmness though he continued to write to her.

Condé died on 5 March 1588. He was popularly supposed to have been poisoned at his wife's instigation, his steward being convicted of the crime and pulled to pieces by four horses. Henri of Navarre was deeply upset, giving loud cries of grief, weeping, bemoaning 'a lost right arm' and reciting the Psalm 'God is my refuge and my strength, in Him will I trust'. Yet his cousin, besides being a poor general had, politically, never been wholly reliable, so that if anything his death strengthened the position of Henri of Navarre, both as leader of the Huguenot party and as heir to the throne; now there was no alternative to the Béarnais.

'For whosoever esteemeth too much of amorous affection, quitteth both riches and wisdom.' Yet if many of Henri of Navarre's friends thought him irresponsible the next move after Coutras was not his but Henri III's. Instead of being beaten as planned, the Duc de Guise had twice defeated the Germans so that the King who had lost much of his own army was at the League's mercy. Paris was now controlled by *Les Seizes*, a junta of fanatic Catholic bourgeois which anticipated the Revolution's Committee of Public Safety and which zealously obeyed Guise. For Henri also events had reached a climax. In March 1588 he wrote to Corisande, 'Soon I will either be mad or a very clever man. This year will be my touchstone....'[60]

Henri III had become even more eccentric; he had developed a passion for cups-and-balls and Rosny once met him 'with a basket hanging from his neck by a ribbon, rather like an itinerant cheesemonger, in which were two or three puppies no bigger than one's fist'.[61] The Paris mob '*enyvrez d'estime pour luy*' thought that their idolized Guise, handsome and soldierly, looked far more of a King than this painted, mincing sodomite. When Duc Henri entered Paris on 9 May 1588 Henri III knew that both his throne and his life were in danger. He dared not trust

Guise while any alliance with Henri of Navarre would set the League against him in murderous earnest. Having ordered Guise not to come to Paris the King was pale with anger when he had to receive 'the Scarred One' who, during a tumultuous entry, had been acclaimed by the mob with cries of 'Hosanna to the Son of David' and 'Long live the pillar of the Church'. The Hôtel de Guise now became more important than the Louvre. At the Sorbonne professors were arguing that 'it is lawful to remove government from princes who are unfitted to rule just as one takes away the stewardship of any other untrustworthy guardian'. Every day Paris grew tenser as clerical demagogues ranted with waxing frenzy against their sovereign and an excited rabble hunted down heretics. Finally, three days later on 12 May, the King's ill-executed attempt to seize the city's strongpoints failed when the trained bands deserted and the mob crying '*Vive Guise*' and led by the Comte de Brissac set up barricades and humiliated the royal troops. Guise quelled the uproar and then demanded concessions which would have left Henri III a mere figurehead; whereupon the despairing Valois fled from his capital. Duc Henri, with his wolfish smile, was now '*le beau Roy de Paris*'.

Eventually His Most Christian Majesty was to decide that there was no remedy other than assassination. Meanwhile, in his refuge at Blois, he plumbed the depths of humiliation appointing this 'Carolingian' pretender Lieutenant-General of the Kingdom and summoning the Estates General which, being an exclusively Leaguer assembly, was promised that the King would not rest until he had extirpated heresy and that no Protestant would ever succeed to his throne. Even so, haughty words about overmighty subjects caused an outcry that Guise should be made Constable of France and Henri III immured in a monastery like the last Merovingian; one enthusiastic duchess hung a pair of golden scissors at her waist so that she could tonsure him.[62] Despite repeated warnings Guise and his brother, the Cardinal de Guise, stayed at Blois; even for them Paris had become dangerously demagogic, and they could not believe that the King would dare to commit murder.

They were sadly mistaken. The Valois and his *mignons* plotted coldly and implacably, deriding suggestions that the arch-enemy be merely seized and imprisoned; 'one does not net wild boar'. The King's special bodyguard, the *Quarante-Cinq*, were adventurers with few qualms about killing. Sinister rumours began to circulate and secret warnings were sent to Guise who dismissed them with his usual arrogance. The plotters decided on the days just before Christmas and, true to his Italian tastes, Henri III chose the knife rather than the pistol. On Friday, 23 December 1588, the King was late for his Council which had been called for seven o'clock that morning. Then the waiting Duc Henri, suddenly grown nervous in these cold hours before dawn, was summoned to the royal bedchamber where in the guttering candlelight he was struck down by ten of the Forty-Five, staggering the entire length of the great room, pouring blood and dragging his murderers with him, before falling at the foot of the King's empty bed. Two hours previously Henri III had personally presented each assassin with a dagger after which he had piously ordered Mass to be said for their intentions, to make certain of success. *'Mon Dieu, qu'il est grand—il paroist encor plus grand mort que vivant,'*[63] said the King, gazing on the Duke's mangled corpse. Next day, in an attic, the Cardinal de Guise fell beneath the halberds of the royal guard. The two bodies were burnt and their ashes scattered in the wind.

Henri III's judgement had been poisoned by his thirst for revenge. Now that its champion was dead he expected the League to collapse— *'morte la bête, mort le venin'*—but instead it gained strength from the 'martyrdom', reacting with terrible violence. From Christmas Day onwards vast processions marched through Paris at night to quench hissing torches in tubs of water as they cried, 'So may God quench the Valois' race' while preachers denounced 'M. de Valois' as another Herod, 'a perjurer, an assassin, a murderer, a perpetrator of sacrilege, a spreader of heresy, a simoniac, a magician, an infidel and a man accursed'. The Guises were mourned as saints whom tearful congregations swore to avenge; it seemed as though the Papacy had blessed the League's holy cause when it excommunicated Henri III for murdering a Cardinal. The *Seize* ruled Paris more firmly than ever, repudiating the King and sending for Guise's brother the Duc de Mayenne. It was rumoured that Catherine de Medici, on her deathbed, realizing that her son was doomed, gave way to despair. When the Queen Mother died three weeks later, enjoying no more respect than 'a dead goat', he had lost his chief support. Not only had Henri III forfeited all hope of making peace between Huguenot and Papist but he had alienated the greater part of his subjects. Politiques and all those Catholics who abominated war rejected a murderer as the symbol of law and order, even if they continued to support him in his vain attempts to check the triumph of total anarchy.

Certainly Henri III, beginning in adversity to rediscover both his innate courage and his political sense, had no illusions as to who was his heir. His rule extended little further than a few towns in the Loire valley so, inevitably, he summoned his cousin, giving him Saumur with its citadel for safe conduct. On 13 April 1589 Henri of Navarre, wearing armour, rode into Plessis-les-Tours with a small troop of horsemen to throw himself at his King's feet. This was not just a flattering gesture or even an act of formal homage but a calculated piece of political showmanship to demonstrate his reverence for the ancient monarchy. Henceforward Henri III always addressed him as *mon frère*, recognizing him as his indisputable successor. The two armies joined forces. The struggle was now between Royalists and Leaguers, between the Crown and the people of France.

The King summoned the *Parlement* of Paris to Tours to underline the legality of his cause—no laws were valid within its jurisdiction unless it registered them—while Henri of Navarre began a furious campaign, storming town after town. Lord Burghley, Queen Elizabeth's Lord High Treasurer, wrote at the end of May: 'At this time the French King's party, by the true subjects of his Crown, both Catholic and Protestant, doth prosper in every place.'[64] Soon they controlled the entire area between the Loire and the Seine and on 30 July Paris was invested by an army which including foreign troops numbered forty thousand. A vengeful Henri III sent a message to Guise's sister, the limping little Duchesse de Montpensier and the same virago who had sworn to tonsure him, that he was going to burn her, whereupon she gaily retorted that the stake was not meant for people like her but for sodomites like him. However, the capital was panic-stricken and though fanatics tried to rally the defence it was plain that only a miracle could save it from falling at the first assault which was planned for Thursday, 1 August.

Dominicans have always been noted for extremism, Savonarola and Pope Pius V, who excommunicated Elizabeth of England, belonged to this Order which staffed the Inquisition and in France formed one of the pillars of the League. A young friar, Jacques Clément, resolved to save his Catholic city from its ungodly foes, in particular from Henri III. On 1 August he obtained access to that haughty and disdainful presence by means of a forged letter; drawing close, on pretext of communicating a secret message, he stabbed the King in the stomach below the navel with a knife which he had concealed in his sleeve. Henri III screaming, 'Oh, this wicked monk has killed me—kill him!'[65] dragged it out and struck the friar in the face before falling. The assassin was immediately cut down; later his body was burnt and his ashes cast into the Seine. The King's wound did not seem mortal but during the night violent pains and fever set in—some contemporaries believed the knife had been poisoned—and he sent for his successor. However lamentable his reign Henri III had too much good taste not to die well. He ordered his courtiers to take an oath of allegiance to his cousin: 'I beseech you as friends and I command you as your King to recognize my brother after my death.' Then he made a prayerful and dignified end. Withal, there was an element of truth in d'Aubigné's sarcastic epitaph: 'He was what you might call a real Frenchman.'[66] Some years later Sir Walter Raleigh expressed the age's wonder at the extinction of the Valois dynasty: 'For after Henry [II] was slaine in sport by Montgomerie we all may remember what became of his foure sonnes, Francis, Charles, Henry and Hercules. Of which although three of them became Kings and were married to beautifull and vertuous Ladies, yet were they, one after another, cast out of the world, without stock or seed.'[67]

Henri of Navarre arrived too late, learning that the King was dead only when the Scots Guard flung themselves at his feet crying, 'Sire, now *you* are our King and our master!' Though he did not shed many tears for his strange predecessor Henri was so shaken at 'finding himself King sooner than he had expected' that he retired to a privy where d'Aubigné steadied him.[68] If two Capetians had acknowledged each other's majesty and Henri III of Navarre was now Henry IV of France most Frenchmen would not recognize him as such. Yet no monarch was ever surer of his divinely appointed right even though, to proclaim it, he now had to ride from battlefield to battlefield.

4. A THEATRE OF MISERY

'La voici l'heureuse journée
Que Dieu a faite à plein desir
Par nous soit ioye demenée
Et prenons en elle plaisir.
O Dieu eternel, ie te prie
Ie te prie ton Roy maintient
O Dieu, ie te prie & reprie
Sauve ton Roy & l'entretien...'
The Huguenot Battle Psalm, tr. Marot[1]

'*Ce venin Espagnol*'
Agrippa d'Aubigné[2]

In 1592 Sir Francis Bacon wrote that

The Kingdom of France which by reason of the seat of the empire
of the west was wont to have the precedence of Europe is now
fallen into those calamities, that, as the prophet saith, '*From the*
crown of the head to the sole of the foot there is no whole place.' The divisions are so many and so intricate, of Protestants and Catholics,
Royalists and Leaguers, Bourbonists and Lorainists, Patriots and
Spanish, as it seemeth God hath some great work to bring to
pass upon that nation; yea the nobility divided from the third

state and the towns from the fields. All of which miseries, truly to speak, have been wrought by Spain and the Spanish faction.[3]

Elsewhere he had spoken, with dry compassion, of France 'which is now a theatre of misery'.[4] Though the country had already suffered pitifully, the years which followed Henri III's death would be among the most terrible in her history.

Heralds might cry *'Le Roy est mort! Vive le Roy!'* but Henri of Navarre had become Henri IV in name alone and soon twenty thousand troops had left the royal camp at St Cloud. The new King had issued an edict on 4 August in which he promised to maintain the Roman Church and innovate nothing in matters of religion until a national assembly could meet to settle the problem; meanwhile the Reform would receive no more than the freedom of worship granted by earlier edicts. As Catholics the overwhelming majority of Frenchmen dared not trust him; only thirty years before England had been ruthlessly torn from the Roman fold by a schismatic Queen. It was plainly impossible that a Protestant Prince who could not be sacramentally consecrated should incarnate the ancient monarchy and become the Eldest Son of the Church. Montaigne may have been justified in suspecting that Henri had always been ready to return to the Old Faith but to do so now would mean political suicide; the League would treat his conversion as a lie while he would lose his loyal Huguenots, those formidable supporters 'whose souls were of iron like their armour', many of them stern old veterans who had in old days ridden with Coligny. As it was the Vicomte de la Trémouille refused to fight for a King who protected idolators, and marched off with nine regiments. Henri's sole course was to fight on under the Politique banner.

Only a sixth of France supported Henri IV. Besides the territory controlled by the League many areas were neutral, including such big cities as Bordeaux and the great Politique fiefs of d'Ornano in Dauphiné and of Damville in Languedoc. Twenty years before, the Sieur François de la Noue, old *Bras de Fer* who despite his age was still one of Henri's most formidable generals, had written in his memoirs of the early Wars of Religion that to attack Paris was a sure means of ending a civil war; *'pour obtenir la paix il faut aporter la guere pres de cette puissante cité'.*[5] The King shared the Iron Arm's opinion, realizing that however scanty his resources he must continue to threaten the capital; a withdrawal to Gascony would cost him his throne. So in mid-August 1589, with an army which had now shrunk to seven thousand men he marched into Normandy where he could control the districts of the Eure and the Oise on which Paris depended for much of her food; though he would be cruelly outnumbered the battle could at least be fought on ground of his own choosing.

The position of the King of France was perilous; the odds were desperate and a single serious defeat meant final ruin. And if small his army was not altogether trustworthy. The Catholics were as numerous as the Huguenots whose prayer meetings angered them and with whom they bickered; despite Henri's assurances of toleration Protestant zealots still expected that his victory would mean the Reform's triumph. While Baron de Givry might fling himself at Henri's feet crying 'You are the King for real men—only cowards will desert you',[6] all too many Papists followed him from the purest self interest like the battered old Marshal de Biron or Marshal d'O, 'a debauchee and a spendthrift and consequently of few scruples'.[7] In the event of failure the Politiques would desert; their lack of fanaticism did not necessarily make for loyalty. Yet Henri's faith in his destiny was absolute; he knew that he was King, that he alone could give his Kingdom peace. Also he had the inestimable advantage of a Gascon temperament and throughout the coming struggle would show all the qualities with which Balzac, no mean observer, credited that amazing race: 'the Gascon character, bold, brave, adventurous, prone to exaggerate the good and belittle the bad aspects of a situation if there is anything to be gained by it, laughing at vice when it serves as a stepping stone.'[8]

The League now reached its zenith, ruling the north and east of France and most cities while thousands flocked to its banners, not merely 'the fiercer and more violent sort of Papists' but moderate Catholics too. It proclaimed the Cardinal de Bourbon King as 'Charles X', issuing edicts and striking coins in his name even if he was Henri's prisoner in the grim custody of Agrippa d'Aubigné. The *Sainte Union* could make an excellent pretence at being the country's lawful government.

The feeble old Cardinal King was only an interim figurehead and Leaguers had good cause to believe that the Crown would soon belong to one of their two great champions, the young Duc de Guise—also Henri's prisoner—or his uncle the Duc de Mayenne. The latter was the League's acknowledged chief, excessively fat and breathlessly ambitious but dangerous enough. There had been thirteen Valois Kings of France, beginning with that Philippe VI whom Edward III had defeated at Crécy, so that while Henri was the admitted heir in blood and a direct descendant of Robert de Clermont, sixth son of St Louis, a Bourbon dynasty would be hardly less a break with tradition than a Guise dynasty. However, despite his much vaunted 'Carolingian' pedigree, as yet 'the false Mayenne' did not quite dare to seize the throne.

There were enemies outside France. Disregarding the Salic Law, which restricted the royal succession to the direct male descent, the Dukes of Lorraine and Savoy made a bid for the French Crown. More alarmingly, so did Philip II of Spain, whose ferocious pikemen could outfight any troops that 'the Man from Béarn' might muster. King Philip was ageing and had seen many of his plans come to nothing; a year ago his Great Armada against England had been destroyed as though by act of God while he had failed humiliatingly in trying to overcome the seemingly endless rebellion in the Low Countries. Indeed the total collapse of her economy would soon put an end to Spain's dominance and though final disaster would be staved off for another fifty years a relentless economic anaemia was already sapping her strength. Yet Philip II remained as coldly determined as always and saw the French succession as a gift from heaven; a Spanish King of France or a client King would recompense him for all his losses, besides setting his yoke firmly on the Dutch neck. He therefore inundated the grateful League with arms and money; later his captains would follow, with *tercios* of pikemen.

This was a war which the French would not be allowed to fight by themselves: it was a battle between Reformation and Counter-Reformation which involved all Europe, just as in the 1930s the Spanish Civil War would become an international conflict between Fascism and Communism. Of the Catholic powers Spain and Rome were bound to come to the League's help as also were small neighbour states like Savoy and Lorraine whose rulers naturally hoped for large territorial gains if the throne was beyond their reach. Among Protestants the Dutch Calvinists of the United Provinces understood very well that a France ruled from Madrid would be their doom. However it was England which gave Henri most assistance. Queen Elizabeth, Philip's wily old enemy, realized just how desperate was the French King's situation and forgetting her usual parsimony sent £200,000 in silver, 70,000 lbs of powder and ammunition and provisions; troops would follow, though her money and munitions were better value than the lamentable English soldiery of the period. England's short term objective was to keep the Norman and Breton ports out of Spanish hands.

Henri captured Dieppe, where he set up his headquarters. Here he could organize the reduction of Normandy and stay within easy reach of England. But Mayenne was following him, slowly yet purposefully, with 33,000 men. The King was outnumbered by more than three to one and had insufficient supplies and no money until the arrival of the English cargo. Most of his staff counselled flight to England. Instead, like Wellington at Torres Vedras, he prepared an impregnable position between Dieppe and the nearby village and castle of Arques on the road from Paris.

The King was an excellent tactician. The bayonet had not yet been invented so infantry consisted of square formations of armoured pikemen who were flanked by musketeers, the former protecting the latter during the lengthy and laborious ritual of reloading. In addition musketeers known as *enfants perdus* were placed well in front, hidden behind hedges or in broken ground to snipe at the advancing enemy. As there was no horse artillery, cavalry were the chief means of breaking enemy squares. Generally the French still favoured lancers who charged in widely spaced lines *en haie* but Henri preferred 'cuirassed pistoleers' like the German Reiters. These wore three-quarters armour—helmet, breast-and-back, thigh and arm plates and high leather jackboots—and carried wheel-lock pistols instead of lances. In most countries they rode in dense squadrons up to the enemy squares where they wheeled their horses in a half turn *en caracole*, fired their pistols at point blank range, and then retired to reload. However, in France it was the practice for them to charge home and use their swords in the ensuing mêlée. Almost invariably such cuirassiers proved superior to lancers, both in hand to hand combat and in smashing enemy formations. Nonetheless a fight was won or lost by the pikemen; one side would eventually wear down its adversaries who were then swept off the field 'by push of pike'.

Henri was a sufficiently good judge of ground to know that he could even the odds in the defile at Arques. Here the road from the south crossed a narrow marshy gap between two hillsides and was commanded by the castle's cannon. Henri dug in on the hillside, guarded the approaches with well placed trenches, earthworks and palisades, and mounted another battery in a chapel by the roadside. Some troops had to be left to man the walls of Dieppe but he made the most of his scanty forces; his pikemen, mainly Swiss, occupied the trenches together with the musketeers while his cavalry were drawn up behind them.

Mayenne appeared on 13 September and finding, after a very leisurely reconnaisance, that Dieppe and its suburbs were strongly fortified decided to batter his way in at Arques by dint of sheer numbers. Over a week after his arrival, on 21 September, the Duke launched his first onslaught when the morning mist prevented the castle's guns from firing. Some of his German pikemen pretended to desert, shouting to the King's Swiss that they could not fight fellow Protestants; as soon as they were let in they treacherously attacked, overruning the front line trenches. The royalist foot began to panic and the chapel battery was lost. Seeing that his front was on the point of disintegrating, Henri, who was fortunately well forward, rode up yelling to his cavalry, 'Are there not fifty noblemen of France who will come and die with their King?' By now Mayenne's horse was attacking on both flanks where a confused sword and pistol mêlée ensued. The royal pikemen rallied while their musketeers fired steadily into the dense mass of enemy cavalry. Suddenly the mist lifted whereupon the castle batteries opened up, scything great gaps in the Leaguer ranks. As the Papist cavalry hastily withdrew the King charged with his infantry, retaking all the lost ground.

Mayenne now recognized that he could not make use of superior numbers on such a narrow front, though he had suffered hardly more than six hundred casualties. He tried threatening Dieppe from the west, without result, made another half-hearted attempt at Arques and finally withdrew on 6 October. During these three weeks of skirmishes, assaults and counter-marches Henri had shown that despite his love of the charge he knew how to fight a defensive campaign.

He had taken the measure of his chief opponent, of the 'sluggishness of the Duc de Mayenne who set about everything very slowly. His flatterers called it gravity. This fault was mainly due to his disposition and was made worse not only by the size of his body, big and fat in dimensions, which in consequence needed plenty of food and plenty of sleep, but also by coldness, and by the torpor resulting from a certain illness which he had contracted in Paris some days after the death of Henri III which, so people say, he had wanted to celebrate in an unseemly way.'[9] Copying their master, his officers were 'tardy, careless and lazy and, however urgent the circumstances, would allow nothing to interfere with their comforts and amusements. The story is told that his First Secretary once left an important dispatch unopened for four whole days.'[10] This sort of leadership and the failure at Arques disheartened his men who began to desert in large numbers.

Mayenne's withdrawal was due to the imminent arrival of La Noue with another Royalist army. In addition four thousand English troops under Peregrine Bertie, Lord Willoughby d'Eresby, had landed at Dieppe together with a Scots regiment. All told the King now had fifteen thousand men. True to old *Bras-de-Fer*'s precept he decided to give Paris a fright. Neither the capital nor Mayenne would expect an attack which, conceivably, might just succeed and which if it did not would at least show the League that it could never afford to disregard Henri.

Even in the sixteenth century Paris bewitched Frenchmen. Montaigne wrote:

I will not forget this, that I can never mutinie so much against France, but I must needes looke on Paris with a favourable eye:

It hath my hart from my infancy, whereof it hath befalne me as of excellent things: the more other faire and stately cities I have seene since, the more hir beauty hath power and doth still usurpingly gaine upon my affection. I love that Citie for her own sake, and more in her onely subsisting and owne being, then when it is full fraught and embellished with forraine pompe and borrowed garish ornaments: I love her so tenderly, that even hir spotts, her blemishes and hir warts are deare unto me. I am no perfect Frenchman but by this great-matchlesse Citie, great in people, great in regard of the felicitie of her situation; but above al, great and incomparable in varitie and diversitie of commodities: The glory of France, and one of the noblest and chiefe ornaments of the world....[11]

A man from the Midi like Montaigne, Henri understood very well the sway his capital exercised over the provinces.

Marching with desperate speed the royal army reached Paris ahead of Mayenne on 31 October, storming and sacking the faubourgs on the left bank the following day. 'This All Saints' Day the King, having a desire to see his city of Paris, climbed to the top of the tower of St Germain des Prés, where a monk conducted him. When he got down he confessed to Marshal Biron that an apprehension had seized him, alone up there with the monk, remembering the knife of Brother Clément, and that never again would he do such a thing without having the monk searched for weapons beforehand.'[12] However, the Seine was impassable, in spite of fierce old La Noue who was nearly drowned trying to ford it, and by 2 November Mayenne and twenty thousand troops had entered to reassure the great city 'which saw itself within two fingers of ruin'. Next day Henri withdrew having tried in vain to engage the Duke in battle. Yet though the gamble had failed it had done his prestige good service.

He returned to conquer Normandy where most of the towns soon submitted save for Rouen and Le Havre while elsewhere in France cities and magnates began to declare for him, among the great Politique feudatories—d'Ornano in Dauphiné, Damville in Languedoc and La Valette in Provence. The winter of 1589–90 was spent in consolidating a position which had been miraculously transformed since that grim march from St Cloud in the autumn. Even so he had insufficient troops. The fearsome campaigning and the need to live off the country had been too much for the ill-equipped English contingent, all but a thousand of whom, true to the inglorious record of Elizabethan expeditionary forces, had died not in battle but of cold and hunger; their commander, Lord Willoughby, had gone home with the broken remnant, writing to Burghley that, 'In my life nothing ever grieved me more but I must endure God's will.'[13] There was no respite for Henri who lived in the saddle or the muddy trenches directing siege after siege. His closest escape was near Meulan where having climbed a church steeple to examine the enemy lines a cannon ball hurtled between his legs, smashing the staircase so that he had to descend by a rope. Yet with all this Herculean striving victory was as far away as ever.

Indeed France was beginning to disintegrate. Among the vultures the Duke of Lorraine hoped for the Three Bishoprics—Metz, Toul and Verdun—and the Duke of Savoy had designs on Provence and Dauphiné. The Duc de Nevers, the Duc de Nemours, the Duc de Mercoeur, all plotted to set up their own independent principalities. Philip II demanded that he be given the title 'Protector of the Kingdom' in recognition of his daughter's claim to the Valois throne as a granddaughter of Henri II. Fortunately neither Philip nor Mayenne were strong enough to triumph. The latter's position was threatened not only by the Spanish interest but by divisions within the League at Paris, between the Catholic lords and *haute bourgeoisie* on the one hand and on the other the mob and the popular preachers who wanted neither King nor nobility but a new social order. This disunity was the salvation of Henri IV.

He was determined to bring Mayenne to battle for by doing so he would challenge not only a rival but the entire Catholic opposition. He deliberately laid siege to Dreux and Mayenne took the bait. On 14 March 1590 the Leaguers engaged the Royalists on the plain of St André between Nonaincourt and Ivry. Mayenne, with his Spanish and Walloon allies under Comte d'Egmont, mustered fifteen thousand foot and four thousand horse, many of the latter being heavy lancers. Henri had eight thousand infantry, his pikemen mainly Swiss veterans, and three thousand cavalry all of whom were pistoleers including a regiment of German Reiters. Both sides drew up their formations in a straight line facing each other and the Leaguers, determined to exploit their numerical superiority, did not even bother to mount a reserve.

The Germans' colonel, Dietrich Schomberg, asked the King to settle his men's arrears of pay whereupon Henri sneered that no brave man asked for money before a battle. However, he later begged the colonel's pardon for such an insult, moving him to tears and protestations of loyalty.

Forgetting his Gascon swagger Henri prayed before his men, like Cromwell at Naseby.

O God, Thou knowest my mind and seest my heart. If it be to my people's good that I should possess the Crown, then do Thou prosper my cause and direct mine arms. But, Lord, if it hath pleased Thee to ordain otherwise or if Thou foreseest that I must be counted among the number of those Kings whom Thou givest in Thy wrath, then take away my life and my Crown; grant that today I may be the victim of Thy holy will so that my death may deliver France from the calamities of war and my blood be the last shed in this quarrel.

Then the Calvinist gave place to the paladin:

My comrades, do you prosper my fortune today so will I do the same for yours. I mean to conquer or die with you. Keep your ranks I beg of you. Should the heat of combat make you fall out, remember to close up at once—that is how battles are won. You must charge between those three trees up there on the right and should you lose sight of ensign, standard or pennon, do not lose sight of my white plume—you will always find it on the road to honour and to victory![14]

The troopers noticed how he spoke with a laughing face.

The combat was of the sort in which Henri excelled, a cavalry battle where infantry and artillery played little part. The few cannon fired several desultory salvoes and then the horsemen on both sides rode forward. The King, near the centre, found himself opposite Mayenne into whose picked squadrons he led his own crack troopers after riding down some Spanish arquebusiers; the Royalist pistoleers charged home with the sword, crashing into the Duke's lancers who found their clumsy weapons useless. Henri was lost sight of in the general mêlée where, shouting 'we must use our pistols—the more against us the more the glory', his white plume did indeed become the Royal battle flag when his standard bearer was shot down; eventually his little phalanx cut right through Mayenne's horse which then disintegrated. After some final confused swordplay the enemy cavalry who had been driven back all along the line by the charge of the Royalist horse turned and fled while arquebusiers fired volley after volley into their pikemen. Fleeing, Mayenne ordered the bridge at Ivry to be broken down behind him so that many of his infantry, who were now running, lost their lives. Henri ordered his exultant troops to spare Frenchmen but to kill foreigners—'*sauvez les François, et main basse sur l'Etranger*'—and about three thousand foot and eight hundred cavalry died in all, among them Egmont. The King suffered few casualties though they included the gallant Schomberg. He had taken nearly a hundred standards and in two hours had wiped out the League's entire army.

Shortly afterwards he sent the good news to La Noue, writing with his usual terse grace: 'Our victory has been absolute; the enemy quite broken, reiters half destroyed, infantry surrendered (Burgundians badly led), ensign and guns taken, and a pursuit to the very gates of Mantes.'[15] Nonetheless if he loved battle and gloried in his victory Henri genuinely hated having to kill Frenchmen.

Paris was defenceless and only thirty-five miles away. It is difficult to understand why Henri did not advance to seize his capital as he had tried to do after Arques. It may have been a mistress who kept him yet he returned to campaign energetically in Normandy for several weeks before laying siege to the great city. Possibly he was taken aback by so complete a victory or he distrusted his Huguenots, some of them grey-headed veterans who had ridden with the martyred Coligny and who were still burning to avenge the massacre of St Bartholomew. Perhaps, always cautious in politics despite his recklessness on the battlefield, he was waiting for the situation to become clearer. Whatever the reason he would later regret bitterly his waste of such an opportunity.

At last the Royalist army, fifteen thousand strong, invested Paris in mid-May 1590. Despite Henri's delay the city was ill prepared for a siege, even if Pantagruel's view—that a cow's wind could overthrow six fathoms of its walls—was no longer applicable. The League's field force had been annihilated and the discredited M. de Mayenne dared not enter, so that the only Catholic magnates in Paris were his young half-brother, the Duc de Nemours, and his sister, that virago Mme de Montpensier. Their garrison numbered no more than eight thousand men and the city's stock of food for a population of three hundred thousand was only sufficient for five weeks. The Spaniards were too busy in the Low Countries for any hope of speedy relief. Nonetheless a new army sprang up, of fanatic citizens of the same mould as those who would repulse the Revolution's enemies in 1793. Other, stranger troops swelled their ranks. 'The Feuillants, Capuchins, and other friars appeared in arms led by the Bishop of Senlis (who according to the moderates is crazed in the head) ... marching around the city bearing a crucifix and a statue of Our Lady as their banners.'[16] Though these thirteen hundred tonsured storm troopers proved more formidable than expected Henri could have fought his way in with ease. However, as Tallemant des Réaux observed, 'Henri IV understood very well that to destroy Paris would be, as one says, to cut off his nose to spite his face.'[17] He knew that his zealous Huguenots were only too keen to take the city by storm and cut the throat of every Catholic inside. 'Furthermore he believed he might be destroying a town whose ruin, like a wound in the heart, could prove mortal for all France.' Wisely the King decided to starve his capital into submission. He spent the siege on the heights which overlook Paris. Here according to a scandalous but probably well-founded tradition he passed the time debauching two young nuns whom he afterwards made abbesses.

Henri IV as a young man, by Antoine Caron

Henri IV in about 1600

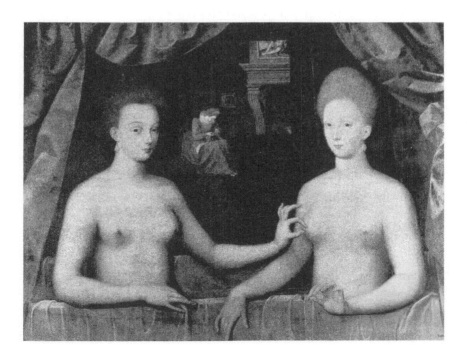

The Duchesse de Villars and Gabrielle d'Estrées in the bath

The rich *Politique* lawyer Pierre de L'Estoile who was in Paris though-out the siege left a grim record in his diary. By 15 June the Spanish ambassador had proposed grinding the bones of the dead to make flour and by 9 July the poor were chasing dogs and eating the grass which grew in the streets. On 15 August L'Estoile found a man dying of hunger at his door with a child who died in his arms. On one occasion he saw a woman eat the skin of a dog. At the end of August 'you could see the poor, dying, eating dead dogs on the street; some ate garbage thrown into the river or rats or the flour made from bones ...' This latter was known as 'the bread of Mme de Montpensier' who recom-mended it without sampling it herself; most of those who did died in agony. The Duchess kept a little lap dog alive until the very end, for a last desperate resource. By that time there were cases of cannibalism and the diarist noted how starving wretches 'began chasing children along the streets as well as dogs'. Thirteen thousand people died of hunger or malnutrition.

The news of this suffering caused Henri genuine distress and he gave a safe conduct to all women, children and scholars and indeed to many others who wished to leave the beleaguered city. When some peasants were caught trying to smuggle food in, instead of hanging them out of hand he rewarded them. Such inconsistency infuriated Queen Elizabeth who wrote to chide him for his lack of purpose. But Henri knew what he was doing; in time tales of mercy would stand him in good stead.

On 27 July 'he seized the Parisians by the throat'[18], capturing the faubourgs by a general midnight assault that was well calculated to cow the citizens. Sully has left a graphic account:

There was not one person who did not think that this immense city would be destroyed either by the fire of the artillery or by the mines kindled in its bowels; never was there a spectacle more capable of inspiring horror. Thick clouds of smoke, through which darted by intervals sparks of fire or long trains of flames, covered all that space of earth, which by the vicissitudes of light and darkness, seemed now plunged in thick shades of night and now swallowed up in a sea of fire. The thunder of the artillery, the clashing of arms, and the cries of the combatants, added to this object all that can be imagined terrible which was still increased by the natural horror of night.[19]

Yet all Henri's efforts to subdue the people of Paris were in vain, '*car il est merveilleusement patient ...*'[20]

The Duke of Parma arrived from the Netherlands with fourteen thousand men and joined Mayenne who had another twelve thousand, and Henri was forced to raise the siege. On 7 September 1590 'the Duc de Mayenne and the Prince of Parma took Lagny from under the King's beard' so that Paris once again enjoyed free access. Henri found it impossible to bring the wily Parmesan to battle, for his pikemen dug in so quickly that it was impossible for cavalry to reach them through the trenches and earthworks. Soon Parma had organized a fleet of small boats which ferried food across the Seine to the all but stricken city. After more fruitless skirmishing the Royalists, exhausted and disheartened, withdrew to winter in northern France, whereupon Parma returned to the Netherlands.

The King had had his first encounter with the greatest soldier in Europe, '*le plus grand Capitaine entre les Estrangers de ce siècle-là*'.[21] Alessandro Farnese, Duke of Parma, black bearded, sober, and of painstaking brilliance was in his mid-forties and had been governor of the Low Countries since 1578; his skill and determination had saved the southern Netherlands for Spain and Catholicism. He was almost unceasingly at war with the United Provinces so that though he had succeeded to his Duchy in 1586 Philip II would not, dared not, let his return home. Parma was nonetheless unshakeably loyal; when his troops' pay did not arrive from Spain he sold his own jewels to find the money. With his terrible but devoted Spanish veterans who had fought under him for over a decade, with his genius for engineering and staff work, and with his instinctive grasp of all strategic and tactical possibilities, Parma was very nearly invincible. Thus Péréfixe ascribed his victories to 'deep reasoning and judicious ordering; he kept the plan of his tactics in his head in such a way, based his movements so carefully on exact maps of the terrain, and pondered so thoroughly over what was going to happen and what he could do that his success was always assured'.[22] Parma provides a yardstick by which to judge Henri's own military abilities.

The King's failure before Paris was a body blow, perhaps the worst reverse of his life. Many royalist squires rode home, even Huguenots. The *Tiers Parti,* that nascent alliance between the more worldly Papists and the former courtiers of Henri III—the political *mignons, le pluspart athées et libertins*—was beginning to take shape. Henri had to find allies to reassure his supporters whether Catholic or Politique, greedy *Tiercelet* or dour Huguenot. He therefore sent the Vicomte de Turenne, as a great nobleman who was also a stalwart Protestant, into England and Germany to beg for help.

The King needed to be consoled. Corisande's sun was setting and he was pursuing the Marquise de La Roche Guyon. The lady's marital fidelity was unconquerable, but she nonetheless inspired one of the most beautiful of his love letters, even if its elegance is hardly matched by its passion:

> My mistress. I am writing this short word to you on the day before a battle. Its outcome is in the hands of God who has already ordained what must happen and what he knows to be expedient for his glory and for my people's salvation. If I lose it you will never see me again for I am not the man to flee or give ground. I can assure you that if I die there my last thought but one will be of you and my very last of God to whom I commend you as also myself. This last of August 1590 by the hand of he who kisses yours and is your servant. Henry.[23]

Her resistance delayed poor Corisande's final congé.

However, after harrying Parma's withdrawal, the King found consolation in Picardy of the most soothing and absorbing kind—Gabrielle d'Estrées, *'qui estoit parfaitement belle et d'une très noble Maison'.*[24] Thus the

delicate Bishop Péréfixe. Tallemant des Réaux put it somewhat differ-
ently: 'This Mme d'Estrées was of the de la Bourdaisière, the family
most prolific of gallant ladies that has ever been in France. One counts
up to 25 or 26 of them, whether nuns or married women, who all made
extravagant love. Which is why people say that the arms of the de la
Bourdaisière are a fistful of whore as by a pleasing chance it happens
that in their arms is a hand grasping a fesse (old *argot* for whore).'[25] Like
her five sisters this charmer of seventeen years was willing enough to
follow the family tradition; with their brother they would one day be
known in Paris as 'the Seven Deadly Sins'. She had probably taken a
lover already, the Duc de Bellegarde, who foolishly introduced the
wonderful girl to his susceptible master. Henri, now thirty-seven, was
at once infatuated when he met her towards the end of 1590. Despite
Matthieu's tale of the King on campaign halting at the gate of the family
château and asking for bread and butter to avoid arousing her father's
suspicions, that nobleman was well pleased by the honour. Soon Henri
was writing passionately to '*la belle Gabrielle*' who was to become the
second of his three great loves. After finding her the King no longer
wrote to Corisande.

All contemporaries testify to Gabrielle's beauty. Her blonde hair was
compared to spun gold while men marvelled at the delicate rose of her
complexion, at the softness of her blue eyes, at her chiselled features,
and at her exquisite figure and shapely limbs. In *La Muse Chasseresse*
the old court huntsman Guillaume du Sable, who was as good a judge
of women as he was of horses or hounds, credited her with 'a mouth
of cinnabar, lips of coral and teeth of ivory' and rhapsodized over her
glorious bust:

> *Une gorge de lys sur un beau sein d'albâtre*
> *Ou deux fermes tetins sont assis et plantés.*

He also admired 'her beautiful double chin' though this Renaissance
perfection is not evident in an early portrait. All these pink and white
charms were accompanied by a high forehead and a Roman nose and

animated by a strong if very feminine personality with gifts of character rather than intellect. Obviously *la belle Gabrielle* was a young woman of dazzling loveliness. She even captivated Agrippa d'Aubigné who admitted that there was nothing lascivious in her *'extreme beauté'*. A besotted Henri soon found a complaisant husband to ensure her accessibility, the Sieur de Liancourt, a rich, elderly widower to whom she was married in June 1592; the marriage was never consummated. However, the skittish girl did not at first altogether relish the exacting role of royal concubine and sought for love elsewhere.

The continuing rivalry of Bellegarde, her old lover and Henri's junior by ten years, brought the King's passion to boiling point. Suspecting infidelity this least faithful of lovers became madly jealous, often writing twice a day to his *belle ange*. By mid-April 1593 he was full of reproach: 'My beautiful love you are indeed to be admired yet why should I praise you? Up to now, aware of my passion, triumph has made you unfaithful. How the truth of all those fine words spoken with so much sweetness—at the foot of your bed on Tuesday when night was falling—has removed all my old illusions! I mention the time and place to refresh your memory ... To end I will tell how sorrow at leaving you so racked my heart that throughout the night I thought I was dying and I am still in pain ...'[26] The same day he wrote again, and the day after too, pleading 'don't fail, my beautiful love, to come on the day you promised. The further I go, the less am I able to bear your absence. You have bewitched me—I admit it—more than I have ever been before.'[27] Shortly afterwards he was writing desperately, 'It is killing me, this dread of your delay ... Jesus! I will see you the day after tomorrow. What joy!' He added thoughtfully, 'Sleep well, my beautiful love, so as to be plump and fresh when you arrive—I have made my own preparations.'[28] No doubt Henri's 'preparations' had made him even more impatient for on the following day he was telling his beautiful love that 'to-morrow I will kiss those lovely hands millions of times—already my pain is soothed by the approach of a moment which I hold dearer than my life, but if you keep me waiting a single day longer I shall die of it ... to spend the month of April away from one's mistress is not to exist'.[29] Next day he lamented, 'I had no news from you yesterday ... it is noon and still I've heard nothing ... when will you learn to keep faith? I don't break my promises like this.' Then he tried pathos: 'The fever came this morning, before I woke. On a sudden impulse, without any real need, I took some medicine which made me so ill that I haven't taken any more.'[30]

In May he had recourse to verse set to music and sent her the following song:

> *Charmante Gabrielle,*
> *Percé de mille dards*
> *Quand la gloire m'apelle*
> *A la suite de Mars,*
> *Cruelle départye,*
> *Malheureux jour*
> *Que ne suis-je sans vie*
> *Ou sans amour....*

'These verses will give you a better idea of my condition, and more agreeably, than any prose,' said Henri in his accompanying letter.[31] It is even just possible that he wrote them himself. The song was to become a popular Royalist anthem.

By now the King had grown so furious that to calm him an alarmed Bellegarde pretended to be in love with the young Mlle de Guise, a ruse which had some success. In June Henri could still write to Gabrielle, from the siege of Dreux: 'Come! Come! Come! My dearest love, honour with your presence he who were he free would journey a thousand miles to throw himself at your feet and never leave them.'[32] However, the relationship was beginning to go more smoothly and in the autumn of this year, 1593, Gabrielle found herself *enceinte* with his child, the future Duc de Vendôme. If unfaithful the King could fall very genuinely in love with his bedfellows; the secret of retaining his affections was as much one of personality as of sex. Nonetheless one is hardly inclined to pity Henri's torments of jealousy over Gabrielle in the light of his heartless treatment of a discarded mistress, Esther Imbert, who being in need had come to St Denis to beg for help. The King was too busy to see her whereupon poor Esther took to her bed and died of sorrow.

Henri IV was formidable even with the scantiest forces and in April 1591 took Chartres, 'the granary of Paris'. Gabrielle was present to felicitate him. Meanwhile all over France lesser campaigns, mostly independent of his direction, were going in favour of the Royalists. His star had begun to re-ascend. Furthermore Turenne had been staggeringly successful in his mission; by the summer the King had nearly twenty thousand fresh foreign troops, Germans, Dutch and English. Turenne was rewarded by a delighted Henri with the hand of the heiress to the semi-independent Duchy of Bouillon.

The English were commanded by a Welshman, Sir Roger Williams, who had been in France with the Royalist armies for over a year and was devoted to Henri. In May 1591 with only six hundred men—most of them English—he had routed two Leaguer regiments besieging Dieppe whereupon the King's ambassador in London commented, 'Glory to God and the said Sir Williams who has not belied by this action the good opinion that all good people of both nations have had of him this long time.'[33] In July of the same year Sir Roger was joined by the Queen's favourite, Robert Devereux, Earl of Essex, young, very handsome and very incompetent, who brought four thousand English troops, mainly ill-trained infantry. They marched to join the King with whom Essex remained until January 1592, showing himself unfailingly brave and foolhardy. He used to hawk in enemy territory and challenged the governor of Rouen to a duel;[34] an angry Elizabeth wrote to him at the end of the year: 'We hear besides, to our no small wonder, how little the King regards the hazard of our men and how you, our General, at all times refuse not to run with them to all service of greatest peril, but even like the forlorn hope of a battle, to bring them to the slaughter.'[35] Surprisingly, this spoilt and incapable young exhibitionist could do no wrong in the eyes of the King who seemed to take a great fancy to him. But Henri had too much Gallic shrewdness in matters of sex not to pamper a doting old woman's darling boy. The Queen's support was gratifyingly continued when Essex returned home. Indeed Dallington claimed in 1598, 'So her Maiestie by defending the oppressed and withstanding his [Philip II's] Forces, deserueth the Title of Protectrix of France, and Deliuerer of the Estates.'

There were many other Englishmen who fought for Henri, like Sir John Norris in Brittany or the ambassador Sir Henry Unton. Inevitably relations between the English and their hereditary enemies sometimes grew strained; when Biron rebuked Williams for his men's slow marching pace the fiery Welshman snapped back that their ancestors had been wont to conquer France at that same pace.[36] Yet almost all of them took a strong liking to the King of France. Thus Sir Henry Unton wrote to Burghley in November 1591: 'He is a most noble, brave Kinge, of greate patience and magnanymitie; not ceremonious, affable, famillier and only followed for this trewe vallour but very much hated for his relligion and threattoned by the Catholiques to forsake him if he converte not.'[37]

Despite his Protestant faith the Royalist cause was everywhere making steady if inconclusive progress. So many bishops rallied to the King that he was able to hold a council of the Gallican Church at Chartres, his excommunication and the Papacy's continued hostility notwithstanding. In August Henri was saddened by news of the death of La Noue, 'the Protestant Bayard', at an obscure siege. In November 1591 old Marshal de Biron and Essex invested Rouen, beginning a struggle which would prove another siege of Paris. This rich city was the capital of Normandy and the key to the entire province. It was defended by a fanatical garrison under a governor, Villars-Brancas, who was one of the League's ablest and most resourceful soldiers.

Sully gives a vignette of the exhausting life which the King led on campaign; on one occasion, after dinner on the day before an assault, Henri 'having a great desire to sleep threw himself down on a bed clothed and booted (the period's great thigh length boots) with his weapons at his side'.[38] Nor was he so strong as might be supposed; the English ambassador could write 'the Kinge hath a weake body and is inclyned to a feaver natuarallie'. The same writer grumbled, 'we never rest, but are on horsebacke almost night and daie'.[39] Furthermore, like the Duke of Wellington, war did not stop Henri's hunting whenever possible.

In Paris the conservative and democratic factions within the League were by now openly, and murderously, hostile to each other. Since Ivry Mayenne's stock had sunk so low that the extremist element had been able to gain control; popular preachers urged 'a bloodletting', attacking all moderates including the *Parlement* of Paris whose lawyers supported Mayenne and a strong Catholic monarchy. All through the summer tempers worsened until the outburst in November by the 'Seize of Paris (A Councell of 16, the most seditious Burgers of the Towne) who strangled M. Brisson a President of the Parliament, the rarest man of his time, and two other lawyers, the one an Aduocate, the other a Procuror …'.[40] The Seize now drew up a list of opponents who were to be murdered or exiled; their ultimate objective was to obtain a weak King who must obey the States General—which would meet every five years—besides guaranteeing various new privileges for commons and clergy. However, Mayenne returned and in December surrounded the Bastille, beheaded four of those responsible for Brisson's murder, dissolved the council of the Seize, and installed moderates in all political offices. But it was impossible for him to eradicate the ferocious preachers with their wild demagogy; soon there was talk of elective monarchy.

The League was now dividing into many factions, all violently inimical. The Cardinal de Bourbon, 'Charles X', had died in May 1590, still in captivity, since when the Leaguers had been unable to agree upon even a nominal candidate for the throne. The Cardinal de Vendôme was the next Catholic Bourbon in succession but received scant consideration. The young Duc de Guise, full of hatred, had escaped in August 1591 and, as Henri predicted, soon quarrelled with Mayenne whose position was also weakened by the 'furious jealousy' which existed between him and the Duc de Nemours. The foreign claimants, those of Lorraine and Spain, continued to press their claims though understandably the Spanish received most attention; they proposed Philip II's daughter Isabella for Queen with Guise as her consort. Philip's primary objective was to weaken France by turning her into a republic or setting up a

King who would be entirely dependent upon him. However, no single faction was able to triumph and nothing could be decided until the States General had met, each party trying to postpone the assembly while consolidating its own strength. This chaotic situation was to last till 1593. The one point upon which all were agreed was the unacceptability of a heretic sovereign, a rejection only made possible by Spanish money: 'The chiefest supporter of these Guisards; and that still gaue oyle to the fire of this rebellion, was the King of Spaine, who ... stood by and looked on, following that Machiauellian maxime, or lesson, which he had learned of that other Philippe of Macedon, to suffer them to ruyne one another, as did the Cities of Greece, and then himselfe to take the aduantage and winne all ...'[41] From the League's emergence under the Balafré until its demise nearly a decade later it was always a child of the Escorial. Agrippa d'Aubigné said no more than the truth when, in *Les Tragiques*, he spoke of '*ce venin Espagnol*'—this Spanish poison.

King Philip decided to relieve Rouen where despite repeated assaults the Royalists were making no progress against M. de Villars-Brancas' sturdy defence. Hearing in December 1592 that Parma was on his way with twenty-three thousand foot and six thousand horse, Henri left most of his troops with Biron to carry on the siege and galloped off with six thousand cavalry and one thousand mounted musketeers so to hinder the Duke that he would not reach Rouen in time to save it. On 3 February 1592, having omitted to make a proper reconnaissance, he unexpectedly made contact with the Spaniards at Aumâle on the north-eastern border of Normandy and had to beat a hasty retreat which he covered personally with a mere handful of troopers—'being the first at everie charge and the last at the retraict which contynued very hotely foure or five hours'[42]—until he was wounded by a bullet in the loins whereupon his little force fled panic-stricken. Henri only stayed in the saddle with difficulty. Fortunately Parma would not waste troops in pursuit, unable to believe that the King of France would fight as a mere captain of light horse. The bullet cut through Henri's jerkin and underclothes but did little more than penetrate the flesh even if he was in considerable pain and had to be carried in a litter for several days. After this skirmish, which might have well proved fatal for France, Parma continued to advance slowly but inexorably, shrugging off every cavalry attack.

Meanwhile at Rouen Villars-Brancas had sallied out, killing many of the besiegers and blowing up their ammunition. After much confused manœuvring Parma and Mayenne relieved Rouen on 21 April. They then advanced to take Caudebec but here Parma was badly wounded by a bullet in the arm and had to take to his bed. Digging in at Yvetot under the command of Mayenne the Catholic army was trapped by Henri, suffering three thousand casualties. It seemed as though the Spaniards and the Leaguers were doomed. '*Vive Dieu!*' joked the King, 'though I may have lost the Kingdom of France at least I possess that of Yvetot,' referring to an imaginary king in a nursery rhyme. However, when all seemed lost for the Spaniards Parma rose from his bed and in an operation of real genius evacuated his troops across the Seine by night. This great general then returned to the Low Countries after reinforcing Paris. He would never again cross swords with Henri for his wound proved mortal and he died in December 1592.

One must admit that Henri IV's calibre as a soldier was small compared to that of the Duke. The King though capable of fighting a defensive battle, as he showed at Arques, was primarily a cavalry soldier with a genius for the charge by which all his victories were won. While he had a good grasp of tactics and a reasonable understanding of strategy his instincts as a *rittmeister*, a captain of horse, always came before his duty as a general, perhaps because of his early years when, too poor to hire infantry, he had had to depend on the mounted Huguenot squirearchy. He was a commander after the school of Prince Rupert of the Rhine and of Murat, even of Lord Cardigan at Balaclava, not of Napoleon. The incident at Aumàle might have happened on only too many other occasions. Frequently his followers reproached him but he would answer, 'I thus play at hazard every day of my life and endure a thousand things which try me sorely, in order to uphold my name for it is far better for me to die sword in hand than to see my Kingdom broken in pieces and I therefore entrust myself and my affairs to God.'

Referring to the near disaster at Aumâle Sir Henry Unton commented glumly, '... wee all wishe he were lesse valliant ... His to much forwardnes doth discourage greately his servants,' and again, 'Her Majestie may make many praie for her if shee please to admonishe the Kinge of his to much indangeringe of himselfe'.[43] A few years later Dallington noted, 'perhaps some wil taxe this hazarding of his owne person, as a matter of imputation, and better befitting a young Prince of Navarre, then a great King of France', concluding that 'a good and discreet Generall should dye of age'.[44] Not even Henri's greatest admirers can claim that he was a 'discreet Generall'.

Certainly the King was a remarkable leader whose bravery and willingness to share every danger endeared him to all and helped unite a most divided and ill-paid following, but in battle he became intoxicated, for he enjoyed soldiering in much the same way as he did hunting. He loved the drama and excitement of war, the rolling kettledrums and shrilling fifes, the jangle of harness and clatter of weapons and the rattle of musketry and thunder of cannon, above all he loved the ecstatic thrill of the charge, wild-eyed horses foaming and neighing, their hooves pounding, and riders yelling with rage as they burst through the black powder smoke to crash into the enemy ranks. No doubt he could fight on foot, as at the taking of Cahors, yet here too he was in the front line rejoicing in the combat. He won many small battles and several large ones, but when faced with the science and staff work of Parma his élan was of no avail. In the final analysis Henri IV was not a really great commander. Nevertheless one must surely agree with his own troops that he was a grand fighting man and truly *'le Roy des braves'*.

He lived in constant peril. Even if, as Montaigne noted, he did not employ a food taster, assassination by poison or the knife was endemic and the League made several attempts to murder him. There was danger too, of a sort, from his very family. Though his pale, inelegant sister Catherine was fond of him, since the age of sixteen she had been in love with a Bourbon cousin of extremely doubtful loyalty, the Comte de Soissons—'a Prince of the bloud and one of the rarest Gentlemen of France'. Corisande, to avenge her replacement by Gabrielle, encouraged both Soissons and her friend Catherine to marry in the teeth of the King's opposition; grimly, Henri warned her, 'I would not have thought it of you and say only this, that I will never forgive anyone who tries to set my sister against me—on this certainty I kiss your hand.'[45] For the suit of Condé's scheming younger brother was far from disinterested; he believed that Henri would destroy himself in which case Catherine would inherit Béarn with all the lands of the d'Albret. Blindly in love, she managed somehow to extort written permission from her brother to marry his would-be heir. Suddenly, in March 1592 during the siege of Rouen, the Count fled from the Royalist camp and rode hard for Pau where Catherine had her chief residence.

The King reacted swiftly. To M. de Ravignan, President of the Council in Béarn, he wrote: 'I am ill pleased by the journey my cousin, the Comte de Soissons, has undertaken. I have only one thing to say to you, that if anything occurs to which you agree or give your help against my wishes, your head will answer.'[46] Meanwhile he dispatched the ever reliable Rosny to Pau to retrieve poor infatuated Catherine's permission to marry. Rosny did so by dint of soothing lies and false promises; though he despised Soissons as a shallow and treacherous schemer he could never afterwards think of this exploit without shame or pain. Understandably Henri has been reproached with ill-treating his sister but he simply could not afford to trust such broken reeds as M. de Soissons.

After Parma's final withdrawal in May 1592 the Royalist army was exhausted and the King unable to mount a campaign on any serious scale though he continued operations in northern France. During this summer old Biron who was wearing the King's white plumed hat for a jest had his head taken clean off his shoulders by a well aimed cannon ball, at the siege of Epernay. In the south and west Leaguers and Royalists fought it out with inconclusive results apart from the Huguenots of Dauphiné who triumphantly routed their Papist enemies and the Duke of Savoy. In fact Henri, the League and Philip II were at the end of their resources and had to accept a military stalemate.

The *Tiers Parti* now asserted itself. Its members were quite ready to transfer an allegiance which was not paying dividends, emerging as a distinct political grouping prepared to consider a Catholic Bourbon like the Cardinal de Vendôme if Henri would not turn Papist. It was an alternative which attracted both Politiques and moderate Leaguers; indeed the latter were actually called Politiques by their extremist colleagues. Henri's inability to conquer by force of arms gave this solution plausibility. The throne would no longer be his should the States General agree upon such a candidate.

Politiques believed that the King must be above religious differences and their concept of monarchy could be reconciled with the emergent Gallican version of Divine Right. Yet while Henri was a declared Politique with a natural predilection for Divine Right, for many years his only completely reliable supporters had been the Huguenots who subscribed to a different philosophy based on the idea, first expressed in Calvin's *Institutes* and then developed in the French *Vindicia contra Tyrannos*, that ultimate political authority rests with the 'inferior magistrates' who can guard the people against an idolatrous King; in France the Huguenot nobles had identified themselves with these 'inferior magistrates', an identification which explains much of French Calvinism's aristocratic appeal. Admittedly there had always been some Huguenot Politiques, such as La Noue, but hitherto they had been rare. Now, despairing of victory, more and more Huguenots became willing to settle for a Politique monarchy and like the *Tiers Parti* urged their Godly Prince to turn idolater. Even the Religion's ministers protested only half-heartedly against his proposed conversion.

Henri remained hesitant. He had been dependent on Huguenot support for so long that to entrust himself to other factions was an unnerving prospect, intellectually and emotionally if not spiritually. The pressure on him became almost unbearable when news arrived that the States General would assemble in Paris in January 1593. Again he declared his readiness to receive 'instructions' in the Roman faith, but he had done this several times before.

Sully gives an account of a private and most revealing conversation which took place in the King's bedchamber at Mantes sometime in 1592. Henri was still in bed and the then M. de Rosny was sitting on his pillow. The King confided that he had not turned Papist for fear of alienating the Huguenots whom he did not want to have to fight 'as my heart could not bear to harm the men who for so long have spent their goods and their lives in my defence, whether nobles or townsmen—it is beyond my power to keep myself from loving them'. Moved to tears by this declaration his henchman though a firm Calvinist urged Henri to let himself be converted for the sake of France, claiming that he knew several ministers who did not dispute that one could be saved in the Catholic as well as in the Protestant faith.[47] The King continued to sound Huguenot reactions: 'What, you agree that one can be saved in the *"religion" de ces Messieurs-là?*' he asked a too tactful minister, laughing somewhat cruelly that 'prudence requires I should be of their creed, not yours, because being of theirs I can be saved according to both them and you, while being of yours I can be saved well enough according to you but not according to them. Prudence dictates that I should follow the most guaranteed road'. But Henri was still not ready, despite hints by the *Tiercelets* that they might desert him or pointed jokes that '*de tous les canons le canon de la Messe estoit le meilleur pour reduire les villes de son Royaume*'.

Luckily King Philip thought that France could be bought and having poured out his gold believed the game was won. In May 1593 his ambassador arrogantly nominated the Infanta Isabella as Queen, adding that her consort must be Archduke Ernst of Habsburg. Mayenne and the Guisards could hardly be expected to swallow this and all save fanatics refused assent by insisting on the Salic Law—inheritance through the direct male line. Too late the Spanish ambassador agreed that Guise might be a fit husband for 'Queen Isabella'. The States General was hopelessly demoralized; it had already been badly shaken by the circulation of such pamphlets as the *Satyre Menipée* which savagely ridiculed the League's hypocrisy and self-seeking. There was little talk of the *Tiers Parti*. Meanwhile Henri's followers were loudly urging their master to be reconciled to the Church; he was told with some exaggeration by d'O, who was 'bored at being a Financier without money',[48] that if he did not do so the States General would elect another King of France within the week.

On 23 July Henri de Bourbon received 'instruction' from a select body of Catholic divines at Mantes. Two days later, clad in white satin from head to foot save for a black hat and mantle, he knelt humbly at the doors of the abbey of St Denis—the French Westminster Abbey—and begged to be taken back into the fold of the Roman Church. The doors were opened and the King entered to kneel again before the Archbishop of Bourges and seven bishops where he recanted his heresy, swearing to live and die in the true faith. Having kissed the Archbishop's ring he was led within to attend mass and receive communion. A political earthquake ensued. As a man the Godless *Tiers Parti* rallied to him, within a fortnight the States General had dispersed, declaring itself incompetent to regulate the Succession, and all over France towns and lords began to declare for Henri IV. A shrewdly conceived truce of three months sharpened the whole country's appetite for peace.

Since childhood Henri's personal beliefs had been the battleground and prize of the Kingdom's most persuasive theologians so that he had become hopelessly confused, seeing virtue in both Calvinism and Catholicism. His conversion has too often been seen as an act of cynical statesmanship, explained by the dry phrase *'Paris vaut bien une messe'*, though there is no proof he ever said it. If he did these apparently damning words were no more than Gascon buffoonery and self mockery. In fact he wept over the gravity of his step and wrote to Gabrielle—whose influence d'Aubigné believed to be decisive—that 'to-morrow I shall make a perilous leap'[49] while to judge from reactions during the preliminary 'instruction' and from his later behaviour under the close scrutiny of courtiers there is excellent reason to suppose that he became a perfectly sincere if hardly sinless Catholic. One of the principal divines who 'instructed' him told the diarist L'Estoile that the King was astonishingly well versed in theology and able to defend his errors but that, though sceptical about the adoration of the Sacrament, purgatory and prayers for the dead, he had suddenly burst into tears and cried out to the Catholic doctors that as he was entrusting them with his immortal soul they must make sure of his salvation.[50]

Henri's religion was one of feeling. Though he had once been a convinced Calvinist, as Montaigne divined he had long been veering towards Rome, possibly under Corisande's influence. No doubt the Roman Church's authority, its disciplining of society and its traditional role as a prop of monarchy appealed strongly to the autocrat in Henri, yet his conversion was, in the last analysis, a matter of temperament. The fresh and vigorous spirituality of Trent had brought a gay and reassuring faith typified by such delightful saints as François de Sales with his dictum 'always condemn the sin, but show mercy to the sinner', a faith which was far more attuned to Henri's warm, earthy nature than the pure but icy grandeur of the Reform. As Athos remarked to the Musketeers, during their famous siege of La Rochelle, that while respecting the Huguenots' courage he deplored their obtuseness in not accepting Catholicism 'that most cheerful and comforting of all religions'.

Huguenot suspicions about *ce notable mutation*[51] were confirmed by Henri's continuing affection for their Ministers; he even asked one to pray for him. In the late 1590s when ill he asked d'Aubigné if he thought he had committed the terrible sin against the Holy Ghost, that persistent denial of inescapable truth for which there is no forgiveness, but he soon regained his peace of mind. Other Protestants, and also agnostics, have since claimed him as a kindred spirit who never really bowed to Rome. They completely fail to understand the man. One must remember that Charles II who changed his faith from Anglican to Presbyterian, from Presbyterian to Anglican, and from Anglican to Catholic, and who lived as a sceptic and a libertine, nevertheless died a spectacularly edifying death with the piety of a Counter-Reformation saint. As always this grandson, a Gascon manqué, who shared his cynicism, his self mockery, his sexual weakness and his lack of gratitude, yet also his realism and fundamental honesty, offers a revealing parallel.

The Royalist cause continued to make progress throughout the winter of 1593–4 though Paris and a substantial part of the Kingdom remained defiant while the great lords clung tenaciously to their fiefs. The Béarnais, as his enemies still called him, decided upon a step of genius, to be crowned, even though Rheims the traditional crowning place of

French Kings was in Leaguer hands; instead of waiting till his right to the Kingdom was beyond dispute he would use the Coronation as an instrument, not as a consummation. In this decision one may discern his unerring political instinct which, surprisingly, was as much that of a lawyer as of a popular leader.

Any balanced estimate of Henri's political motives must emphasize his quite remarkable respect, indeed reverence, for the law. Before its unification in the Code Napoléon the French legal system was a disunited collection of separate jurisdictions, each one with its own *Parlement* or court of justice and totally independent of each other. Only royal *ordonnances* (edicts by the King in Council) had a universal application throughout the Kingdom and even then only after they had been registered by each *Parlement*. North of the Loire in the lands of the Languedoil the *Loi Coutumier* (traditional Common Law) prevailed, whereas south of the Loire, the lands of the Languedoc were subject to Roman Law. The practice of Roman Law makes able politicians, and notwithstanding the advent of the Code Napoléon most great French political figures have come from the Midi. In pre-Revolutionary France all *Parlements* whether in the Languedoc or the Languedoil wielded immense influence and prestige as custodians of the law and as champions of good government. Significantly *La Robe* was the means by which the bourgeoisie entered the nobility; both legal office and titles of nobility could be purchased by them. Henri took pains to cultivate this *noblesse de la robe* with its *habitude parlementaire*. As a true man of the south he himself was not only a natural politician but fully aware of the law's strength and of the vital interdependence between the *Parlements* and the monarchy. Hence his conscious championship of fundamental laws and the careful legality which underlay nearly all his public actions; never once did he act illegally. He therefore calculated that the impact of his coronation would be legal as well as psychological, especially in the heartland of the *Loi Coutumier* which was largely held by Leaguers. To put on the Crown would be both a sacramental confirmation and a seal of legality.[52]

Not only was Rheims in Leaguer hands but so was its sacred ampulla, brought from heaven by an angel and containing the oil which had consecrated almost all French Kings since 496. Luckily the monks of St Martin at Tours produced another *sainte ampoule* which, so they claimed, was even older and just as miraculous. The ceremony took place at Chartres on 25 February 1594. No setting more sublime can be imagined than the cathedral with its soaring spire, jewelled windows and mysterious carvings. Surrounded by six spiritual and six lay peers of France, Henri de Bourbon, after devoutly kissing the sword of Charlemagne, lay prostrate before the altar naked save for a crimson satin shirt while the Bishop of Chartres prayed over him and then anointed him on the head, on the chest, between the shoulders, on the elbows and in the elbow joints, saying each time '*ungo te in Regem*'. Then he stood to be vested in the dalmatic, the tunic and the chasuble—the first two of blue velvet sewn with gold lilies, the latter of cloth of gold damascened with pomegranates—after which he knelt again to be anointed in the palms of the hands. The gloves, the violet velvet boots, the ring and the sceptre were presented to him by the great lords and finally the Bishop took the Crown from the altar and placed it on his head whereupon this glittering being was enthroned while the vast congregation shouted '*Vive le Roy! Vive le Roy! Vive eternellement le Roy!*' Then 'hautboys, bugles, trumpets, fifes and drums' sounded, cannon roared out salutes, musketeers fired volley after volley, heralds threw fistfuls of gold and silver coins among the crowd, and the *Te Deum* was sung. There followed a Pontifical High Mass at which the King communicated. The joyous and triumphant day ended with the Coronation banquet.[53]

Anointed like Saul, Henri was now an all but magic figure, an archetype from mythology. Heir to the God Kings of the pagan Franks he was also a sharer in the sacrificing Christian priesthood; alone of French laymen he had received Communion in both kinds and worn the chasuble in which a priest celebrates Mass. With the mentality of his period, little removed from that of the Middle Ages, the psychological impact upon him and upon all Frenchmen was profound. This splendid and awe inspiring sacrament, of which the modern English form is only a pallid shadow, had consecrated Henri's divine election to be King no less than St Louis, than Charlemagne, than Clovis. His destiny had been made holy. He had become France herself.

It is hard to exaggerate the veneration of pre-Revolutionary Frenchmen for their ancient monarchy, that charismatic rock upon which depended all law and all society, almost as Tridentine Catholicism depended upon the Pope. Within a week the League was collapsing. It testifies to Henri's shrewd judgement that throughout this year of 1594 those lawyers who had purchased office in districts governed by the League flocked to the King to make sure of their status. The most fanatic Leaguer sensed that something extraordinary had happened at Chartres. It was more than a hallowing, more than an affirmation of the law. Something had returned which had not been known in France for over thirty years— monarchy. No less than the landing of Charles II in England in 1660, the Coronation of Henri IV marked a Restoration.

5. THE HEALING HANDS
OF A KING

'For the last kings of the house of Valois drew drye the brookes and Channells of this pleasant Meadowe, and that when the Sunne in the Lyon (I mean the Ciuill Warrs) most parched the same, and so dissipated the Mowen grasse thereof, as they left all in ruine to the succeeding house of Bourbon.'

Fynes Moryson[1]

'But as for warring any longer for Religion, the Frenchman vtterly disclaymes it, hee is at last growne wise, marry, he hath bought it somewhat deare.'

Sir Robert Dallington[2]

In Paris on Easter Sunday 1594 Henri IV publicly touched for the Evil—scrofula, that disease whose sores could only be healed by the consecrated hands of a King.[3] For the sixteenth century there was no greater testimony to the validity of his Kingship. He now began to cure the ills of the entire realm. His first task was to reunite his divided people and bring them peace.

He had ridden quietly into his capital nearly three weeks before, at 7 o'clock in the morning of Tuesday 18 March, his troops picketing crossroads and other strongpoints. In Mayenne's absence its governor, that hitherto staunch Leaguer the Comte de Cossé-Brissac, had sold it for the rank of Marshal, various governorships and a large down payment in cash. Henri was lucky to make himself master of Paris so easily; the garrison included five thousand Spaniards while the Seize had perhaps twelve thousand men under arms yet hardly a drop of blood was spilt. The streets were nervously silent till the King came to the Pont Notre Dame when the crowd began to cheer and cry *'Vive le Roy!'* Henri exclaimed with emotion, 'I can see very well that these poor people have been tyrannized.' Dismounting at the cathedral he allowed himself to be all but mobbed by his joyful new subjects before attending a mass in thanksgiving which ended with fervent singing of the *Te Deum*. As former Leaguer leaders rode through the streets shouting news of a pardon for the whole city and scattering copies of a Royal proclamation which declared a general amnesty, enthusiasm rose until the bells pealed and all Paris rang with relieved cries of *'Vive le Roy! Vive la paix!'* The King 'returned to the Louvre where he found his Officers and his Dinner ready as if he had always remained there'.[4] That same afternoon the Spanish troops marched out of Paris, unmolested. Henri watched them pass and when their ambassador—who went with them—saluted he raised his hat and bowed, saying, 'My compliments to your King—go away at a good time and don't come back!' That evening 'the calm was so profound that nothing interrupted it but the ringing of the bells, the bonfires and the dances which were made through all streets, even till midnight'.[5]

This must have been a sweet day indeed. 'Is it not passing brave to be a King and ride in triumph through Persepolis?' Yet Henri had no desire for vengeance. He pardoned everyone, even the Seize, though a hundred and twenty Leaguers were banished. Those lionesses, Mmes de Nemours and de Montpensier were understandably nervous; the latter, noted for her 'evil, seditious and tempestuous spirit', contemplated suicide, but Henri sent word that he had taken them under his protection. When he visited the two duchesses they were so overcome by his kindness and affability that Mme de Montpensier, who was of course Mayenne's sister, exclaimed how she wished her brother had been in Paris to admit the King. *'Ventre St-Gris,'* laughed Henri, 'he might have made me wait a long time—I would not have got here so quickly!' The

Parisians' new-found loyalty amused the King. When a former Leaguer told him gracefully that what was Caesar's had been rendered to Caesar Henri quipped that it hadn't been rendered (*rendu*) at all but sold (*vendu*). Pardon and purchase were his panacea.

The most fanatic Papists were gratified by the King's edifying and unflagging observance of the Church's feasts and ceremonies, even if to please the English ambassador he had removed from Notre Dame horrific placards which depicted the martyrdom of Catholics in England. He attended mass at all the great churches, listening to sermons with seemingly keen interest and worshipping with a fine show of reverence. Within a few weeks many of the clerical demagogues had either left Paris or been won over. When on 22 April the theologians of the Sorbonne signed a declaration recognizing the King's orthodoxy it was with the approval of most of the Paris clergy, though in the provinces many priests remained obdurate until such time as the Papacy should absolve him, notably among the Jesuits and that most noble and disinterested of all religious orders, the Carthusians.

The mob soon began to idolize this hard-living King of great lusts and great laughter who, with his stream of jests, was so admirably equipped to be a Parisian hero; one must remember that Henri's *mots* were invariably illumined by a charming grin, sometimes rueful but always comical. Within a few months Catholic Paris was able to relish the spectacle of the erstwhile heretic monster disporting himself with his mistress. Gabrielle's child was born in June 1594, a son who was given the martial name of César. On the evening of Thursday, 15 September she and the King triumphantly entered Paris by torchlight to be welcomed with shouts of applause, Gabrielle gleaming in a litter, the King on a great grey horse and wearing grey velvet slashed with gold, and his usual white plumed hat. Preceded by marching troops, accompanied by a splendid escort of cavalry and mounted nobles, they rode to hear yet another *Te Deum* at Notre Dame which the members of the *Parlement* attended in their red robes. Henri's somewhat brutal comment on his loving subjects, perhaps made during this occasion, was that the people are 'an animal which lets itself be led by the nose, especially Parisians'.

But the King did more than reassure the clergy and woo the rabble. To the delight of the lawyers he speedily re-established the *Parlement*, the *Chambre de Comptes* and the *Cour des Aides*, in their lawful authority, besides confirming anxious appointees of the League in their posts; Henri had not forgotten the *Parlement*'s brave stand the previous summer when it had condemned any attempt to set aside the Salic Law. The *Parlement* of Paris now spoke for the capital's entire bourgeoisie by depriving Mayenne of his title of Lieutenant-General and revoking the acts of the States General of 1593. Well-to-do bourgeois in every town of the Kingdom noted the Parisian lawyers' confident loyalty.

As might be expected the League's firmest adherents were the great *appanagistes*, including the Politiques, though by the end of 1594 Villars-Brancas, '*l'un des plus braves hommes de ces temps là*',[6] had traded Rouen and Leaguer Normandy for the post of Admiral and a pension, Montmorency had surrendered Languedoc to become Constable of France with lavish emolument, and Guise had yielded up Champagne for the governorship of Picardy and similar sums. However, the majority preferred to retain a defiant independence, notably Mayenne in Burgundy, Joyeuse—that former Capuchin friar—in the upper Languedoc, Nemours in the Lyonnais, Epernon in Provence and Mercoeur in Brittany: 'As for Monsieur de Mercoeure, hee playd the good Kitchin Doctor, of whom Rablais speaketh, who gaue his patient the necke and bones to tyre upon, and kept the wings himselfe; for he left them all France tyred, and tewed, as bare as a birdes bone, and kept Bretaigne, one of the fattest wings of the Countrey to himselfe, purposing to haue entituled himselfe Duke thereof'.[7] Most magnates had like ambitions. Henri was still weak and they were encouraged by the certainty of full-scale war between France and Spain. The fact that the entire countryside was ravaged by plundering bands of armed and murderous peasants was even more harmful to the authority of the King than it was to that of the nobles.

The sole class to rally as a whole to Henri were the bourgeoisie; his careful respect for law and favouring of the *noblesse de la robe*, his policy of everywhere upholding the rights and privileges of *Parlements* and municipalities and of confirming officials in their posts did not escape their notice while instinctively they preferred government under the ancient monarchy to arbitrary rule by upstart princelings. Steadily they undermined the magnates' authority, town after town rebelling, as did Dijon in February 1595 where, led by their mayor, armed citizens overcame Mayenne's troops after fierce fighting and then handed the town over to the Royalists. Their desertion of the Leaguer cause—which was now hardly more than a cloak for neo-feudalism—would continue on an increasing scale throughout 1594 and 1595, often in concert with the King's officers. Ultimately the bourgeois destroyed the nobles' ability to resist Henri.

Paris was still dangerous. Early in 1595 a young scholar Jean Chastel, like a second friar Clement, obtained an interview with the King at the Louvre and then, in the candlelight, struck wildly at him with a knife; always agile Henri recoiled so quickly that though pouring blood he had only received a cleft lip and a broken tooth, Chastel being seized before he could strike again. The King urged mercy but the lawyers, who had had a bad fright, were pitiless; when he had been racked, the public executioner burnt off the poor lunatic's hand with the knife in it, and he was torn with red hot pincers, after which he was pulled in pieces by four horses—finally his mangled quarters were burnt, their ashes scattered in the wind. This excruciating agony was watched with vociferous approval by Henri's new admirers, the Paris mob. Chastel had been a pupil of the Jesuits, who were dedicated to the service of the Papacy and therefore among the most genuine of the hard line Leaguers. They were blamed, unjustly, for the attempted murder, an accusation which resulted in their expulsion from France against the King's wishes 'as disturbers of the public peace and corrupters of youth'.

On 16 January 1595 Henri formally declared war on Spain. He had not done so before to avoid the onslaught of Philip II's full military might, still directed against the United Provinces, and to leave a breathing space in which to win over as many Leaguers as possible. The King hoped for considerable advantages from this declaration; it would appeal to national pride, it would reassure the Reform that he had not made a secret pact against them with Philip, while the

Leaguers would be branded as Quislings. In addition he hoped that England and the Dutch would now co-operate with him to the utmost. Money was borrowed from the Grand Duke of Tuscany, the entire muster of the nobility was summoned province by province, and his most formidable followers, the Duc de Longueville, the Duc de Bouillon (Turenne), the Admiral de Villars-Brancas, the Constable de Montmorency and the new Marshal de Biron—old Biron's son— were ordered to make ready. True to his aggressive nature the King intended to carry the offensive into enemy territory, to invade the Low Countries and Franche Comté.

He did not neglect domestic affairs. His Council was in permanent session, while the Huguenots were to be further reassured by the *Parlement*'s re-registration of the edict of 1577 which had given them the maximum freedom of worship allowed hitherto. To make a show of national unity Princes of the Blood and high officers of State were summoned to discuss the proposed hostilities before the formal declaration of war.

Philip II was old, in failing health and bankrupt, but reacted fiercely. Never one to stay on the defensive he quickly found money to pay troops and, though the French had some initial successes, by the summer the Spaniards were attacking on five fronts. Philip actually hoped to wrest the throne from Henri whom he still called contemptuously 'the man from Béarn'. Fuentes, his governor in the Netherlands, drove the French back sparing neither prisoners of war nor civilians; whole villages were put to the sword and Leaguer deserters, like Admiral de Villars-Brancas taken after his defeat at Dourlens, were butchered in cold blood. The Dutch could give little help while Elizabeth, who had no wish to see a strong France, withdrew her troops. Money to wage war and buy Leaguer magnates was almost unobtainable as the Council of Finance remained as incompetent and corrupt as ever. In Brittany and the Lyonnais Spanish troops buttressed the *appanagistes* while in Provence Epernon was aided by the Duke of Savoy. The most dangerous threat of all came from the east.

Don Fernando de Velasco, Constable of Castile and Governor of Milan, had brought up his troops from the Milanese to the Franche

Comté and was now entering Leaguer Burgundy, Mayenne's territory, breathing fire and slaughter. Henri advanced carefully towards him, bringing men and munitions to reinforce the young Marshal de Biron. Though the King had no intention of repeating his rash conduct of three years before at Aumâle, he was caught in a similar situation through no fault of his own. Near Fontenay-le-Français on 5 June 1595, after an apparently thorough reconnaissance had discovered only a few Spanish horse, he and Biron rode ahead with a small force of cavalry. Suddenly they found themselves facing the entire enemy army under the Constable and Mayenne. A fast Turkish horse was got ready for Henri to escape but that embodiment of the *furia francese* growled, 'I want help, not advice—there's more danger in running than in chasing.'

Biron with a handful of men had been cut off and surrounded so the King, not even waiting to don his helmet, charged to the Marshal's rescue. In the thick of the mêlée Henri was several times nearly shot or cut down yet nonetheless he drove back the enemy who withdrew in confusion to the main Spanish army which was a little way off. During this struggle he found time to save one of his officers, M. de la Curée, who was without armour; a shout of '*Garde, la Curée*' caused the latter to turn just in time to parry a lance thrust which would otherwise have skewered him. Henri's own life was saved by M. de Mainville; an enemy trooper slashing at the King was shot by this faithful gentleman with a steel bullet which went through his head and whistled past Henri with a noise the King swore he would never forget. Biron, begrimed with blood and dust but always in the front rank, also routed his opponents. Then the Marshal and Henri, who was still bareheaded, reformed their tiny squadrons of battered cuirassiers to charge a second time, against eight hundred Spanish cavalry, with less success. Luckily the vanguard of the Royal army now arrived whereupon the King advanced purposefully with fresh troops. However, the enemy retreated, harassed by Henri for some miles. Mayenne had fought well and bravely but the Constable's inaction in the face of Henri's pugnacious resolution lost the Spaniards their greatest opportunity of the war. That evening Velasco withdrew his troops to Franche Comté. Writing to his sister Catherine after the battle, Henri told her, 'you were very near becoming my heiress'.[8] Elsewhere he commented that in this fight of Fontenay-le-Français he had to fight not merely for victory but for very life itself.

In the north the Spaniards still had the advantage with their victory at Dourlens in July, where the French lost three thousand men, and with their capture of Cambrai in October after a long siege. The odds were suddenly and dramatically redressed. King Philip had 'set the Popes on also to kindle this fire who were but Barkers, and could not bite; their leaden Buls did but butt; they could not hurt; abler to curse then to kill...'.[9] All the same the Papacy's hostility was a great thorn in Henri's side. Since November 1593 the Duc de Nevers had been in Rome trying to persuade Clement VIII to absolve Henri IV. For his Most Christian Majesty was excommunicate as a relapsed heretic and had he been some humble prisoner of the Inquisition would have died at the stake. Agents of Spain and the League lobbied vigorously against absolution, enlisting theologians and canon lawyers to prove its impossibility, and claiming that Henri would renege once he was firmly established on the French throne. For two years the rival lobbies wrangled to such an extent that the exasperated Pope, who found the decision a difficult one and who was not encouraged by the expulsion of the Jesuits, cried out that they were making his life a misery. Eventually Henri prevailed. The Papacy had grown increasingly resentful of the Church's interests being identified with those of Spanish *realpolitik* while Clement, forceful and independent, realized that most French Catholics supported the Bourbon. There was even a threat of schism, that he, Clement VIII, might lose France as Clement VII had lost England. Furthermore Henri was supported by the saint, Philip Neri, and by a redoubtable member of the latter's Oratory, the historian Baronius. The Pope deeply respected St Philip's combination of supernatural foresight with shrewd commonsense, while Baronius was his own confessor. The Spaniards could hardly hope to outgun such other-worldly artillery and on 17 September 1595 despite many protests Clement agreed to a ceremony of absolution. Henri was symbolically scourged by proxy in the persons of two French envoys kneeling at the feet of the Grand Penitentiary and his assistant who admistered the token whipping—a ritual tapping on the shoulders with wands while the penitents, who later compared the sensation to being trampled on by a mouse, recited the *Miserere*—after which he was absolved. The King of France was once more the Church's Eldest Son, and the Holy Catholic League, that earlier Vichy, was stripped of its last shabby rags.

Six days later Mayenne negotiated a truce with Henri, to be confirmed in January of the following year; for his submission the would-be King of Burgundy received over three million livres—a vast sum—three *places de sûreté* and the governorship of the Île de France (excepting Paris). Just as Guise and Montmorency had done Henri good service against dissident lords so Mayenne was to perform prodigies against his former allies, the Spaniards. When he came to Monceaux to make his submission Gabrielle met him at the gateway and brought him in to Henri who, beaming, exclaimed 'my cousin, is it really you or am I dreaming?' They dined together most amicably, with Gabrielle and her sister Diane. Next day the King took the Duke for a walk in the park at such a rapid pace that the fat, gouty Mayenne began to pant, red-faced and sweating. Henri halted, embraced him, grasped his hand and said 'this is all the vengeance you will ever suffer from me!' After which Mayenne was installed in a summer-house to recover his breath before being taken back by Rosny to the château where two bottles of his favourite Arbois wine were waiting for him. Soon the fierce Nemours and Joyeuse had also yielded in return for money and governorships; the latter eventually returned to his friary as 'Frère Ange'. Epernon was more stubborn but in March 1596, defeated by Guise and deserted by the towns of Provence, he too gave way for similar compensations. Of the *appanagistes* Mercoeur alone remained, maintained in Brittany by Spanish troops and the existence of a genuine separatist tradition. Elsewhere in France every important city had recognized Henri IV by the summer of 1596.

Philip II gave up hope of overrunning France, Henri of striking deep into the Netherlands; the war became a struggle for border towns and strong points. Accordingly, on 8 November 1595, Henri who had taken charge in Picardy invested La Fère which was the advance supply depot for Spanish troops operating in France, a town filled with artillery, munitions and stores which Philip could not afford to lose. Surrounded by a marsh and defended by a resolute garrison it was all but impregnable, so Henri began a blockade. In March 1596 the Cardinal-Archduke Albert of Austria, Fuentes' successor as Governor of the Low Countries, tried to relieve La Fère; failing, he unexpectedly attacked Calais which he took on 17 April, much to the envy of Elizabeth of England who still hankered after her sister's lost jewel. The wily old Queen had offered to relieve the port if Henri would let her keep it as a pledge for monies owed her but the King said he would as soon be bitten by a lion as by a lioness. Soon Ham and Guines had also fallen but Henri hung on at La Fère, even if all northern France lay open to invasion, summoning the *Ban* and the *Arrière Ban*, the old feudal muster of the nobility. At last on 22 May the town surrendered, enabling the King to reorganize the defence of his frontier provinces where he busied himself repairing city walls, installing artillery, re-stocking supplies, and relieving and reinforcing garrisons.

Meanwhile the entire country remained a prey to brigandage. The destruction wrought by 'friendly armies was no less dreadful than that by enemies, with wholesale rape, arson and pillage.' Roving Leaguers in Poitou liked to hang their captives from the sails of windmills but the worst atrocities were committed by men of no allegiance. When the Baron de Fontenelle took the little town of Penmarch all males had their throats cut and all women over sixteen were raped; he had an aristocratic loathing of peasants, boasting that he had killed five thousand and how he loved the smell of corpses. It was small wonder that the miserable toilers in the fields revolted. In the Limousin, in 1594 the *Croquants* (so called after the village of Croc) were no longer armed with just 'stakes hardened in the fire but were nearly all arquebusiers, musketeers or pikemen' and, led by a handful of bourgeois renegades, nursed wild dreams of setting up a democratic republic on the Swiss model; in August 1595 twenty thousand *Croquants* shouting '*Liberté! Liberté! Vive le Tiers État!*' fought an inconclusive battle with an army of vengeful nobles, after which they dispersed, sadly and hopelessly.

Henri himself felt sorry for them, saying that were he a peasant he would have been a Croquant. Even in those regions which were free from Spaniards, Leaguers or a *jacquerie*, there was still a daily threat of red ruin from swarming bandits.

The fillip which the Absolution had given to morale in the previous autumn was paralleled in the spring by the signing of an offensive and defensive alliance with England against Spain, a league later joined by the Dutch, even if in the event the French were to receive little help from these dog-in-the-manger allies. The Cardinal-Archduke was unable to mount a fresh onslaught having suffered disastrous casualties when attacking the Dutch, while Spain was further weakened by the loss of a second Armada and by the English raid on Cadiz. King Philip's American silver had at last been overpledged and his treasury was finally exhausted. Henri now received a badly needed breathing space.

He too did not know where to turn for funds. Gabrielle's generous nature, her love for Henri and her love for France, showed itself in these difficult days; the siege of La Fère had only been brought to a successful conclusion because of her diamonds which she gave as security for a further loan from the Grand Duke of Tuscany; later, during the siege of Amiens, she would sacrifice the greater part of her resources. A contemporary historian wrote that 'this lady knew how to keep the affections of that great prince, so that he was as faithful to her as she was to him, for he looked at no other woman and it would be difficult to say which of the two was the fonder'.[10] Her marriage with Liancourt had been annulled and Henri had created her Marquise de Monceaux in her own right. D'Aubigné noted with admiration how she reigned at court without making enemies, unlike most royal mistresses.[11] However, all Gabrielle's sacrifices could not remedy the King's poverty.

In April 1596 he had written to Rosny:

I would like to tell you of the state in which I find myself, which is such that I am facing the enemy but do not have a horse on which I can fight nor a full suit of armour to put on my back;

my shirts are all torn, my doublets out-at-elbow; my saucepan is often empty and for two days I have been eating where I may, my sutlers saying they have nothing to serve at my table, all this because I have had no money for six months. So ponder well if I deserve to be treated in such a way; whether I must longer allow the financiers and treasurers to make me die of hunger while they keep their own tables dainty and well served; whether my household should be in such need while theirs are in wealth and plenty, and whether you are not surely obliged to help me loyally as I pray you.[12]

Indeed the historian Legrain saw Henri in a dirty white coat, worn and soiled by his armour and with ragged sleeves, and in stockings torn and in holes.[13]

The nobles had their own solution. They would provide a really large and well paid army on condition that their governorships should become permanent and hereditary fiefs whose possessors would owe the Crown nothing more than formal homage. It was the high water-mark of French neo-feudalism. Acceptance of their offer, made in this desperate year of 1596 and supported by the entire nobility including Princes of the Blood like the Duc de Montpensier, would have reduced the King of France to a *roi fainéant*, his country to a mosaic of petty principalities.

After rejecting this poisoned suggestion, so terrifying in its implications, Henri knew that only Rosny could find money—if it was to be found at all in France. The financial machinery of the Kingdom was an Augean Stable, the preserve for too many years of venal officials, greedy courtiers and tax farmers of mammoth appetite, who all slandered the incorruptible Marquis with unrelenting savagery. Despite literally Herculean efforts Rosny's success, though remarkable enough, did not produce sufficient revenue for the bottomless abyss of Henri's needs; every sou went on war or on winning Leaguer magnates. Yet France was already groaning under terrible taxes; 'the King's poore people are already with these ciuill Warres so spoyled and impoeuerished, as there is nothing to be had'.[14] To try and raise more might well break her back.

Henri dared not summon the States General whose meetings under Henri III had invariably ended in tumultuous dissension; in any case it was a purely consultative body which could do little more than voice grievances. He therefore called the old feudal *Assemblée de Notables*. In October they met at Rouen, nine from the clergy, nineteen from the nobility, fifty-two from the bourgeoisie, all men of genuine power and influence; the large number from the Third Estate, mostly members of the *Parlements*, indicates Henri's continuing reliance on this class. His opening address made a profound impression.:

> If I wanted to acquire the title of orator I would have learned some fine, long harangue and would have spoken it to you gravely enough. But, gentlemen, my desire is to attain to two more glorious titles, which are to call myself liberator and restorer of this State. For which end I have summoned you. You know to your cost, as I do to mine, that when God called me to the Crown, I found France not only almost ruined, but almost entirely lost to Frenchmen. By the grace of God, by the prayers and by the good advice of those of my servants who do not follow the soldier's profession; by the sword of my brave and generous nobility, among whom I do not take special account of princes, but only of our finest title, the honour of a nobleman (*foy de gentilhomme*); by my toils and troubles, I have preserved her from this fate. Together we must now save her from ruin. Share with me, my dear subjects, in this second glory, as you have already shared in the first. I have not summoned you as did my predecessors, simply to approve their wishes. I have brought you together to hear your advice, to consider it, to follow it, in short to put myself in guardianship under your hands, an ambition which is not often found among kings who are greybeards and victorious. But the fierce love which I bear my subjects, the keen desire that I

have to add those two fine titles to that of King, makes it seem to me both pleasant and honourable.[15]

Corisande d'Andoins, Comtesse de Guiche, with her daughter, Catherine de Gramont, later Comtesse de Lauzun

Henri IV receiving the portrait of Marie de Medicis, by Rubens

The whole tone is in striking contrast to the godlike condescension of his grandson Louis XIV. Yet Henri IV was no less of a despot. Gabrielle asked him afterwards if he had really said that he would place himself under the *Notables'* tutelage, '*Ventre St Gris,*' growled the King, 'it's true, but I said it with my sword at my side.' His brand of absolutism was tempered by tact and moderation—he cared little for show, only for substance.

Even so the *Notables*, according to Rosny, tried to put their sovereign under tutelage. Inspired by the example of England, in January 1597 they demanded the establishment of a *Conseil de Raison* to superintend the expenses of government which were to be divided into two, those of the nation and those of the King, the latter to include the cost of war. This separation of revenue and prerogative would have hamstrung the Royal power at a time when an anarchic France needed the firmest hand possible. The King's Council were horrified but, on Rosny's advice, Henri agreed to set up the Council. After three months its members found the appalling complexity of the country's financial system and the obstruction by officials and by taxpayers to be quite unmanageable. Humbly they went to the King, admitting that they had presumed beyond their capacity, and surrendered their powers. If, as some authorities suggest, this story is a fabrication of Rosny it is nonetheless an excellent illustration of the way in which Henri preferred to rule. He wished to establish the monarchy on a genuinely popular basis while retaining absolute power.

During 1597 Amiens, the capital of Picardy, was the focal point of the war. Henri was preparing to attack Arras and meant to use this rich market town, which was the centre of Franco-Flemish trade, as a supply base, filling it with cannon and munitions. Early in the morning of 11 March forty Spanish troopers disguised as peasants and led by a veteran officer, Don Hernan Teillo de Portocarrero, entered one of the gates at Amiens whose portcullis they blocked with a farm cart whereupon a detachment of their comrades nearby rushed into the town; the governor panicked and soon Amiens was in the hands of the Spaniards who sacked and plundered it for three days.

This appalling news reached Henri at Paris in the dark hours before dawn on 12 March when he was in a deep sleep after dancing at a ball. Leaping out of bed the King cried, 'I will have that town back or die,' adding, 'I have been King of France long enough—I must become King of Navarre again.' Gabrielle was weeping. 'My mistress,' he told her, 'we must dry our tears and mount our horses to fight another war.' Most of the *Notables* from Rouen were in Paris so that same morning he summoned them, together with the chief officials of the *Parlement*, demanding money with which to replace the supplies and armaments lost at Amiens. He spent the afternoon with the Constable de Montmorency, planning the campaign and giving orders to found new cannon. Then, in the late afternoon, *ce Roy Vaillant* swung into the saddle and rode out of Paris on his great warhorse at the head of his troops, banners flying, drums beating and the mob roaring applause. This day which had begun with news of a national disaster had ended with a triumphant procession.

His capital he left in charge of the Constable—'a great Perswader of the Peace, of no real Capacitye but of greatest Swaye in Court by reason of his Place and Quallitie'.[16] *En route* north the King calmed the terrified populace, fortifying towns and villages, and, most important, settling arrears of pay with many disgruntled garrisons. Assembling his army near Amiens he suddenly made a surprise attack on Arras but was unsuccessful. After blocking all access from the north he entrusted the siege of Amiens, which was now garrisoned by four thousand five hundred Spanish troops under the brave Teillo, to Biron. Henri then returned to Paris, in mid-April.

Here the *Parlement* was objecting to the new taxes. Henri made yet another impassioned speech, swearing that he preferred to die rather than to let France be destroyed: 'I beg of you, unite, for if people will give me an army I will willingly give my life to save you and restore the State.' But these rich and selfish lawyers remained obstinate so, after trying every possible means of persuasion he reluctantly forced them to register the necessary edicts by that ultimate legal sanction, a *lit de justice* or Royal session of the *Parlement* presided over by the King in person whose presence procured automatic registration.

During the summer the Spaniards attempted, unsuccessfully, to seize other French towns as far south as Poitiers, while continuing to support Mercoeur in Brittany; at the same moment the Duke of Savoy threatened Dauphiné. No help save promises came from England and the Dutch. Henri persevered with his investment of Amiens during which he found the time to create France's first standing army, placing the three veteran corps of Picardy, Champagne and Navarre—commonly called Gascony—on a permanent basis together with new regiments from the northern provinces and that of Piedmont, each of twelve hundred picked musketeers and pikemen, many of whom were needy scions of the nobility; there were also the Royal Guards and various regiments of mercenaries—mainly Swiss—while cavalry consisted of four thousand *Gensdarmes d'Ordonnance*, the precursors of the redoubtable *Maison du Roi*. Thus began the glorious tradition of the pre-Napoleonic Grande Armée. By July Amiens was completely blockaded by earthworks; on 17th of the month Teillo led a sortie which was repulsed, Henri himself helping to drive the Spaniards out of his trenches, fighting on foot with a pike. The garrison suffered many casualties and was further weakened by famine and disease. On 3 September the gallant Teillo was killed by an arquebus bullet. The Spanish relief force was delayed from sheer lack of money but at last in mid-September the Cardinal-Archduke reached the Somme and the alarmed besiegers prepared to defend their earthworks; the King, as on so many other occasions, prayed publicly before his troops. However, despite treacherous advice from Biron on where to attack, the Cardinal's attempts to cross the river were beaten back by the King and Mayenne whereupon Albert retreated to the Low Countries. Henri joked that the Cardinal of Austria had come like a soldier and gone home like a priest. Amiens surrendered on 25 September; Henri was merciful to the Spanish garrison, treating them with the utmost courtesy.

Spain's Savoyard allies then suffered several defeats at the hands of Lesdiguières—that future Marshal and Constable of France who had begun his career as a simple archer—while the Dutch were increasingly successful in the Low Countries. Yet another Armada, destined for Ireland, was destroyed by storms and everywhere the Spanish war effort faltered. It was stalemate. 'There rested now no appearance of the League in France but only the Duke of Mercoeur, yet keeping a corner of Brittany.'[17] However, by early 1598 even the Celtic Duchy had at last begun to revolt against Mercoeur who for the usual inducements surrendered in March, his daughter and heiress being betrothed to the King's small son, César, soon created Duc de Vendôme. Gabrielle's intervention was largely responsible for the gift of such merciful terms to the rebel whom Henri called 'the Duke of Mercury'. For the past year the Papacy had been trying to reconcile His Most Catholic Majesty with His Most Christian Majesty; now 'the King of Spain finding the forces both of his body and mind to diminish by a languor which after-wards degenerated into a horrible malady' became anxious for peace. On 2 May 1598 a treaty was signed at Vervins which confirmed that of Câteau-Cambresis, France retaining the frontiers of 1559 and regaining Calais and all her other lost towns 'which might be called the Keys of France'. It was a genuine if unspectacular triumph for Henri. Within a few months Philip II was dead after 'a perpetual flux of blood through all the conduits of his body', thwarted but unbroken, cursed by Europe yet a hero to all true Spaniards.

Henri had taken other steps to ensure peace, at home. On 13 April 1598 the Edict of Nantes—promulgated when the King was presiding over the Estates of Brittany—gave the Religion remarkably gener-ous terms. The Huguenots received liberty of conscience, freedom of worship in the châteaux of Protestant lords, in every town where their faith was already established, and at the least in two towns in every bailiwick; in addition those who were royal officials or great nobles could hold services in their lodgings. They were eligible for any public office and obtained *chambres mi-parties* in the *Parlements*, their legal rights as citizens being fully guaranteed. More ominously, they retained two hundred fortified *places de sûreté* maintained at the Crown's expense, though defended by their own Protestant garrisons, and the right to hold assemblies whose representatives might meet to present the King with their grievances. This was indeed a state within a state, with political and military independence.

The motives which dictated Henri IV's religious settlement have so often been misinterpreted that the Edict is usually seen either as the triumph of common sense over bigotry or as an early essay in ecumenism. On the other hand, while Henri has been regarded as the protector of his former co-religionists from Catholic persecution in contrast to his grandson Louis XIV, some Protestants consider the Edict to be lacking in generosity. However, if Henri IV is seriously criticized for his settlement it is because he accepted the existence of a Calvinist republic within the Kingdom of France, a major political error which had to be set right by Richelieu. It is rarely appreciated how limited was the King's freedom of action.

In fact the Huguenots, though no more numerous—there were less than eight hundred congregations where there had been two thousand in 1562—were far more formidable than in Coligny's day; thirty years of savage war had forged an indomitable fighting tradition embodied in a large corps of dedicated and highly professional officers, of whom the majority were in no sense Politiques, while between them the three thousand five hundred noblemen of Protestant France could muster twenty-five thousand troops. Until Henri's conversion they had looked forward to a Calvinist monarchy which would eventually impose the Reform on the entire Kingdom; England provided a reassuring blue-print. In June 1594 a general assembly of the Religion at Sainte Foy divided France into nine administrative circles which were to levy taxes and maintain troops, an organization tantamount to a Republic; there was talk of electing a Protector on the model of the Dutch Stadtholder, an office to which such potentates as Bouillon and La Trémouille aspired, no less dangerous than Leaguer magnates. 'As for Religion, it hath onely been the cloke and shaddowe of their ambitious pretences,' discerned the percipient Dallington.[18] In 1596 during the siege of La Fère when the King refused to accept their proposed new organization these two lords rode off with their regiments. Fortunately du Plessis-Mornay, the Religion's moral and intellectual leader, did not cease to urge restraint. By early 1598, as peace with Spain came in sight, Huguenot extremists were mobilizing to begin yet another War of Religion. It was this which finally made up Henri's mind and extorted the Edict of Nantes, to be proclaimed perpetual and irrevocable.

He had never underestimated the danger and always taken good care to favour his Protestant nobles. Several, like Rosny, Lesdiguières, and du Plessis-Mornay, were among his most trusted servants, Bouillon owed his duchy to him as did La Trémouille while even d'Aubigné received his meed of flattery when he appeared at La Fère in mourning for his wife (he cried over her death every night for three years); Agrippa was astonished to be greeted warmly by the King who having embraced him ordered Gabrielle to do likewise and then to let him hold little César in his arms after which they listened tactfully to his enthusiastic suggestion of taking the baby back to the Saintonge to be brought up as a good Calvinist. It is, incidentally, in such a context that one must see Henri's dramatic requests for Huguenot prayers after his conversion to Catholicism.

While it is true that the Papists were far stronger, that Henri IV was now undisputed King of France, and that the Reform's military power might have been broken, as Richelieu was to break it thirty years later, France simply could not afford another civil war at this particular moment. Henri believed he had an alternative and his timing was perfect; most Frenchmen had had their fill of fighting for the sake of religion. There was of course a furious outcry against the Edict among the more intolerant Catholics whom the King answered when he addressed the *Parlement* of Paris 'as a father of a family in ordinary clothes speaking frankly with his children'. He asked them to register the Edict for the sake of peace, reminding them that he spoke as the Eldest Son of the Church who loved the Roman faith just as much as they did. 'I am the one upholder of religion.... I am King, I speak as King and I must be obeyed.' He recommended the example of the Duc de Mayenne's loyal obedience and told the *Parlement* that they should be grateful to their King for saving France. If they did what he asked they would be doing it not only for him but for themselves. Not even the most obstinate bigot dared resist such appeals and the Edict was duly registered on 25 February 1599 without recourse to a *lit de justice*, though the provincial

Parlements held out longer. Henri told that of Toulouse that it still had 'a Spaniard in its belly'.

The English traveller and pedant, Sir Robert Dallington, a future Master of Charterhouse, saw Henri on several occasions in 1598 and described him vividly in 'The View of Fraunce'.

> This King then, of whom now by course I am to relate, is about 48 yeeres of age, his stature small, his haire almost all white, or rather grisled, his colour fresh and youthfull, his nature stirring and full of life, like a true French man. One of his owne people describeth him thus: 'He is of such an extremely liuely and actiue disposition that to what soeuer he applyes himselfe, to that he entirely employes all his powers, seldome doing aboue one thing at once. To ioyne a tedious deliberation with an earnest and pressing affayre he cannot endure: Hee executes and deliberates both together. But in Councels that require tract of time, to say the truth, hee hath neede of helpe. He hath an admirable sharpnesse of wit.'

Dallington's informant added that 'though by his Phisiognomy, his fashion & maner of behauiour, ye would judge him leger and inconstant, yet is no man more firmly constant than he'.[19] Actually Henri was three years younger though his white hairs made him seem older. The King's own description of himself was: 'I am all Gray without but you shall find me Gold within'[20]—a fair enough judgement on the contrast between his plain grey doublet and warm, emotional heart.

He was beginning to enjoy Paris. One of his more bizarre new friends was the fabulously rich tax farmer Sebastien Zamet, a naturalized Italian from Lucca who once described himself as 'lord of 1,700,000 crowns' when asked to state his claim to nobility; he had begun his career as Catherine de Medici's shoemaker and then become a court money-lender. Henri liked Zamet's 'facetious and merry' company and often dined and gambled or gave intimate little supper parties for his mistresses in the financier's luxurious house in the Marais. One is reminded of Edward VII's predilection for Jewish millionaires. L'Estoile noted that on 23 February 1597 the King and Gabrielle attended 'a sorcerers' masked ball', how Henri kissed 'his friend' everywhere they went and how they danced all night, returning to the Louvre at 8 o'clock in the the morning.[21]

The King's ménage with Gabrielle was now on a permanent basis, even if he had other women; a certain Mme des Essarts presented him with two bastards but he remained emotionally faithful. D'Aubigné jokingly referred to the Court as *'La Cour de la belle Gabrielle'*:

> The Duchesse de Beaufort made very modest use of the power she had over the King but those near to her saw nothing to criticize in this. Here we may discuss their love so far as respect and propriety allow. Among our Kings' mistresses there have seldom been seen women who have not brought upon themselves the hatred of the great, by taking anything they covet or bringing disfavour upon those who do not worship them or by forwarding their relatives' interest, debts, dues and feuds. It was a marvel how this woman, in whose extraordinary beauty there was nothing lascivious, could live as a queen rather than a concubine for so many years and yet make so few enemies. The needs of the State were her only foes….[22]

'His Gabrielle' was a familiar figure in Paris, receiving near regal honours—though asked her name by a bystander a Royal archer could reply loudly, 'that's no one, only the King's whore'. She was seen everywhere with Henri who 'went through Paris having this lady by his side; he took her with him to hunt and caressed her before all the world'. They rode together hand in hand, she riding astride like a man, especially resplendent in her favourite green, her golden hair studded with diamonds and it was she who presided over every ball and court function.[23]

Yet though the King was devoted to his unwed spouse, by now Gabrielle's looks were somewhat full blown and she had acquired that 'lovely double chin'. Sir Henry Unton, the English ambassador, met her in February 1595 and was unimpressed. He wrote to Queen Elizabeth that 'She was attyred in a playne Sattayne Gowne, with a Velvet Hood all over her Head (to keape away the Weather from her) which became her verie ill; and, in my Opinion she is altered verie much for the worse in her Complection and Favor, yeat verie grosselye painted ...' Upon Union's unctuously showing his Queen's portrait to the King, Henri beheld it 'with Passion and Admiration', crying, 'I surrender' and kissing it with gusto again and again.[24] A subtler diplomat than Unton—who died of the Purple Fever shortly afterwards[25]—met her two years later, Sir Robert Cecil, Queen Elizabeth's Secretary of State, the future Earl of Salisbury and James I's Lord Treasurer. This grave, sensitive little hunchback, who was a coldly accurate judge of humanity, received a very different impression of Gabrielle when he saw her in March 1598: 'She is great with child and truly a fair and delicate woman. I staid little with her; and yet she is very well spoken and very courteous ...'[26]

Unton had also reported how Henri 'used many affectionate Wordes in her Commendation; among others, that she never intermeddled with his Affayres and had a tractable Spyrite, whearin he spake not amiss for she is heald to be incapable of Affaires and very simple'.[27] Gabrielle's power over the King derived from her ability to bring him the bourgeois joys of home and family for she had born other children since César. Nonetheless she was shrewd enough to urge him to employ Rosny, despite her dislike for that farouche bureaucrat. When absent Henri continued to send her a spate of letters in his exuberant, graceful hand and curious spelling with its excess of 'y's. On 29 October he described a joyful afternoon that he had spent with his children and told her how much happiness she had given him. Earlier that month he had written, 'I cannot throw off my melancholy humour and think I will take medicine on Tuesday though nothing can do me more good than the sight of you, the one remedy for all my sadnesses.'[28]

Eventually Henri resolved to make her his Queen. He wanted a more substantial heir than little Condé or the egregious Soissons and decided to legitimize young César; it was no accident that the latter's birth had been greeted by a *Te Deum*, that he had been affianced to Mercoeur's daughter and created a duke with a title born by Henri's father. Gabrielle was given increasingly greater rank, becoming first Marquise de Monceaux, then Duchesse de Beaufort, then Duchesse d'Étampes and a Peeress of France, in preparation for the ultimate honour. By 1598, driven on by her relatives rather than by her own ambition, she had begun to give herself indisputably regal airs. On occasions she was waited on at dinner by the young Duchesse de Guise, who might herself have been Queen had the League triumphed, while the baptism of her second son Alexandre de Vendôme was performed with honours reserved for a Son of France. Rosny's flat refusal to pay, on the grounds that there were no Sons of France and his complaints to the King culminated in a tearful scene with Gabrielle who called him a lackey; for once she had gone too far, Henri retorting that he preferred to lose ten mistresses like her rather than one servant like Rosny. But normally her power over the King was complete. When he resisted her wishes she would weep and faint or, as when he objected to making her father Master-General of the Ordnance, threaten to enter a convent. Once Rosny brought news that her coach had been involved in an accident whereupon Henri trembled and turned pale, something which he never did in battle. Despite Rosny's plain-spoken warnings the King was determined to marry her and asked the Papacy for an annulment from Marguerite, that worst of wives, who was living at the château of Usson in the Auvergne, in disreputable retirement after many picaresque and lecherous adventures; she had wandered the roads with strange lovers and been captured by bandits, and she too was turning fat, adding the vices of the table to those of the bed. However, though ready enough to accept an advantageous settlement should he wish to marry some foreign daughter of a Ruling House, the last French Princess of the Valois would not make way for a whore from Picardy, that *bagasse* (slut) as she called her.

Indeed Henri himself expected trouble from such a marriage; he actually asked Rosny if he thought the nobility would rise in revolt. While César, who much resembled his father, would have made an excellent dauphin his legal position as heir to the throne would have been even more doubtful than that of his younger brother, for he was born of a double adultery, not merely of a single like Alexandre; at his birth Gabrielle had still been Liancourt's wife. Yet the King's heart could rule his head in the most important matters of state and in token of betrothal he gave her his coronation ring, a great square-cut diamond.

At Sancy on Tuesday 6 April Henri took leave of Gabrielle, who was big with child, for he wished to spend Easter at Fontainebleau in a suitably edifying fashion, without scandal. His concubine was in tears as if knowing she would never see him again and the King wept from sympathy. Gabrielle had always suffered from melancholy and from wild irrational fears; she was a prey to astrologers who invariably prophesied she would die an early death unwed, predictions which caused her to lie awake whole nights in tears. After leaving Henri she went on to Paris by barge where she dined at the house of Zamet, 'ce fameux Financier', where she began to feel unwell. On the next day, Maundy Thursday, her labour began accompanied by terrible convulsions and on Good Friday her stillborn child had to be cut out of her while she suffered such dreadful agony that her face was horribly disfigured, turning literally black. She died on the morning of Holy Saturday. Sinister rumours of poison began to circulate but the real cause of her death was puerperal convulsions. She was buried with much sad pomp by a stricken Henri who gave her the obsequies of a Queen, the court walking in procession behind her cortège to St Denis; for a week the King wore black and then changed to the violet of half mourning. Of all his mistresses 'Charmante Gabrielle' brought him most happiness. To his sister he wrote that 'the roots of love within me are dead and will never spring up anew'.[29]

This sorrow struck while he was wrestling with the thorny problem of Savoy, which was to be further complicated by the treachery of an old and valued friend. Since 1588 Duke Charles Emmanuel I, *Il Grande*, a pallid hunchback who was nonetheless a tough and formidable soldier, had been occupying the Marquisate of Saluzzo which he had seized from France with no other justification than force of arms. Some years later an English ambassador wrote: 'Among the princes of Italy may also be reckoned the Duke of Savoy; but as the chief of them, not only for the largeness of his territory and multitude of subjects (though in treasure perchance Florence exceeds him) but for the nobleness of his extraction also, the rest being descended, for the most part, either from merchants or the pope's bastards.'[30] Henri dealt carefully with the wily Duke who was a long-standing ally of Spain and Philip III's brother-in-law, and so desperately ambitious that he would one day propose himself as a candidate for the Holy Roman Empire. At Vervins the question of Saluzzo had been referred to Papal arbitration, with small result. Charles Emmanuel hoped to win Spanish support and procrastinated for as long as possible, visiting France with a great train of courtiers to negotiate insincerely while suborning French lords on whom he showered gold in the vain hope of overthrowing Henri. Without the Duke's knowledge Savoyard agents commissioned a fashionable innkeeper to poison the King, the woman Nicole Mignon whose husband was one of the Royal cooks; the plot was discovered and Mme Nicole burnt alive in the Place de Grève. Henri indignantly rejected a suggestion that he should keep the Duke a prisoner until he surrendered Saluzzo.

Charles Emmanuel's most dangerous ally was the King's best general, the Duc de Biron, whom Henri described to Elizabeth as '*le plus trenchant instrument de mes victoires*'. The old Marshal de Biron *le boiteux*—the lame one—whom Brantôme called 'France's oldest and greatest captain',[31] had frequently warned his son to keep himself under better control unless he wanted 'to go home and plant cabbages'. This son, now in his late thirties, owed everything to Henri who had created him a Marshal in 1594, and a Duke and a Peer of France in 1598, for though a wild debauchee and greedily avaricious he was a fine soldier like his father and no less brave, only lacking the old warrior's brutal common sense. Though a professed atheist, he had also an unwholesome weakness for the occult, consulting not merely astrologers but magicians and necromancers. Proud as Lucifer, crazed by ambition, Charles de Biron could not reconcile himself to accepting a mere fellow campaigner for his sovereign; intimacy had bred a jealous contempt instead of friendship. Even so, right to the end Henri remained attached to this strange, troubled spirit who had suffered thirty-two wounds in his cause.

By June 1600, the date stipulated for its return by the preceding February's Treaty of Paris, Charles Emmanuel was still clinging defiantly to Saluzzo, so Henri, who 'was not to be gulled by gilded shadows',[32] invaded Savoy, dividing his army between Biron and Lesdiguières; the former was watched by officers loyal to the King who was already suspicious of him. Rosny, having succeeded Gabrielle's father as Master-General of the Ordnance, had cast whole batteries of cannon which now battered down hitherto impregnable castles in which the Duke had placed his trust. Throughout the campaign Biron was consistently treacherous, sending full details of the French plans to Savoy in the way that he had given information to the Cardinal-Archduke during the Spanish war. Several times he plotted Henri's murder and once told the governor of a besieged Savoyard fortress to train his guns on a spot which he would reconnoitre with the King; at the last moment his nerve broke—and he warned Henri of the danger.

Though Charles Emmanuel had no troops, snow made it a hard campaign when winter set in, and even before that the mountain paths were bad enough. Henri grumbled in a letter: 'Yesterday it was necessary to dismount 20 times and today the road was 20 times worse. France is much indebted to me because I work very hard for her.'[33] However, his discomfort was amply compensated; all of what would become French Savoy was almost completely overrun, as far as Lake Geneva. Spain and the Papacy did not wish to see a French invasion of Piedmont and, after arbitration by Clement VIII, peace was signed at Lyons on 17 January 1601. The Duke retained Saluzzo which was strategically worthless but surrendered all his lands on the Rhône; Bresse, Bugey, the Pays de Gex and Valromey. The King wrote that the Peace of Lyons was 'a purge in the Savoyard entrails but thank God the hand holding the goblet is steady so he must drain it'.[34] Henceforward Savoy turned its attention to Italy; as Charles Emmanuel put it 'Italy is an artichoke which the House of Savoy must eat leaf by leaf.' Franche Comté was now isolated, and Henri's new territories all but blocked communications between the Spanish Netherlands and Spain's possessions in northern Italy; the 'Spanish Road' might be cut at will. On the other hand France could protect Lyons and menace Milan, a threat even more effective after

Henri's treaty with the Swiss Cantons in December 1601 which gave French troops free passage through the Alpine passes.

Biron now made a partial confession, a feigned repentance which so moved Henri that he merely asked him to dismiss his Savoyard agents. But the haughty Marshal spurned forgiveness, still hoping to implement his devil's bargain with Spain and Savoy; he would murder Henri and exterminate the Bourbons, and elective monarchy would be installed in France which was to be partitioned and he, Biron, would receive his governorship of Burgundy as an independent principality. He bided his time.

The Peace of Lyons had ended a quarter of a century's campaigning which left Henri with the outlook and habits of a soldier: 'For his valour and princelike courage it is such, to say truly, as neuer any of his Precedessors, Kings of France, were matchable to him, who, for the space of almost thirty yeeres, hath, as one would say, neuer beene vnarmed, without his foote in the stirrop and his lance in the rest, hath beene himselfe in person, the formost in all perils and last out of the field ...'.[38] Other monarchs have been to war and ventured their persons in battle but few have handled a pike in the trenches, taken a hand in street fighting or pistolled their way through a cavalry mêlée with such gusto. Certainly no French ruler ever fought to more lasting effect. In the teeth of fierce opposition the Bourbon had won a crown and founded a dynasty, had ended religious war and made peace between Catholic and Protestant, had expelled a foreign invader and restored his country's boundaries, and in addition had taken the first step for a hundred years towards establishing the frontiers of modern France. For nearly half a century war had meant only humiliation for France; she had grown accustomed to being beaten in the field, invaded and occupied, or rent by sordid struggles within herself. Now she had faced her foes abroad as an equal and had overcome them. Henri IV, 'that valiant King' had given his country a taste of glory. This heady tonic brought new self-confidence and new vigour. He now had to show that he was a ruler who could bring prosperity as well as victory.

6. *L*A BELLE ET DOUCE FRANCE

'Je feray qu'il n'y aura point de laboureur en mon Royaume qui n'ait moyen d'avoir une poule dans son pot.'

Henri IV[1]

'The Noble Kingdom of France shall prosper and triumph this Year in all Pleasures and Delights, so that Foreign Nations shall willingly retire thither. Presents of Nosegays and Feasts on Birth-days, and Saints-days, Treats, Pastimes and a thousand Sports, shall keep up the Mirth. There will be plenty of delicious Wines; many Radishes in Lymosin; store of Chestnuts in Perigord and Dauphiné; a deal of Olives in Languedoc; whole shoals of Sand in Olone; a world of Fish in the Sea; swarms of Stars in the Firmament; abundance of Salt at Brouage; and prodigious quantities of Corn, Pulse, Kitchen Herbs, Flowers, Fruit, Butter, Cheese, Milk, and other Dairy Goods. No Plague, no War, no Vexation. A Fart for Poverty, hang Sorrow, cast away Care. Old Gold, such as your Double Ducats, Rose-Nobles, Angels, Spankers, Spur Royals, and Well-wool'd Sheeps of Berry will once more be in fashion, with plenty of Seraphs and Crowns with a Sun upon them …'.

Rabelais' 'Pantagruelian Prognostication'[2]

So early as 1580 a contemporary had reckoned that eight hundred thousand Frenchmen had died in battle or massacre, that nine cities had been razed to the ground, that two hundred and fifty villages had been burned down, that a multitude of dwellings had been destroyed. This was before the advent of the League and the Spanish invasions. Nearly twenty years of civil strife and bloodshed had considerably increased the terrible account when peace came in 1598. Those whose lives and property had survived staggered beneath the back-breaking taxation which the King was forced to impose, and were bled white by robber barons, brigands, or armed mobs of desperate peasantry, while trade, agriculture and industry had been everywhere disrupted. On his return to England in 1598 Dallington wrote confirming that La Noue's lament of some years previously was still justified: 'More then halfe the Noblesse is perished, the people diminished, the Treasure exhausted, the debts increased, good Order ouerthrowen, Religion languished, maner debauched, Iustice corrupted, and the men diuided.'[3]

The impact of this frightful devastation was sharpened for all classes by chronic and perennial inflation. Between the late fifteenth century and 1600 prices throughout western Europe rose at least six times, a spiral which accelerated in the last decades of the sixteenth century. Without realizing what was happening, noblemen found themselves suddenly impoverished overnight; it has been estimated that one half of seignorial land in France changed hands by purchase during the Wars of Religion. The King himself publicly mourned the decline of a nobility whose proper function was to serve the Crown in arms, declaring that many 'good and ancient families' had been ruined. The bourgeoisie suffered equally though at least its members were not debarred from 'vile trade' and had a chance to recoup their losses. For the poor, the artisans and the peasants, even the bare necessities of daily life were almost beyond reach.

Yet France was nearly the most populous country in Europe, with a population estimated at about 16 millions, compared with 20 millions in the German speaking lands, 13 millions in Italy, 10 millions in Spain and Portugal, and 4½ millions in England.[4] Further, it was an especially sad irony that every Frenchman knew his country, 'lovely, gentle France', to be the most beautiful and richly endowed in all Christendom. Half a century before, Rabelais had painted his picture of her as she should be in 'The most Certain, True and Infallible Pantagruelian Prognostication for the Year that's to Come, and Ever and Aye' which Henri may well have read. Like every man of the Renaissance the King believed in a past Golden Age which might come again. Before describing his greatest achievement it is vital to examine in some detail his attitude towards the problem of restoring France to her full health.

Henri IV saw his role as that of healer rather than rebuilder. The task has in retrospect a superficial resemblance to that of Bonaparte after the Revolution. But the Revolution made a clean sweep of the old institutions and administrative machinery, displacing the social classes upon which they rested, so that Napoleon could build from the ground up; in addition he controlled a mighty military machine, his authority being unchallenged. Henri was in a very different position. First, the traditional establishment and its institutions were still in working order and irremovably entrenched, staffed by those lawyers and municipal officials whom he could not afford to alienate. Each of the privileged Estates (or social classes), nobles and clergy as well as the so-called 'fourth Estate' of lawyers, believed that its organization and functions were sacrosanct, in much the same way as politicians, trade unionists and the Press in modern Britain. Secondly, he was far from being undisputed master of his Kingdom, even if he was undisputed King. He had pacified, not conquered his enemies; they had been fought into submission or bought but not destroyed. Magnates remained powerful: 'Gouernours and Lieutenants generall of Cities and Prouinces, are as it were Viceroyes & Regents of these places committed to them.'[5] Many of these were the great Leaguer lords who had large funds at their disposal being the price of their submission. Others like Biron and Bouillon still dreamt of independent principalities. At the same time there was a latent threat of aggression from the Religion with its para-military organization. Not least there remained a residue of Leaguer fanatics who had gone underground, dangerous bigots who could never accept that Henri was genuine in his Catholicism; in each year of his reign there would be a plot to murder him, and the wings of that strong life were always plumed with the feathers of death. To have tried to reconstruct the Kingdom in a new form would have ended in the disintegration of France.

Moreover he was tied by what amounted to an unformulated but far more binding Magna Carta, the Fundamental Law of France, which ordained the inviolability of these traditional institutions and of the rights and privileges of the Estates, a concept which was tantamount to an unwritten constitution. Though Absolutism would not be defined (by Bossuet) until the end of the seventeenth century, by 1600 there already existed a tacit distinction between absolute monarchy and despotism; even if he was above the law a King must still respect it and must always honour his subjects' legal rights. For this reason, however much of an autocrat he may have been in his secret heart and however often he may have unobtrusively overridden obstructive local franchises, Henri was scrupulously careful to observe the letter of the law and to avoid any appearance of acting arbitrarily. Hence his most undespotic pleadings with the *Parlements* and his perfectly sincere reluctance to resort to the ultimate sanction of a *lit de justice;* thus, to ensure the registration of the Edict of Nantes with as little discord as possible he personally addressed each *Parlement* with strong but flattering words. Not only did he never once act illegally, but he was a stickler for legal form. Henri IV knew very well that if the dauntingly complex and antiquated machinery of the divinely ordained state was to function at all it was necessary for the King himself to be the first lawyer in the land and himself be seen to keep the law.

There is a certain parallel with the Tudor system of managing and co-operating with the Houses of Parliament in England instead of coercing them, a system whose abandonment by the Stuarts later led to the overthrow of the English monarchy; indeed the French monarchy's despotic, and therefore illegal, treatment of the *Parlements* in the eighteenth century would be one of the root causes of the Revolution. Unfortunately the French Crown's unchallengeable position—for there was no means of withholding taxes—ensured a steady petrification which must inevitably end in self-destruction. However, while it worked, and particularly when Henri made it work, the *Ancien Régime* gave France a remarkable sense of national unity with the soundest foundation possible, that of mutual self-interest; chairman and shareholders alike were determined that their company should show a profit. If the *Parlements* could not resist the Royal demands they were nevertheless safety valves for opposition and were operated as such by the King because the law which they enshrined was very much a reality, even if indefinable; the concept was a rationalization of tradition, a tool to preserve the living, organic continuity of government and society which, like the British constitution, had quite as much strength as any carefully expounded written code. The Bourbon had won his throne by his championship of this law; he could only hope to retain it by faithfully adhering to the same law. The Henrician Restoration therefore precluded any radical change, let alone revolution.

Throughout the reign taxes were levied with impeccable legality. Henri has been criticized for not keeping his promise to summon the States General and for having recourse instead to the Assembly of Notables, but he was within his rights in not doing so; it cannot be too strongly emphasized that the States General was an extraordinary assembly which was only to be called in times of national crisis, which was never a French equivalent of the English Houses of Parliament or of the Spanish Cortes and which, as has already been shown, possessed no authority either to grant or withhold taxes. The States simply constituted a safety valve for popular grievances, a cumbersome and dangerous safety valve moreover, which frequently exploded. For the King to have summoned it would have served no purpose whatever, constitutional or administrative, national or popular, but would have merely hindered the recovery of France.

Finally it should never be forgotten that however modern the appeal of his personality, Henri's education and outlook were essentially those of the Renaissance, not of the Enlightenment; the sixteenth century produced no 'benevolent despots', even though Voltaire might later claim him as one, no revolutionary monarchs like Peter the Great or Frederick II in the eighteenth century, for the Renaissance always looked back, never forward. Its very name defines it as a *re*-birth of something old, not the introduction of something new. Taught to prefer the art and letters of Antiquity, bred on Plutarch and Livy, great rulers of this period such as Philip II, Elizabeth of England or Henri IV, regarded themselves as upholders and maintainers, never as innovators or founders. All saw their reforms as a return to some pristine model of the past. It was such an attitude of mind which caused Henri to describe himself to the Assembly of Notables as 'Liberator and Restorer of the French State'.

He had always possessed the knack of picking a good staff. In the field it had been the Birons, La Trémouille, Crillon—'*braves des braves*'—with other redoubtable warriors, and now in time of peace he showed the same flair. Ability, regardless of past loyalties, was the sole criterion for membership of Henri's Council, whose number he reduced to twelve, together with four Secretaries of State in charge of correspondence; the latter's principal function was to expedite, to ensure that the King's commands were carried out with the maximum speed. Throughout the period of reconstruction which began in 1598 and only ended with Henri's death, the key men in the Council were Villeroy, Jeannin, Bellièvre, Sillery and of course Rosny. Sir George Carew, who was British ambassador in France from 1605 until 1609, drew up 'a relation of the state of France' for James I when he returned, an early example of a valedictory dispatch which contains shrewd comments on these men; most of them were lawyers, and as a legal man himself Carew was particularly well qualified to appraise their capabilities.

Nicolas de Neufville, Seigneur de Villeroy, 'by his long experience in matters of state is held to be the dean in chapter of all the statesmen in Christendom, having attained to a great age, still vigorous and healthy, not decaying in his judgement or senses anything ... upon his advice and counsel the king chiefly relieth ...'. A Secretary of State, Villeroy who looked after all diplomatic correspondence was largely responsible for the successful negotiations at Vervins and Lyons, although he had once been a ferocious Leaguer, remaining 'in matters of religion very obstinate and very ignorant, a great friend to the see of Rome'.[6] Pierre

Jeannin, another foreign affairs expert and formerly *President* of the Dijon *Parlement*, had likewise been a staunch member of the League. The Chancellors were Pomponne de Bellièvre, also a man of great age (for the time)—he had been born in 1529—and Nicholas Brulart de Sillery who succeeded him in 1605; the latter, a former Councillor of the Paris *Parlement*, was another diplomat whose 'plausible proceedings with all men, and his obsequious secondings of the king's humours hath brought him to the height of authority'.[7] Finally there was the Huguenot Rosny who dominated the Council and was cordially disliked by his colleagues. Maximilien de Béthune, Baron and then Marquis de Rosny, and finally in 1606 Duc de Sully and Peer of France, had been born in 1560. He belonged to a modest if ancient family of the *petite noblesse* of Picardy but was inordinately proud of his birth; Sir George could class him with the obviously bourgeois Sillery as 'being raised to their greatness from very mean estate'.[8]

Sully (as he will be called henceforward) was a singularly unappealing figure in his private life. Avaricious to the extent that he jilted his fiancée to marry a richer girl, he had been enabled by a miser's fanaticism for small economies to amass a considerable fortune in the Wars from systematic plunder supplemented by shrewd dealing in horses. Bald, bearded like a patriarch, he affected extraordinary headgear of the sort which must have inspired Ben Jonson's line—'Thou look'st like anti-Christ, in that lewd hat.'[9] Tallemant, embalmer of scandal, imputed even more ludicrous eccentricities: 'One of his follies was dancing. Each evening until Henri IV's death a man named Le Roche, valet of the Chamber to the King, played the dances of the day while M. de Sully danced them by himself with I don't know what extravagant hat upon his head which he normally wore when he was in his private closet,' all this in front of a few privileged spectators.[10] His vanity extended to altering, in his notoriously untrustworthy memoirs, letters the King had written him so that they should seem more intimate and flattering, though an English historian overstated this weakness when he wrote 'Of the fantastic and discredited imaginations of Sully little use could be made'.[11] Like Malvolio, his coxcomb's pride made him quarrelsome, and his vile manners won him a host of foes to whom he showed himself malicious and vindictive.

Yet Henri saw through this unpromising mixture of faults, discerning the gold which underlay all the vanity, greed and boorishness, for he had known Sully since he was a boy; when only sixteen he had escaped with the King from Paris, and after that had fought in most of his major campaigns, showing himself a steady if hardly dashing soldier. Henri had grown accustomed to asking his blunt but always excellent advice, and where his master's interests were involved Sully was indefatigable and unshakeably loyal. During the war with Spain he had wrung desperately needed funds out of the treasury, in the teeth of corrupt officials, while the triumphant conquest of Savoy was due to the cannon he had manufactured as Master-General of the Ordnance, an early example of his flair for productive organization in which he could show the dynamism of a Beaverbrook. Since 1598 he had been *Grand Voyer* or Master of the Posts and Highways which would soon show a remarkable improvement. In 1599 Henri IV made the most important appointment of his reign; the unwieldy Council of Finance was abolished and the Kingdom's financial affairs placed under the control of a single Superintendent—Sully.

Henri now had a gifted and reliable team of administrators to whom he could delegate power with complete confidence. As a man of action he disliked any 'tedious deliberation' and so, according to the invaluable Dallington, 'In affayres of Iustice, of his Reuenues, forayne Negotiations, Dispatches and gouernment of the State, hee credites others, and meddles little himselfe.'[12] He would always listen to unwelcome arguments; 'his Maiestie hath generally this commendation, which is very laudable in a Prince, he can endure that any man should tell him the truth though of himselfe,' continued Dallington, while Carew noted 'those councellors of his who are the most potent with him, as Villeroy and Sully, govern him by terror rather than by obsequiousness'.[13] The most frequent criticism of his lieutenants was social. Thus Dallington again: 'And sure, it is a lamentable case, or at least misbeseeming in a goodly Countrey, and full of Nobilitie, that the State should be gouerned, and all matters managed by them of the *robba longa*, Aduocates and Procureurs, and Penne & Inkehorne Gentlemen, and the Noblesse themselues for want of learning, not to haue imployment.'[14] Alas, all too many French noblemen were incapable of desk work having been educated in the belief that 'A man of War should haue no more learning than to bee able to write his owne name'.[15] But the King's ministers were all the better for being *novi homines* who owed everything to the Royal favour.

However, the problems posed by the *noblesse* had to receive Henri's personal attention. The turbulent, not to say murderous, temper of 'our warlike nobility' was savagely expressed in duels which were not the smallsword minuets of eighteenth-century affairs of honour but brutish combats to the death whose ferocity was bloodily demonstrated by the classic 'duel of the hat' between Messieurs Bazanez and Lagarde Vallon. The former having sent the latter a fine hat and dared him to wear it, Lagarde Vallon donned it immediately, rushed out and, after finding Bazanez and giving him the lie, slashed his skull open with a broadsword before running him through and through, shouting each time 'for the tassel!' 'for the plumes!' Though weakened from loss of blood Bazanez suddenly rallied to cut his opponent down and then stab him fourteen times with a poignard as he lay on the ground while Lagarde Vallon managed to crack his skull with his sword pommel and bite off half his chin. At last they fainted but, amazingly, both survived, Lagarde Vallon continuing to challenge enemies with such insults as, 'I have made ashes of your house, raped your wife, and hanged your children, and am at your service.' Often these combats were miniature pitched battles, like those of *The Three Musketeers*, for the seconds usually joined in as well. What might be described as 'the officer class' was seriously depleted; during 1607 not less than four thousand noblemen perished in duals of this sort.[16] This might well be considered a blessing, but tradition and contemporary social thought still insisted on regarding the *noblesse de épée* as the most valuable members of society. Hence in 1602, badgered by Sully, the King issued the Edict of Blois whereby duellists were declared guilty of '*lèse majesté*', incurring the death penalty. Even so Henri's sentiment that he was the first nobleman of France as well as its

King, caused him to issue no less than seven thousand pardons for this peccadillo, an attitude reminiscent of Kaiser William II's ruling that any officer who fought a duel would be court martialled while any officer who refused to fight one would be cashiered. However, Henri had at least shown that he knew how to control such perennial bloodletting.

His real concern was that the nobility should not harm the community at large, that affairs of honour should not burgeon into small scale civil wars when the lords began to prey on farmers and townsmen. In 1607 the King lent cannon to the Sieur de Fontange whose daughter had been abducted by a neighbouring lord so that he could batter down the walls of her kidnapper's château. Likewise Henri was merciless to robber barons. Some of these, like Captain Guillery, whose elegant slogan was 'Peace to noblemen, death to provosts and archers, and a purse from the merchants', lived in richly furnished castles deep in the forest from where they emerged to slay and plunder; Guillery was only defeated in 1604 after a full-scale cavalry battle, and similar bands of outlaw noblemen continued to ravage the countryside throughout the reign. The true significance of the *Croquants* had been to show the fundamental hostility between seigneur and peasant. One of the King's more responsible gestures was to prohibit nobles to ride over ripening crops when they were hunting; he would not allow them any pretensions to be above the law. During the Wars such lords had acquired a taste for life at court, for entertainment and Valois luxuries, and the King welcomed their dancing attendance on him at the Louvre rather than disrupting local society or challenging his authority. This formula was, of course, carried to excess at Versailles by his grandson, who ultimately ruined the French nobility.

Above all, Henri imposed his will upon the greater magnates. Formerly, provincial governorships had been tantamount to semi-independent fiefs ruled by princely warlords. Henceforward the King insisted on appointing every town governor and garrison commander, controlling all troop movements and military supplies. No longer would he pay for private armies, and even Marshal de Lesdiguières was forced to relinquish many of his powers as Lieutenant-General of the infantry regiments. Henri was determined to be obeyed even if he still preferred to lead rather than to drive. To the truculent Duc d'Epernon he wrote: 'Your letter is that of a man who is angry—I am not so yet and I pray you don't make me.'[17] By the end of his reign the nobility were tamed, including the magnates. Henri had overcome if not eradicated neo-feudalism.

Fear of the overmighty subject dictated his harsh treatment of his sister. Catherine was now an eccentric old maid of over forty, a tiresome, sickly bluestocking who lacked both her mother's beauty and her mother's steel, though she clung stubbornly to her Protestant faith and enabled Huguenot courtiers to hold services in the Louvre. In 1598 Robert Cecil described her thus: 'She was well painted, ill dressed and strangely jewelled.'[18] Péréfixe recalled that she was 'more agreeable than fair, having one leg a little short. She was very spiritual, loved learning, and knew much for a woman; but was an obstinate Huguenot.'[19] Yet if odd and frustrated she genuinely loved her brother whom she addressed as *'mon bon et brave Roy'*. However she still held with pitiful obstinacy to her love for the worthless Soissons whose own fidelity was purely venal. In 1599 her loyal friend, the formidable Vicomtesse de Rohan—who had once told Henri she was too poor to be his wife and too well born to be his mistress—secretly published a sharp attack on the King's heartless treatment of his sister in refusing to let her marry Soissons: 'And still this diamond of firmness, this Béarnais marble, opposes it without the least sign of changing, of sorrow or of pity.' At last Henri decided to marry off the unhappy woman and his eye lit upon the Catholic Duc de Bar, heir to Charles III of Lorraine and a most eligible prince— politically. The Pope thereupon insisted on Catherine turning Papist, an impossibility. However, Henri promised her she could keep her faith and then browbeat his bastard half-brother, Antoine de Bourbon, the somewhat disreputable Archbishop of Rouen, into marrying the couple in his private chamber. Alas, once at Bar Catherine's unsympathetic father-in-law tried to force her conversion, sending away her beloved ministers and ladies. Callously Henri refused to intervene; he had to think of his image as Eldest Son of the Church. So, 'This Princess died three years after with sadness and melancholy to see herself live in a discontented manner with her husband who daily pressed her to turn Catholic.'[20] Undeniably Henri's treatment of his poor sister was unkind but he could never forget the patient, vulpine Soissons who waited grimly for Catherine like la Fontaine's fox who waited for the crow to drop the piece of cheese. For similar reasons the King prevented children of the Guise clan from contracting profitable marriages and had their parents 'live in court, so they practise not in other places; and there by play and other unthriftiness they grow poor'.[21]

The loss of Gabrielle's services drove Henri into a frenzy of whoring; in the days that followed her death he rutted with at least two ladies of the court and one lady of the town, a professional prostitute called *La Glandée*—the Glandered One. While a slave to sensuality Henri was far from being the Great Lover of legend. The sad truth is that for all his charm and warmth he did not know how to love properly or to make women love him which was why he was so often cuckolded by his mistresses; with the possible exception of Corisande, now growing fat and red faced in her forgotten retirement, he showed that he was almost incapable of loving a woman for herself. It was inevitable that he would one day fall victim to his own lust and be caught by a thoroughly dangerous woman. This happened less than two months after Gabrielle's burial when he met the last of his three great concubines.

He had fallen into a real wasp's nest. Henriette d'Entragues was eighteen years old, daughter to François d'Entragues, Governor of Orléans, a ruthless adventurer who had married Marie Touchet, once mistress of Charles IX. This simple baker's daughter was known for her soft, amiable nature—her motto was *'je charme tout'*—but her bastard Valois son, Charles d'Auvergne, was no less ferocious than his terrifying father. His beautiful half-sister Henriette was almost as savage in her own way. A slim brunette, with a disturbing bosom and a small round face whose greatest charm was a pair of flashing black eyes, she at once infatuated Henri with her sulky yet lively grace, provoking airs and cruel, amusing wit. Instinctively this youthful combination of Anne Boleyn and Becky Sharp, an archetypal gold-digger, knew how to exploit the King's wild jealousies. He had been ready to marry Gabrielle d'Estrées so there was no reason why he should not make Henriette his Queen instead. Advised and encouraged by her father she laid careful plans.

Everything went as she hoped. She had already taken lovers, the Prince de Joinville and the Duc de Bellegarde, Henri's old rival for Gabrielle's favours, who despite his yellow face—he was known as *Feuillemorte* (Dead Leaf)—was famed for his conquests. The King caught the Prince and the Duke fighting a duel over Mlle d'Entragues, much to his fury and her delight. The seductive young termagant played him like a salmon till he was ready to be gaffed: 'She had certainly many charms, nor had she less spirit and cunning. Her refusals did more and more provoke the King's passion.'[22] Thus on 5 August 1599 he visited her in Paris bringing a gift, a magnificent pearl necklace, but Henriette who was playing for really high stakes refused it with hauteur whereupon Henri—obviously to the secret amusement of those who told the story to L'Estoile—carefully replaced the necklace in its case; next day he sent her a big box of crystallized apricots. She continued to blow hot and cold until at last, as planned, the desperate King literally bought her from her fond father who asked for the title of Marshal although he had never seen a battle, a large sum in cash to be paid down immediately, and a document promising that should Henriette have a son by the King he would marry her as soon as he was divorced and then legitimize the child. As Sully put it, 'The Lady was no novice ... she demanded no less than one hundred thousand crowns for the price of her favours.' In the face of Sully's frantic disapproval, Henri agreed to everything save the title of Marshal; the document, in which Henri swore to keep the bargain 'before God on our faith and word as a King', was dated 1 October 1599.[23] This sordid transaction was perhaps the most disgraceful and irresponsible in his entire career—to satisfy his lust he had once more jeopardized the future of the French monarchy.

However, he was just as capable of playing a double game in love as in war. When news of his annulment from Margot arrived on 17 October he allowed his envoys to proceed with negotiations for the hand of a Tuscan princess, not so much from a sense of duty to the nation as from a need to arrive at an advantageous agreement over the vast sums he owed to Grand Duke Ferdinand de Medici who had financed his campaigns against the Spaniard. The Florentine marriage took on even more financial importance when further debts were incurred to subsidize the campaign against Charles Emmanuel of Savoy. During the latter's visit to Henri in late 1599 and early 1600 Henriette was among those whom he tried to bribe, giving her presents and promising to stop the Medici marriage. Henri got wind of this and on 21 April 1600 wrote angrily to the woman he now called 'my own heart' demanding that she send back both his ring and his promise and reproaching her with a wicked nature and with ingratitude—he had made her Marquise de Verneuil, a title which was accompanied by a splendid château. Despite this disillusionment they were soon living together again and only the longed for pregnancy prevented the new Marquise from accompanying him on the Savoy campaign.

Henriette might well have become Queen but for a thunderbolt—in the literal sense. Far gone with child, she was resting in her bedchamber at Fontainebleau in June 1600 when the room was struck by lightning which actually passed under her bed. Terror and shock made her miscarry, dropping a dead boy who had he lived would have been Dauphin. The King now regarded his promise as invalidated, even if Mme de Verneuil did not, and in October he was married to Marie de Medici, the twenty-seven-year-old daughter of His Serene Highness, the late Francesco I, Grand Duke of Tuscany, by an Austrian Archduchess. It was a sound choice. Her uncle, the present Grand Duke, was anti-Spanish, respected by the Pope, and fabulously rich besides being able to exert invaluable pressure on the Florentine money market. The wedding was celebrated by proxy at Florence; ironically the Duc de Bellegarde deputized for Henri; some years after his death the occasion was portrayed exuberantly and inaccurately—the King is shown as present—by Rubens. Marie then sailed for France, accompanied by a fleet of Tuscan galleys. All this time her husband was living with Henriette, as though nothing had happened, while writing graceful and apparently love-sick letters to the Queen he had never seen.

Although thoroughly desirable from a political point of view, Queen Marie was less desirable for her personal charms. Fortunately among the multitude of female types for which the King had a weakness was one for fat goddesses of the sort immortalized by Rubens, steatopygous charmers with deep, dimpled rolls of silky pink flesh and bright golden tresses—there is a certain kinship with the old English barmaid. Marie de Medici was of this kind with wits and character to match, those of a vulgar mare, selfish, overbearing, opinionated and irredeemably stupid; she had inherited none of that Medici subtlety and brilliance which had been so evident in her formidable relative and predecessor. However, at first her true qualities were not apparent. By 8 December she had reached Lyons where the King arrived on the evening of the next day, having galloped through the pouring rain after saying a fond farewell to Henriette. As soon as he had supped he was in bed with his spouse. Marie, who was at least a full-blooded Italian and had waited too long for a husband, performed so well during the consummation that afterwards the King boasted of her prowess to his appreciative cronies. After a month's marital bliss he left Lyons and rode hard for Paris where he lovingly rejoined Henriette. Here with some apprehension he waited for his Queen who was making a slow and leisurely state progress towards her new home.

The horrified noblewoman whom Henri had entrusted with the task of informing Queen Marie that Mme de Verneuil would be one of her ladies-in-waiting, took to her bed with a feigned illness. By now an angry Queen had learnt all about Henriette and the Royal sex life. When the dread moment finally came and a spitting Henriette was introduced by some intrepid dowager Henri blurted out, 'She has been my mistress—now she is going to be your most biddable and obedient servant.' Unfortunately 'the most biddable and obedient servant' continued to scowl viciously at the Queen, whom she later described as 'your fat Florentine banker', who had ruined all her fine hopes, refusing to curtsey whereupon the King had to push her down by main force to kneel before an infuriated Queen. This did not bode well for Henri's naïve belief that he might obtain a harmonious *ménage à trois*. He also appointed another old friend lady-in-waiting, the Marquise de Guercheville, who had once refused to sleep with him, saying, 'I'm making you a lady of honour because you really are one.'

He continued to sleep with both Marie and Henriette who both gave him children. However, after a year of this strenuous relationship the Queen triumphed, and on 27 September 1601 she bore a Dauphin; 'the birth was very hard and the infant laboured till he was all of a purple colour'.[24] The King was beside himself with happiness and the child was given the name of Louis, 'so sweet and dear to France for the memory of the great St Lewis and of the good King Lewis XII, father of the people'.[25] Throughout France cannon roared, *Te Deums* thundered and a delighted country danced and sang with joyful relief that the dynasty's future was secure. It is ironical in view of his legendary lack of interest in sex that the future Louis XIII should have had such a begetting. Marie went on to give Henri a legitimate quiverful, while Henriette continued to produce proofs of his affection.

With all these distractions the King did not neglect his cares of state. He and Sully laboured to increase the Royal revenues. It is impossible to exaggerate the nightmare complexity of the *Ancien Régime* taxation system with its crazy mosaic of regional and social variations in assessment and imposition, its host of levies, dues and tariffs, ordinary and extraordinary, direct and indirect, sometimes nominal, sometimes crushing and frequently self-defeating, and its hydra-headed multitude of exemptions, the whole administered by a battening host of greedy officials; Dallington shuddered at 'the infinite number in all France, vpon which they lye, as thicke as the Grassehoppers in Aegypt'.[26] Why this chaotic system could not be simplified was of course a question of fundamental law; the rights of those who levied taxes had to be protected no less than the rights of those who were exempt from them, official posts being sacrosanct. All that Henri and Sully could hope to do was to try to work this fantastically cumbersome and antiquated engine: it was a question of oil rather than spare parts, let alone of new machinery.

They had first to combat the now almost traditional practices of embezzlement and plain theft which devoured the greater part of the revenue, and to force those who collected monies due to the King to pay them into his treasury. Much of the Royal income from indirect taxes reached him through the agency of 'farmers' whom the impossible system made indispensable; at least they had an incentive to extract the maximum from the unfortunate taxpayer. By cutting their percentage Sully made an immediate profit without impairing the tax farmers' greedy industry. Unlawful exemptions were set aside and corrupt assessments readjusted. In the words of Péréfixe the Superintendent of Finance 'had so well bridled both the gatherers and the farmers that they could no longer devour those great morsels they did heretofore'.[27]

Sir George Carew was full of admiration:

When Sully came first to the managing of the revenues, he found (as he himself told me) all things out of order, full of robbery, of officers full of confusion, no treasure, no munition, no furniture for the king's houses and the crown indebted three hundred million; that is three millions of pounds sterling. Since that time, that in February 1608, he had acquitted one hundred and thirty millions of that debt, redeeming the most part of the revenues of the crown that were mortgaged; that he had brought good store of treasure into the Bastille, filled most of the arsenals with munition, furnished most of the king's houses with tapestry and other movables; and where the farms of the whole realm amounted then but to 800,000 l. sterling, this year 1609, he had let them out for 1,000,000 l. and that without exacting any more upon the people than was paid before, but only by reducing that to the king's coffers which was embezzled by under-officers.[28]

To appreciate the true magnitude of Sully's achievement it is necessary to know a little about the cumbersome machinery which he had to use. The principal direct tax was the *Taille*. In the misleadingly named *pays d'élection* this was an arbitrarily assessed percentage of farm income, but in the *pays d'état*, where taxes were voted by the province's Estates, a specified percentage of a man's actual property. As the nobility and

clergy were exempt and many of the richer bourgeois managed to purchase exemption the *Taille* fell almost exclusively on the bowed backs
of the peasantry, causing much misery and hardship. Carew must have
had this most hated of all taxes in mind when he accused the French
King of 'sharing the booty gotten from the common people … with
the clergy, nobility, gentry and officers of justice…'.[29]

Yet, while he proudly proclaimed himself to be the first nobleman
in France, Henri was also conscious that he was 'father of his people';
he cared for his peasants genuinely if unsentimentally. In 1600 the King
told Charles Emmanuel of Savoy: 'Should God let me live longer I will
see that no peasant in my realm is without the means to have a chicken
in his pot.'[30] Indeed this wish for a chicken in every pot every Sunday
is one of the most enduring of the legends of Henri IV. He knew that
France depended on the *laboureur;* hearing, in 1610, that Royal troops
in Champagne were pillaging a district he shouted with fury. 'Leave at
once, give the orders—you'll answer for it.' Henri told his officers wildly,
'What! if you ruin the people who feed me, who supply the needs of the
state, who then is going to pay your pensions, gentlemen? Vive Dieu!
to rob my people is to rob me.'[31] This is why in the eighteenth century
Henri IV was described as the only French King whose memory was
kept green by the poor.

The most important of the indirect taxes was the *Gabelle*, a duty
on salt which for no reason save tradition varied widely from province
to province; in some regions prices were twenty-five times the cost of
production while the salt had to be purchased from licensed warehouses
who provided two qualities—one for the table, the other for pickling. The
collection of this infuriating tax was organized by the 'Farmers-General'
who in turn employed subfarmers, each deducting a handsome profit.
The farmers also collected another tax similar to the *Gabelle*, the *Aides*
or duties on wine and cider. In addition there were the *Douanes*, customs
levied at internal as well as external frontiers; merchandise entering a
province, and sometimes certain towns, had to pay duty—goods from
the Kingdom's borders might be mulcted as much as forty times before
reaching Paris. Assessment and collection of all these taxes was dictated

by no fixed standards or practice and often decided by such irresponsible factors as opposition from local magnates—or the lack of it—or, more usually, sheer crass inefficiency.

Another source of revenue was the much decried *Paulette*. Offices and titles were already being sold, just as in Jacobean England one could buy a peerage or a baronetcy. However, in 1604, on the advice of a lawyer named Paulet, the French Crown decreed that in future any office which was bought became the buyer's absolute property in return for an annual payment of one sixtieth of the purchase price and could then be re-sold, bequeathed or inherited; such property also conferred the privileges of nobility including tax exemption. Many contemporaries were horrified by this apparently spendthrift measure. Dallington considered it 'a very dangerous & hurtfull Marchandise, both for the Prince and subiect'[32] while 'touching this selling of offices' commented Sir George Carew, 'many suppose that the king receives greater prejudice therein than the profit or gain he draws thereout is worth'.[33] No doubt Henri regarded the *Paulette* as a temporary expedient. Yet there were at least some arguments in its favour. A new nobility of hereditary magistrates was created to balance the old feudal nobility, an innovation which also furthered Henri's policy of favouring the lawyers and the upper bourgeoisie. In addition it made for social mobility. Before the Revolution almost every rich self-made man could and did buy a title; professional pedigree forgers provided him with impeccably feudal ancestors. Indeed the class structure of the *Ancien Régime* was far less rigid than is generally supposed, the aristocratic origins of perhaps most of the nobility resting on make believe rather than genuine blue blood. This was a direct consequence of the *Paulette*.

Sully was responsible for implementing reforms; most of these were simple economies of which his talents as a miser made him the ideal enforcer. He combined the functions of Minister of Finance, Minister of the Interior, Minister of Transport and Minister of Works and was regarded as a sort of Prime Minister, although unlike Richelieu or Mazarin he did not control foreign policy. A glutton for work, rising at four in the morning to begin an exhausting day, he never spared himself. Nor did he spare others in his demands for properly audited accounts and detailed returns. His committees of privilege examined the nobles' rights to pensions and exemptions, to Crown lands and revenues, demanding full restitution where these had been usurped. These, together with his sternness, his meanness and his gauche arrogance made him the most hated man in France. Soissons thought to dispose of him by a duel but Henri 'caused it to be notified that whosoever should attempt Sully should find the king's own person for his second'.[34]

Henri's employment of this unpleasant minister enabled him to avoid much of the odium incurred by unpopular policies, as Carew understood very well: '... the King supporting Sully in all his rough courses, which he hath taken for the encreasing of the revenues of his crown, he hath found great profit thereby himself. But Sully hath thereby made himself extremely odious to great and small ...'.[35] In fact Henri was surprisingly thrifty. Carew wrote:

> He is excellent also in his oeconomical faculty, or looking into matters of profit; omitting no means or advantage of enriching his realm generally, nor of drawing the best offices and inheritances to his children both legitimate and natural. In way of liberality he payeth more pensions than ever any of his predecessors did; and therein also he useth great art and need to furnish the sums requisite thereto, out of means little burdensome to himself, and distributeth them with great choice to persons of importance who may either serve him in his occasions or at least be concerned by the means thereof, from being busy in attempting against himself.[36]

Dallington was almost shocked by this thriftiness: 'For my part, I thinke he giues S.P.Q.R. not *Senatus populoque Romano*: that is, to all sorts of people, but *Si Peu Que Rien*, so little, as scarse any at all. They say, that the chamber of Accounts, is to examine the Kings gifts: and if they find any vnmeasurable, to shorten them.' Henri 'makes money with his teeth saith the Frenchman, meaning his sparing of great and superfluous expence at his table'.[37] In fact like so many of his fellow countrymen he was careful rather than mean.

By 1602 the French nobility was angrily discontented. Powers which it had to come to consider as a right during the last forty years were being whittled away so that its members could no longer live like princes. Not only had they lost their private armies and their fiefs but tax reforms, examination of privileges and the enforcement of the laws were seriously, indeed ruinously, hurting their pocket while the price rise still continued; every magnate was affected, finding it harder each day to maintain his lordly state. Insult went with injury. If the King's measures were irksome, as implemented by Sully and his minions they were outrageous. Moreover, great nobles resented their exclusion from the King's Council and from centres of influence in time of peace, together with the unpalatable fact that positions of real power were kept for upstarts like Sully or for those pretentious, grasping bourgeois who came from nowhere yet whom the King so obviously favoured. Therefore if the end of anarchy also meant the end of neo-feudalism they preferred anarchy. No doubt Henri was a great King, but a nobleman had to live, and live furthermore in the style to which he was accustomed. There was a leader to weld their hot, fierce resentment into a really dangerous opposition which would strike back at the tyrant—Biron. With malevolent industry that implacable though secret enemy approached every disaffected element in France, every foe of Henri at home and abroad; Spain, Charles Emmanuel, intransigent Leaguers, the Huguenots and their chieftains, independent-minded towns, and even Henriette, that little viper in the King's bosom who wished to spite her lover for jilting her. Above all the Marshal sought to rouse the entire nobility, whether a Prince of the Blood like Soissons, an overmighty Protestant lord like Bouillon, or some hedge-squire's ragged cadet reduced to beggary by the disappearance of his sole income—loot. The nobles were about to turn on Henri and rend him, about to destroy France as a nation. It was the crisis of the restoration.

Biron's chief abettor was his bosom friend, that picturesque ruffian, Charles, Comte d'Auvergne, a violent, malicious but subtle intriguer. The son of Charles IX was always in need of money to pay for his vices and dissipations. Not only did he make life a hell for his neighbours in Paris by his practical jokes and outrages but he never paid his lackeys who instead were told to go out into the streets and rob passers-by. An adventurer like this was only too pleased to help topple a King from his throne.

However, the plotters misjudged both the temper and the unity of the disaffected nobility. While the mood of its members was undeniably savage and though their nostalgia for the old, undisciplined days was keen enough, they were not prepared to risk their necks against so formidable an opponent as Henri IV without some tangible prospect of success. Not only were the firmness and efficiency which they so detested forbidding but his position was growing steadily stronger. As early as 1598 Dallington had noted that 'ye daily heare his owne Subiects speake of him more liberally',[38] and the birth of the Dauphin in 1601 had been another powerful psychological asset. In addition there were certain magnates who appeared to be wholeheartedly loyal. Such odds were far too great for a cautious trimmer like Soissons while the Protestant lords would never move unless they had the entire Religion behind them. In 1601 the Duc de Bouillon summoned the nine commanding officers of the Huguenots' military organization to meet him secretly and then put forward Biron's plan, an unholy alliance of the disaffected, which would share France between its members once Henri had been overthrown; the realm was to be divided into a number of principalities and free towns. D'Aubigné who was one of the nine spoke passionately against the proposal, arguing that idolaters never kept their bargains and that the Religion might well find itself in worse case than it was at present. (Henri once said that the word of d'Aubigné discontented was as good as another man's gratitude.) The nine rejected the Duke's proposal outright; he was given to understand that no support would be forthcoming from his co-religionists.

Nonetheless, Biron, encouraged by Spanish agents, was undeterred. During a mission to England in 1601, with ill-mannered effrontery he lamented the death of Elizabeth's favourite, the Earl of Essex—who had been executed the previous year for an attempted coup d'état—to the Queen's face, whereupon the angry old woman gave him a sharp lecture on presumption and told him to take warning by the fate of Essex, pointing at the Earl's weathered mask which was still rotting on Tower Bridge.[39] But the Marshal blundered arrogantly on to his doom until his bubble burst in the spring of 1602. His former private secretary, the Sieur de La Fin, 'a lively cunning intriguing fellow', took fright and laid damning evidence before the authorities. He had kept drafts of the Marshal's most treasonable correspondence by burning blank sheets of paper in their place in the fire in Biron's bedchamber; his master, lying on the bed, was too lazy to supervise the burning. The plot which these revealed was capable of becoming a dangerous reality, despite the general lack of support from the nobility; when the time came Spain and Savoy would mass troops on the frontiers while Biron and Auvergne with their friends and relatives would raise disaffected areas of France.

Yet even now the King was reluctant to destroy the old comrade who had so often played Marshal Ney to his own Napoleon. In June Biron was invited to Fontainebleau where Henri walked him round the great garden, in all the soothing beauty of early summer, offering him a pardon if he would confess his treason. The Marshal refused violently, shouting he had no need of forgiveness as he had not committed any crime. Next morning, that of Thursday 13 June, the King again took him into the gardens for the same purpose and was again rebuffed. Just before midnight Biron and Auvergne, who had finally realized their peril and were trying to escape, were arrested. For the last time Henri tried to save his friend, saying, 'Marshal, remember what I told you!' But the traitor whom pride had brought to the brink of insanity remained coldly silent. 'Good night, *Baron* de Biron,' ended the King grimly; his use of the Marshal's old title implied that he had meant to strip him of all his dignities.

His trial on 17 July 1602 was both grandiose and horrific, the last act in a fallen hero's self-destruction publicly played out against a back-cloth of splendid pageantry. He was brought before the Great Chamber of the *Parlement* of Paris to which his fellow Peers of France had been summoned, an assembly which, as well as being the highest court of law in the land, was also the French equivalent of the House of Lords and no less dignified or daunting. However, the Marshal-Duke's fellow Peers refused the summons (a precedent which lost them their legal and political voice for ever) so Biron was tried before twenty-seven judges, red robed, befurred and bonneted; it was an eloquent confrontation between the old and the new nobility; He rallied sufficiently to make a moving speech which owed more to art than to logic for he accused La Fin of having set on paper what he had merely pondered, in a hellish plot to bring him to his doom. But the judges, coldly dispassionate, were not to be deflected from that damning indictment. The Marshal was found guilty of High Treason and sentenced to be beheaded in the Place de Grève. Instead of showing a veteran's cool indifference Biron raved and ranted, shrieking that the King owed his throne to him. The spectacle was as embarrassing as it was tragic. He had been destroyed by pride but his pride was that of a man who was mentally ill. His execution on 31 July was macabre to a degree. Henri spared him the torment of a death in public so the end came in the courtyard of the Bastille. Here, the half-crazed Marshal was led out to die at 5 o'clock in the afternoon. He behaved like a maniac, raging against fortune and refusing to have his eyes bandaged or his hair bound up; when at last he was dragged to the block the unnerved headsman struck him on the base of the skull and finally his head when hacked off bounced three times, spurting out far more blood than did his trunk.[40] This frightful scene was an oddly fitting end for a devotee of witchcraft. The King commented sadly, 'I would have given 200,000 crowns that he had left room to pardon him. He did me good service though I saved his life three times.'

Auvergne was soon released, and escaped scot free. Henri was much criticized for this leniency to the bastard Valois who was hardly less guilty than Biron; it was said that he could not resist Henriette's pleading for her half-brother. However, it is much more likely, as the Marshal de Bassompierre suggested, that Henri had not forgotten the deathbed of Charles IX who had commended his son to his protection. The King only killed when it was unavoidable. And Biron's lurid end had caught the popular imagination, deterring many disaffected noblemen.

It even caught the popular imagination in England where a parallel was drawn with the fall of Essex. In 1608 George Chapman—whose translation of Homer was one day to be so admired by Keats—published his masterpiece: 'The Conspiracie and Tragedie of Charles Duke of Byron, Marshall of France. Acted lately in two playes.' Biron was cast as a figure of Satanic grandeur, a fallen archangel whom the King does his best to save. Thus, he warns the Duke against an Iago-like La Fin:

> Why suffer you that ill aboding vermin
> To breed so near your bosom? be assured
> His haunts are ominous; not the throats of ravens
> Spent on infected houses, howls of dogs,
> When no sound stirs, at midnight; apparitions
> And strokes of spirits, clad in black men's shapes,
> Or ugly women's; the adverse decrees
> of constellations, nor security
> In vicious peace, are surer fatal ushers
> of femall mischiefs and mortalities
> Than this prodigious fiend is, where he fawns;
> Lafiend, and not La Fin, he should be call'd.

But in the end the King cries:

> Come you are an atheist, Byron, and a traitor
> Both foul and damnable. Thy innocent self?
> No leper is so buried quick in ulcers
> As thy corrupted soul.

Not only did Chapman tell the story with remarkable accuracy, but he also portrayed the French court, even Henriette. After a masque Henri exclaims:

> This show hath pleased me well, for that it figures
> The reconcilement of my Queen and mistress.

Indeed, when the two plays were first performed in 1607—before the English court—the horrified French Ambassador had its actors arrested whereupon various offending passages, which included an entire act, were removed. Nevertheless. 'The Conspiracie and Tragedie' shows that Henri had his admirers in Jacobean England, Chapman depicting him as a model sovereign, wise and humane, with an exalted concept of kingship and its responsibilities:

> He should be born grey-headed that will bear
> The sword of Empire.[41]

Henri IV knew that if France were to prosper much more was needed than more efficient methods of taxation. Mercantilism, the theory of economics then universally accepted and to which Henri and Sully both subscribed, had an oddly modern flavour except that capital was identified exclusively with gold and silver of which it was necessary for a country to earn and keep the greatest possible share. The maximum of goods must be exported, the minimum imported; hence though little importance was attached to internal, domestic trade, home industries were keenly fostered. To achieve prosperity state aid was therefore essential, together with high customs walls and a numerous and hardworking population. Few financial ministers of the period were able to put the theory into practice with such devotion and success as Sully. That he was able to do so was in large part due to his Royal master.

Sully gave French agriculture a golden encomium: *'le labourage et le pastourage estoient les deux mamelles dont la France estoit alimentée et les vrais mines et trésors du Pérou'*—tillage and pasture were the two paps from which

France took her nourishment and the true mines and treasures of Peru. Undeniably the Kingdom's greatest source of wealth lay in its crops and livestock but its unscientific husbandry left much to be desired. In 1600 Olivier de Serres published a revolutionary treatise on agriculture, the *Théâtre d'agriculture des champs*. On his model farm at Pradel in Languedoc this Huguenot squire tried to make better use of the soil, sowing grass where normally land was left to lie fallow, introducing root crops for winter fodder, and importing hops from England and maize from Italy. His book caused a sensation and so impressed Henri (who shared his grandson Charles' enthusiasm for science) that to popularize it a part was read to him every day at dinner; as he always dined in public, when not only courtiers but any curious sightseer might watch him, no more effective promotion exercise could be imagined. Disappointingly, de Serres' innovations were adopted by only a few enthusiasts; too many nobles took no interest in their *domaines* while the peasants, conservative as always, clung stubbornly to the old, wasteful ways. In certain areas Dutch experts were engaged to drain fen and march land but this too was on a very limited scale. Even so peaceful conditions and the natural industry of the French peasant were quite sufficient to win abundant harvests from their country's rich earth. Thus Carew could write that by 1608 France was exporting grain to the extent that it 'robbeth all Spain of their silver and gold that is brought thither out of their Indies'.[42]

To encourage trade communications were improved. Waterways— the period's railways—received special attention, locks and quays being installed along the rivers while canals were dug, notably the junction between the Seine and the Loire. Roads were repaired and provision made for maintenance; as *Grand Voyer* Sully ordered elms to be planted at the roadside—like Napoleon's poplars—trees which the peasants called 'Rosnys' for many years. Such measures increased the yield from internal tariffs, for Sully was not sufficiently daring to give trade a far more powerful stimulus by abolishing them. Nevertheless his measures gave considerable benefit to both external and internal trade; though the latter was of small interest to the government it nonetheless flourished, adding to the Kingdom's general prosperity.

Like all good Mercantilists the King and Sully were anxious to limit imports of manufactured goods as well as of raw materials. During the recent breakdown of society there had been a widespread collapse in the production of many indispensable articles; in the 1590s the English had exploited the situation, sending shiploads of old hats and cast-off boots into Normandy where they sold at exorbitant prices. With the advent of peace French crafts and industries quickly re-established themselves, but this was not enough for the government who wished to reduce the import of foreign luxuries. Many new ideas came from Henri's former *valet-de-chambre*, Bartelemy de Laffemas, another Huguenot who in 1601 founded a Chamber of Commerce: 'It was said that under his leadership the Commission de Commerce had 150 meetings in little more than two years between 1601 and 1604. Silk manufacture, horse breeding, linen and fustian manufacture, gilt leatherwork on the Spanish model, glass, tiles, tapestry, rich textiles in the south, river and canal works, shipbuilding and general inventions were only a few of the matters investigated.'[43] The King summoned Olivier de Serres to Paris to discuss the revival of the silk industry; mulberry trees were introduced from Italy as well as skilled Florentine silk weavers, and if progress was small it was substantial, forming a foundation for the great French silk industries of Louis XIV's reign. Other luxury industries which were founded during this period were the Gobelin tapestry looms—in those days tapestry took the place of wallpaper—and the Savonnerie carpet manufactory, besides glass blowing and pottery. Mirror glass and lace making also prospered. Such basic products as wool and cloth likewise received attention, as did the primitive iron and steel industry, lead piping and even fresh water fisheries. Mineral resources were scientifically investigated and after deposits of gold, silver, lead, copper, iron and tin had been founded Henri created the office of Grand Master of the Mines. Royal forests were reclaimed and replanted. A flood of edicts issued from the King's Council, dealing with a bewildering multitude of projects. None of the country's natural resources was neglected. While it must be admitted that many of these schemes never reached fruition they were nonetheless the basis of much prosperity in later reigns.

Nor was commercial diplomacy neglected. A spectacularly profitable treaty with Turkey obtained special privileges for French traders in the rich Levantine ports, including resident consuls, besides allowing French smacks to fish in North African waters. In 1604 a tariff war with Spain, who desperately needed French imports closed very much in France's favour, while treaties with James I put an end to English piracy in the Channel and gave French and English merchants equal rights in each other's country. In Germany an understanding was reached with the still powerful Hansa. By the strict Mercantilist creed these were no mean gains.

There is a tendency to regard Sully as an earlier Colbert—Louis XIV's financial wizard who created the prosperity which made possible the Grand Siècle—and therefore to underestimate Henri's contribution. As David Ogg says, 'In comparison with Colbert Sully was little better than a painstaking clerk.' On the other hand, unlike Louis, Henri IV did far more than merely support and encourage his minster. While one must not make the mistake of belittling the latter's role, it is nonetheless true that, despite his brilliance as organizer and administrator, Sully undeniably lacked his Royal master's fertile, creative imagination, his enthusiastic response to new ideas. In fact the economic achievements of Henri's reign were the product of a joint effort, of a partnership between King and minister. Thus it was Henri whose interest was largely responsible for the re-establishment of the silk industry, who preached the agricultural revolution of Olivier de Serres. Indeed in the matter of colonies the King showed himself to be a more enterprising and at the same time more orthodox Mercantilist than Sully who regarded them as a waste of money.

The French had been visiting Canada for fish and furs since 1534 but they had never settled. Then, in 1597 Henri gave the Marquis de la Roche a commission as Lieutenant-General with orders to found a colony but the expedition was unsuccessful. Other attempts proved equally fruitless until 1608 when the heroic explorer Samuel de Champlain, who had fought in the Royal armies against Spain and whom the new King knew personally, managed to establish a tiny but lasting settlement of fur traders at Quebec. Throughout all the failures and setbacks Henri continued to encourage the would-be colonists in the face of Sully's dour scepticism. This foundation of what eventually became a Franco-American culture was certainly no mean achievement. Its immediate significance, however, is to show that the King was sufficiently open minded to adopt and further economic projects which were not those of his great minister.

Many books discuss the economic restoration of France under Henri IV, but few convey the immense extent and feverish tempo of the sheer work involved, nor the surprisingly modern degree of state intervention; commissions sat constantly to investigate problems of finance, administration and technology, new laws were enacted every month, laws which the King, that natural lawyer, not only read but helped to draft. If he disliked long debates, nevertheless it was he who ultimately had to take all the decisions; despite his women and his hunting Henri IV was his own first minister, his own Richelieu or Mazarin. Indeed in many respects he was strikingly like a modern Prime Minister or President. The only other French ruler to possess his thoroughness and his capacity for work, and perhaps too his legal sense, was Napoleon.

Henri was nonetheless deeply appreciative of Sully's loyal service, rewarding his bearish henchman with the highest dignities; he was made Governor of the Bastille in 1602, Governor of Poitou in 1603 and at last Duke and Peer of France. These honours were accompanied by suitable emoluments while the new Duke was allowed to indulge his avarice to the full, amassing a vast fortune; no one can deny that he earned every sou. Indeed some of Henri's panegyrists were inclined to eulogize Sully, like Péréfixe who described him as 'a man of good order, exact, a good husband, a keeper of his word; not prodigal nor proud, nor carried away by vain follies or expenses, or play, or women, or any other things not convenient for a man Entrusted with such an Employment'.[44] Tallemant's sneers were nearer the mark: 'There was never any Superintendent so crabbed and surly.'[45] Sully's lack of personal charm makes all the more commendable the support of Henri, that lover of good fellowship.

Certain magnates still dared to plot against the King. First, there was the amateurish scheme of the Prince de Joinville, youngest of the sons of Guise and of whom Sully commented 'nothing could be more light, more whimsical and more unsteady'. The King was contemptuously merciful, merely banishing this foolish young lord: 'Here is the prodigal son himself, I shall use him like a child and pardon him for yours and Monsieur de Rosny's sake,' he told his parents. The conspiracy of 1604 between the Comte d'Auvergne and the d'Entragues, father and daughter, was a much more dangerous business; their project was that Henriette and her children would flee to Spain whereupon Philip III would recognize Henriette's son as King of France as soon as Henri had been assassinated. The King's she-wolf mistress resolved to avenge herself in this way when in the summer of 1604 her father was ordered to surrender that infamous Promise of Marriage (which had been concealed in a bottle). Two attempts were made to ambush Henri but both failed and then Henriette's sister informed the authorities. Auvergne and Entragues were condemned to death in February 1605 while Henriette was confined to a convent. However, the King could never be stern with women for very long, even if his mistress's perfidy must have wounded him cruelly. Yet the true extent of her involvement was uncertain and for all her malice it is unlikely that she would have connived at murder; indeed, infuriated by her half-brother's attempts to incriminate her this woman 'whom disgrace could not humble, whose insolence detection could not abate', demanded 'justice for myself, mercy for my father, and a rope for my brother'. Moreover it had been a very ineffectual conspiracy. Soon, fond as ever of her 'beauty, wit and sprightliness', Henri forgave Henriette though she never quite regained her old influence.

Much more formidable were the intrigues of the Duc de Bouillon who was not only supported by a swarm of relatives and vassals in the Limousin but had some hope of stirring up his co-religionists in 1605, the year in which the Edict of Nantes stipulated they must surrender their *places de sûreté*. The Huguenots were neither so realistic nor so tractable as they had been in 1601. When their general assembly met at Châtelherault at the end of July 1605 it was proposed that future meetings should be held in camera, that resolutions should be kept secret, and that members of the Religion should strive to implement such resolutions whatever the cost to their own lives or property. The proposal was motivated by a determination to retain the *places de sûreté* which formed the foundation of the Reform's para-military organization; its implementation would have made the Protestants of France more of a state-within-a-state than ever, removing all Royal influence. The King immediately recognized the danger, while realizing that the proposal stemmed from fear and insecurity rather than from any genuinely aggressive intent. He therefore sent Sully, himself a sound if flexible Calvinist, to the assembly as Royal commissioner. This plain-spoken advocate argued bluntly enough but was all the more persuasive for his rough realism; the assembly rejected the proposal in return for Henri's guarantee that the Reform might continue to occupy its *places de sûreté* for a further seven years. Mishandled, Huguenot apprehensions could have resulted in yet another War of Religion; they were to do so during the next reign. As it was Carew noted in 1609, 'The body of those of the reformed religion is a great thorn in his foot, being not only constrained to tolerate them as a different regiment from the rest of his realm, but to give fortresses into their hands also, and to pay for keeping them against himself.'[46]

There remained Bouillon. The King marched into the Limousin in the autumn of 1605, blowing up his strongholds and hanging his adherents. The Duke had taken refuge in his town of Sedan, which then constituted an independent principality, but at the end of March 1606 Henri arrived there with an army and fifty cannon, to receive Bouillon's humble submission and surrender. The last challenge to the Royal authority had been successfully averted; the Bourbon had completed his political restoration of the French monarchy.

The magnitude of Henri's achievement in restoring good government and prosperity to France may be judged by comparing it with the legacy of Philip II in Spain and of Elizabeth and James I in England. Of the three great national monarchies of western Europe France alone managed to adapt her traditional administrative system to the problems of the price rise, and this after thirty years of war and destruction. In contrast Philip II ruined Spain while the Tudor and Stuart failure to 'live of their own' kept England weak until the final overthrow of monarchical government in 1689.

Only France weathered the adverse economic conditions of the period, so that she was able to exploit her resources fully and reach that plateau of splendour which was the Grand Siècle, a grandeur which might never have been achieved but for the restoration of the French state by Henri IV.

These are the dry bones of his achievement. But he had done something more. Any student of French history in the seventeenth and eighteenth centuries is familiar with all too many accounts of the peasant's miserable existence, of their brutish life of hunger and of backbreaking toil. Yet Henri's reign does seem to have been kinder to them, at any rate in some parts of France. Years later an old abbé could write with a naïve lyricism of the countryside of Touraine as it had been in 1609, a description which is vividly at variance with the stark scenes depicted by La Bruyère or painted by Le Nain:

The picture I keep of things as they were in those days still fills me with happiness. I see again, with the keenest pleasure, the beauty of the countryside as it was then; it seems to me that meadows were greener than they are now, that trees bore more fruit. Nothing was so sweet as to listen to the cooing of the birds, the lowing of kine, or the songs of the shepherds. Flocks were driven to the fields in safety while the peasants ploughed the land to sow wheat which tax gatherers and soldiers never plundered. They had goods and possessions sufficient enough and slept in their own beds. When it came to harvest time how pleasant it was to see troops of reapers, each one stooped by the other, working the furrows and garnering bunches of corn which the stronger tied for the rest to load as sheaves into the carts; afterwards children who had been watching the flocks far away were able to glean ears of corn which a feigned carelessness had left for them. Rosy village maidens cut the corn side by side with the boys and from time to time their toil was broken by a rustic meal taken in the shade of some apple or pear tree whose branches were laden with fruit to fill their laps.... After the harvest the peasants chose a holiday when they could all meet which they called 'the harvest gosling' (such was its name in the district). They invited not just friends but their masters too and were overjoyed if these took the trouble to come.... When our good people celebrated their children's marriages it was a delight to see how they dressed; for beside the bride's finery, never less than a red gown and a head-dress trimmed with tinsel and glass beads, the parents were clad in their own pleated blue dresses which they had taken out from chests scented with lavender, dried roses and rosemary. I speak of men as much as of women for they too had their pleated cloaks which they wore over their shoulders with high stiff collars like those of certain monks. Peasant girls, their hair neatly arranged, flaunted parti-coloured petticoats. Nor were wedding favours lacking; everyone wore them at his belt or on his shoulder. Then there was a concert with bagpipes, flutes and hautboys and, after a sumptuous banquet, country dancing which lasted until nightfall.... No one grumbled about unjust taxes; everybody paid his due cheerfully and I never remember hearing of soldiers plundering a parish, let alone laying waste entire provinces as merciless enemies have so often done since.... Thus it was at the close of the reign of good Henri IV, whose end was the end of so many good things and the beginning of so many bad, for an angry demon took away the life of that great prince.

Perhaps the idyll of the abbé de Marolles existed only in an old man's nostalgia, perhaps it was some chimera from a long mourned youth. Nonetheless the French folk memory undeniably looked back—and still does—to Henri's reign as an oasis of plenty. It, like the good abbé, realizes that here was a King who did at least try and did partially succeed in making come true that golden dream which was and is *la belle et douce France.*[47]

7. HENRICIAN MAJESTY

'Thus, as bright sunshine by its radiance and its heat lights up the skies, warms the earth, makes plants green again, gives colour to the flowers and ripens fruit, so do true kings by the wisdom of their rule and by their bounty hearten men's spirits, spread confidence, cause sweet hope to be reborn everywhere, protect their peoples from foreign invaders, and fructify and multiply their goods.'

attributed by Sully to Henri IV.[1]

'... he even took delight in balls and sometimes danced, though, to speak the truth, with more spirit than gracefulness.'

Péréfixe[2]

Though he came from the ancient line of Capet and was a Son of St Louis, Henri IV was nonetheless the founder of a new dynasty. By nature unceremonious he yet knew that if the advent of the Bourbons was to be dignified with fitting majesty he could not afford to neglect the trappings of royalty; ceremony, fine buildings and martial pomp were indispensable. For the first ten years of his reign France was at war, so that his courtiers were sabre-rattling cavaliers, while a Parisian monarch had been succeeded by one whose accent and tastes were markedly pro-vincial; the Béarnais retained his southern tones, spoke Gascon to his Gascons, loved Jurançon wine and the cuisine of Pau. Often he rode in from the field, without bothering to change clothes which were tattered and sweaty after days in the saddle, to what was in spirit a cavalry mess whose habitués delighted in Rabelaisian wit, drank hard, swore hard, laughed, swaggered and boasted uproariously. Some ladies found the atmosphere so overpoweringly masculine as to be distasteful, even if a lusty heterosexual activity had ousted transvestist *divertissements*. When peace came and armour gave place to ermine the King's courtiers were still 'his gallant Men for War', his old captains and marshals who like their master felt most at ease in jackboots and a leather coat, the entourage of a Napoleon rather than a Louis XIV.

Many historians have stigmatized this court as a bear garden, a cross between barracks and bawdy house. That staunch champion of Henri III, M. Philippe Erlanger, maintains that 'the survivors of the old reign found it hard to accustom themselves to the violence and vulgarity which had replaced the former refinements. There was no trace, nowadays, of courtesy and politeness. Feasts degenerated into orgies, banquets into drunken brawls, masquerades gave rise to pitched battles, and even court ballets were full of ribaldry'.[3] Critics are fond of citing the Italian Marquise de Rambouillet's flight to the rue Saint Thomas du Louvre where her hôtel became Paris' first true *salon*. But Valois affectation or bluestocking preciosity are hardly good yardsticks. Other European courts of the period were far more debauched or else ludicrously pompous. The drunken buffoonery of that of England under James I was notorious while the Elector of Saxony could sit gorging at his table for eight hours with no comment other than emptying a *stein* over a page's head; brass bands were invented at this time to drown the noise of eating at German courts. At the other extreme, courtiers of Elizabeth I or Charles I knelt when their sovereign passed by, while the ridiculous etiquette of Spain actually caused the death of Philip III who died from erysipelas made fatal by the heat in his chamber; it was beneath any grandee's dignity to open a window.

The Louvre and Tuileries of Henri IV lacked neither grace nor splendour; in some ways his court was remarkably like that of his grandson Charles II at Whitehall. Hunting and whoring did not preclude balls, ballets or the play. Though the exquisite conceits and exotic manners of the Valois had departed and though Henri was irrepressibly friendly and informal, the monarch's public actions were performed with glittering mediaeval ceremony, gilded by the last rays of the Renaissance, a symbolic ritual indispensable to a hierarchic society. Also, sinner that he was, the King attended Mass with decorous pomp, The essential rhythm of court life remained unchanged; there had simply been a violent and somewhat self-conscious reaction against the effeminate or the perverse, a reaction which if a trifle over virile must have seemed no more than a fresh healthy breeze sweeping through some stuffy, scented, overheated boudoir. The Valois pantomime was remembered only as a feverish, noxious dream.

Some found the King's lack of stateliness disconcerting. A dowager who had known the disdainful Henri III sniffed when she first met his successor: 'I have seen the King but not His Majesty.'[4] Dallington was quite shocked:

Hee is naturally very affable and familiar, and more (we strangers thinke) then fits the Maiesty of a great King of France.... Familiarity breeds contempt and contempt treason.... You saw here in *Orleans*, when the Italian Commedians were to play before him, how himselfe came whifling with a small wand to scowre the coast and make place for the rascall Players (for indeed these were the worst company, and such as in their owne Countrey are out of request): you have not seene in the Innes of Court, a Hall better made, a thing, methought, most derogatory to the Maiesty of a King of France.[5]

Yet on occasion Henri could be stately enough, for he understood the magic of pomp. With republicans it was especially effective. When the forty ambassadors of the Swiss Cantons were received by him on 16 October 1602 an awed L'Estoile noted how: 'The great chamber of the Louvre was guarded by two ranks of Scots in line, and each flight of the Louvre's staircase was similarly guarded by two ranks of Archers in line, and outside, as far as the rue St Honoré, by companies of the Regiment of Guards.' The ambassadors found Henri on his throne, surrounded by Princes of the Blood and great officers of state, all richly dressed but outshone by the King:

> His Majesty was magnificently and sumptuously dressed, more so than anyone had ever seen him, with an aigrette of diamonds of incalculable value in his hat, which was black and white, with a scarf of the same colours completely covered in diamonds. On seeing them enter His Majesty rose, doffing his hat to them, and then sat down and replaced his hat whereupon they came forward, bowing, to kiss the hand which His Majesty rested on his knee while with the other he shook their hands in turn and clapped them on the shoulder.[6]

Henri never practised the hauteur of his grandson Louis XIV. Anyone who saluted him received an affable nod, the King raising his hat with a '*Serviteur Jacques, Serviteur*;' he always employed the old fashion of Christian or family name instead of 'Monsieur'. He liked to dress plainly: 'For he ordinarily wore gray Cloaths, with a Doublet of sattin or Taffata, without slashing, Lace or Embroydery.' The famous white plume of Navarre in his wide brimmed hat was his sole affectation. He had no use for a hairdresser and like James I of England was careless about washing, for this was an unclean age. He stank abominably; on her wedding night, Marie drenched herself in scent but nonetheless suffered horribly while Henriette once told him, 'You smell like carrion.' Years later Louis XIII's friendliest compliment was, 'I'm near my father—I smell his armpit.'[7] However, the legend of Henri's chewing garlic like fruit so that his breath felled an ox at twenty paces is apocryphal even if he had a fondness for onion soup. His teeth were bad, stopped with lead and gold, and in later years he had to wear glasses, crudely ground crystal lenses with clumsy silver frames. Indeed his appearance must have been far from impressive for he was so small that despite his agility he always needed a mounting block to climb on to his horse.

Yet this rough, shabby, bespectacled, garrulous little man with his provincial accent and his clowning was renowned for both irresistible charm and a power of terrifying. He fashioned his manners towards his subjects with careful precision. Carew understood him very well:

> For his parts of manners and conversation, they are very sweet and pleasing, nothing sanguinary, not swollen with pride but with an excellent temperament he seemeth to equal himself to the meanest of his subjects in hearing and talking with them, and with the greatest and most potent he retaineth such a majesty, as makes them tremble, not only at his words, but also at his looks and countenances.[8]

If he gave his word it was as *'Foy de Gentilhomme'*; 'we are all noblemen', he would say to his lords and gentry, even in the presence of Princes of the Blood. Undoubtedly he played to the gallery. When an aged non-entity, M. de la Vieuville, a former *maître d'hôtel* to the Duc de Nevers, unctuously lamented his unworthiness to receive the St Esprit which his patron had obtained for him, the King answered, 'Yes, I know very well, I know very well, but my nephew begged me.' A dignitary sinking on his knees to deliver a graceful harangue knelt on a sharp-pointed cobblestone and shrieked out, 'F———!' 'Good! that's the best thing you could say; I don't want any more speeches—you'll spoil what you've just said,' interrupted Henri.[9] Orators who referred to heroes of antiquity were reminded that like the King himself at that particular moment such heroes had suffered from hunger and he wanted his dinner. And when some great lady came upon Henri relieving himself in a flower bed in the gardens of the Louvre the monarch greeted her with *'Passe, ma belle, je le tiens!'* However, he met his match in his confessor, Fr Coton. 'What would you do if one put you into bed with Mme la Marquise?' asked Henri, grinning and pointing at Henriette. 'Sire, I know what I ought to do but I don't know what I would do,' countered that subtle Jesuit. The King was on excellent terms with the Paris mob and roamed the streets of his capital—which he once described as 'a nest of cuckolds'—with little or no escort.

He could laugh at himself. The bad relations between Henri and Marie frequently erupted into noisy squabbles, to the joy of gossip mongers. L'Estoile records how on 26 January 1607 'there was played at the Hôtel de Bourgogne a pleasant farce which was attended by the King, the Queen, and most of the princes, and lords and ladies of the court. It was about a husband and wife who were always quarrelling....' Everyone understood the unsubtle allusions in what was obviously a riotous performance which ended with three lawyers who had been called in to arbitrate being carried off to Hell by three devils. The legal fraternity were unamused by this dénouement and committed the entire cast to prison but Henri ordered their release commenting that, 'If one must speak of insult he had received more than anyone yet he pardoned them all and pardoned them willingly because they had made him laugh till he cried.'[10]

Once, hearing that he had been called a miser, Henri retorted, 'I do three things very unlike a miser—I make war, I make love, and I build.' Carew accounted 'his buildings at Paris, St Germains, Fountainebleau, Monceaux and other places very huge and stately' to be among those things which contributed to the court's 'chiefest splendour'. His most famous structures were the beloved château 'in our delightful wilderness of Fontainebleau' and the great gallery of vast length between the Louvre and the Tuileries. At Fontainebleau there were two courtyards, a 'gallery of Diana', a 'gallery of the deer', and many gardens beside the great canal which were furnished with bronze statues and fountains. English travellers particularly appreciated these gardens. Of Fontainebleau Fynes Moryson wrote: 'And it is built (with Kingly Magnificence) of Free stone, diuided into foure Court-yards, with a large Garden which was then [1595] somewhat wild and vnmanured.'[11] Another English traveller visited it, in 1608, the eccentric Thomas Coryate, by trade courtier, scholar and buffoon, that 'Odcombe leg stretcher' from Somerset who hung up his shoes in his parish church after his first great journey. He told his readers that 'This Palace hath his name from the faire springs and fountaines, wherewith it is most abundantly watered that I neuer saw so sweete a place before; neither doe I thinke that all Christendome can yeeld the like for abundance of pleasant springs.' He was more taken with the gardens than Moryson: 'For most of the borders of each knot is made of Box, cut very low, and kept in very good order. The walkes about the gardens are many, whereof some are very long and of a conuenient breadth, being fairely sanded, and kept very cleane. One among the rest is inclosed with two very lofty hedges, most exquisitely made of filbird trees and fine fruits, and many curious arbours are made therein. By most of these walkes there runne very pleasant riuers, full of sundry delicate fishes.' Coryate wondered at the tame storks and ostriches and also when 'I was let in at a dore to a faire greene garden, where I saw pheasants of diuers sorts, vnto which there doth repaire at some seasons such a multitude of wild pheasants from the forrest, and woodes, and groues thereabout, that it is thought there are not so few as a thousand of them.'[12] Henri himself loved to stroll in his gardens.

However, it was the Louvre which such travellers admired most. In 1599 Dallington marvelled: 'From this Palace the King is building a Galery, which runnes along the riuer East and West, and his purpose is, it shall passe ouer the towne ditch with an Arch, and so continue to the Twilleries ... so both these buildings shall bee vnited into one: which if euer it be done, will be the greatest and goodliest Palace of Europe.'[13] Coryate, who saw the gallery when it had been almost completed was no less impressed:

> After this I went into a place which for such a kind of roome excelleth in my opinion, not only al those that are now in the world, but also whatsoeuer were since the creation thereof, euen a gallery, a perfect description whereof wil require a large volume. It is deuided into three parts, two sides at both the ends, and one very large and spacious walke. One of the sides when I was there, was almost ended, hauing in it many goodly pictures of some of the Kings and Queenes of France, made most exactly in wainscot, and drawen out very liuely in oyle workes vpon

the same. The roofe of most glittering and admirable beauty, wherein is much antique worke, with the picture of God and the Angels, the Sunne, the Moone, the Starres, the Planets, and other Celestiall signes. Yea so vnspeakably faire it is, that a man can hardly comprehend it in his mind, that hath not first seene it with his bodily eyes.[14]

Henri also finished the Louvre's little gallery, begun by Catherine de Medici. At the Tuileries he created an orangery besides, in Coryate's opinion, 'the fairest garden for length of delectable walkes that euer I saw, but for variety of delicate fonts and springes much inferior to the Kings garden at Fountaine Beleau'.[15] The Parisians were especially impressed by his palace outside the capital, at St Germain-en-Laye, where he built a succession of magnificent terraces overlooking the Seine.

Henri's measures to enhance the new dynasty's majesty went further than building palaces and embraced town planning and public health. Streets were widened and paved; indeed Coryate had thought that 'many of the streetes are the durtiest, and so consequently the most stinking of all that euer I saw in any citie in my life'.[16] The water supply was improved and a number of hospitals built, notably the Charité, the Aide Dieu and the Samaritaine. (These measures, together with stringent by-laws and nursing by religious orders, so abated the hitherto chronic menace of plague that in 1705 a Parisian wrote that there had been no serious outbreak of endemic disease for a century.)[17] Attempts were made to raise the standard of ordinary housing. The most revolutionary project, begun in 1605 was a great new square on a grid pattern, the Place Royale, which had thirty-five *pavillons* and arcades. On a similar scale was the Place Dauphine which contained a *bourse* or exchange. In the last two years of his reign Henri was busy with a plan for an entire new district, the immense 'Porte et Place de France', which was to have twenty-four streets (named after the provinces and regions of France), food markets, and public gardens open to all; the King wished to rehouse the poor of Paris and give them work, but the project was abandoned at his death though Richelieu later built eleven of the streets. Henri's most enduring monument is the Pont Neuf on which work commenced in 1604.

The family life of Henri IV might have been decorous enough for The Grand Turk—for His Most Christian Majesty it was a scandal. Not only did he avail himself of many women but, markedly philoprogenitive, rejoiced at the birth of each new child whosoever its mother. One is again reminded of Charles II who would drive through a disapproving London with his Queen and his mistress in the same coach. However, Charles possessed a more docile wife than his grandfather for Marie was no Catherine of Braganza; Henri 'found thorns even in his Nuptial bed'.[18] Between them Marie de Medici and Henriette d'Entragues made the royal *ménage* a perfect hell; the marriage of two strong personalities often leads to friction—the marriage of three produced an impossible situation. Henriette continued to insist that she should have been Queen and that the Dauphin was a bastard, pretensions which infuriated Marie: 'These scandalous disorders extremely offended the Queen; and the Pride of the Marchioness more furiously incensed her: for she spoke alwaies of her in terms either injurious or disdainful: sometimes not forbearing to say, that if she had Justice, she should hold the place of that fat Banker ...'.[19] As for Marie: 'She had so great an aversion for the marchioness of Verneuil, that she would hardly deign to pronounce her name.'[20] Sully condoled with 'this unhappy prince exposed to the fury of two women, who agreed in nothing but in separately conspiring to destroy his quiet'.[21] The two termagants' frequent pregnancies exacerbated these storms of feminine savagery which overshadowed every aspect of court life. Thus when the Queen wished to dance a ballet with her ladies Henriette insisted on taking part, to Marie's tearful fury. (This spectacle, ironically named 'Ballet of the Virtues', was described as both beautiful and dangerous by the Papal Nuncio who added smugly that he dared not look at it, but only blink as one does at the sun.) So late as 1609 Henriette was making 'her continual constant profession, that she never intended to live with this king as his concubine but as his wife (and accordingly suffereth him not now to have any further use of her body)'.[22]

It seems that Henri's dependence on Henriette, which Sully analysed as 'one of those unhappy diseases of the mind that, like a slow poison, preyed upon the principles of life', was as much mental as physical; if in a fit of revulsion she could refer to herself as *la beste du Roy*, he nonetheless delighted in her amusing company. In fact her power stemmed from the combination of a fascinating personality with sexual expertise. Yet, like a true whore, Henriette however skilled in bed, was fundamentally cold; her sole passion was greed, greed for money and place. Even so there were many occasions when she broke with the King, having quarrelled bitterly, and left court only to return after furious remonstrances. Thus '... this prince suffered all the insolence, the caprices, and any qualities of temper, that a proud and ambitious woman is capable of showing'.[23] In addition he underwent such torments of jealousy that she once told him: 'As you grow older you are becoming so mistrustful and so suspicious that there is no means of living with you.'[24]

Unfortunately Henriette's allurements, 'the charms of her conversation, her sprightly wit, her repartees so poignant yet so full of delicacy and spirit' were not exactly emulated by Marie as Henri once explained, rather pathetically, to Sully: 'I find nothing of all this at home,' said he to me, 'I receive neither society, amusement, nor content from my wife; her conversation is unpleasing, her temper harsh, she never accommodates herself to my humour, nor shares in any of my cares; when I enter her apartment, and offer to approach her with tenderness, or begin to talk familiarly with her, she receives me with so cold and forbidding an air, that I quit her in disgust, and am obliged to seek consolation elsewhere.'[25] Péréfixe draws a picture no less dismal: 'She was alwaies in contention with the King: she exasperated him continually by her complaints, and by her reproaches: and when he thought to find with her some sweetness to ease the great labours of his spirit he encountered nothing but Gall and Bitterness.'[26] She wept and nagged to such an extent that on some nights Henri had to flee from their bed and take refuge in that of one of his Gentlemen. Sometimes she even made a truce with Henriette who would then refuse to sleep with him, to his rage and consternation for her physical hold remained strong for many years; in 1608 he was writing, 'Good-night my soul, I kiss your breasts a million times.'[27]

With all this strife Marie was nevertheless the Queen and mother of the Dauphin and therefore enjoyed Henri's loyalty if not his fidelity. In his own eccentric way he seems to have been quite fond of her. Sully tells how when he went to bring their Majesties presents early in the morning of New Year's Day 1606, the King gently pushed Marie, saying, 'Awake, you dormouse, give me a kiss, and groan no more, for all our little quarrells are already forgot by me; I am solicitous to keep your mind easy, lest your health should suffer during your pregnancy …'.[28] To so shrewd an observer as Carew Marie could seem wholly decorous:

The queen is a lady adorned with much beauty and comeliness of body, and with much beauty and virtue of mind; very observant in all exercises of her religion; and very charitable in performing towards the poor works of mercy; governing the young women and ladies about her with gravity, and causing them to spend their time in works of their needle, and thereby containing them from those disorders, which commonly follow idleness and vanity. Her main and sole opposition is against the marquise de Verneuil, who being of an excellent, pleasant and witty entertainment, maintaineth still a strong hold in the king's affections; and the queen by her eagerness doth work herself some disadvantage….[29]

Marie was no paragon, however, and if Sully was an ally against their common foe, the Queen's wilfulness and stupidity were nevertheless only too evident in her chief friends and favourites. These were the Concini 'who were continually filling her ears with malicious stories and giving her bad advice'. Marie had brought from Florence a scrawny, black avised, hysterical young woman, Leonora Galigai, daughter of a prostitute and a carpenter, together with a foppish pederast, Concino Concini, who was hardly less plebeian and quite as illiterate and unscrupulous. This precious pair, clinging like greedy leeches, contrived to make themselves indispensable to the Queen and obnoxious to everyone else, including Henri—'just as a little but vexatious Mouse may furiously trouble and turmoile the noble Lyon'.[30] He insisted that they return to Italy but Marie made a devil's bargain with Henriette who, in return for the post of Mistress of the Robes, persuaded the King to let them stay. Leonora had married her Concino and the two embarked upon a career which would culminate with his assassination when Marshal and virtual ruler of France and her own burning as a witch in the Place de Grève. 'The Common opinion was that these two persons conjoyntly laboured so long as the King lived, to conserve a spleen in the spirit of the Queen, and to make her always troublesome and humoursome towards him; in such manner, that for seven or eight years together, if he had one day of peace and quiet with her, he had ten of discontent and vexation.'[31]

One, two or even half a dozen women could never have satisfied Henri IV. There was Jacqueline de Beuil, a pink and white blonde doll in her early twenties who was 'something of a glutton but agreeable'[32] and quite brainless. An orphan, this young lady belonged to that over-sexed family, the Babou de la Bourdaisière and was therefore related to poor Gabrielle d'Estrées. According to L'Estoile, when in 1604 by the King's connivance she married a complaisant courtier, Philippe de Césy, she slept with her husband the first night and then with Henri the night after while her spouse lodged above them in an attic over the Royal bedchamber. Tallemant has a still more scandalous version: 'They were married in the morning. The King, being impatient and not relishing the idea that someone else should take a maidenhead for which he himself was paying, would not let Césy sleep with his wife that evening or see her henceforward.'[33] The new acquisition, now known as the Comtesse de Moret, slept with the King—intermittently—for several years and bore him a son. Bishop Péréfixe, who could hardly approve what he termed 'excessive voluptuousness' and to which he attributed Henri's gout, declared with half-hearted bravado that there were 'many other Ladies who held it a glory to have some charm for so great a King'.[34] Indeed tradition credits him with more than sixty conquests though it would need a Leporello to list them all. It is sometimes said cynically in

France that when a man is young he explores the physical mysteries of woman but when he is older he explores her spiritual mysteries. Certainly Henri never reached the second stage.

The King adored his children. He caused an uproar in 1604 when he insisted that his bastards by Henriette should be brought up at St Germain-en-Laye with the Dauphin and his issue by Marie. Though he worshipped his father, the future Louis XIII resented such an affront from a very early age, refusing to recognize his half-brothers. Sometimes it was necessary to chastise this solemn young prince and on one occasion the Queen rebuked Henri for beating Louis, whom normally she herself treated with unnatural coldness and severity, crying: 'Ah! You don't smack your bastards like that!' 'As for my bastards,' replied the King, 'anyone can smack *them* when they play the fool but nobody but me can smack *him*!' (This may have been the occasion when Louis had fired a pistol—fortunately loaded only with powder—at a nobleman he disliked.) Henri was not altogether happy with his heir even if he was fond of him. Carew reported of the Dauphin: 'He is yet heavy and dull in conceit and discourse, and timorous and dastardly in his courage; at which the king hath been much troubled, when he hath seen or heard the tokens of it, saying, *"Fault il donc que je soy père d'un poltron?"* but his education is like to polish and amend both these faults'.[35] Coryate has a particularly colourful portrait: 'The Dolphin ... was about seuen yeares old when I was at the Court. His face full and fat-cheeked, his haire black, his looke vigorous and courageous, which argues a bold and liuely spirit. His speech quick, so that his worde's seeme to flow from him with a voluble grace. His doublet and hose were of red Sattin, laced with gold lace.'[36] There were three sons by Marie, the second being the Duke of Orléans—'a maruailous full faced child'—who died in infancy, and the third the worthless, pusillanimous Gaston d'Orléans who would live to plague his brother and who, of course, was Marie's favourite; of the daughters Elizabeth became the consort of Philip IV of Spain and Henriette Marie married Charles I of England. Mme de Verneuil's children were Gaston Henri, born a month after the Dauphin and created Bishop of Metz and Abbot of St Germain at seven years old, and a daughter Gabrielle; both were officially legitimized. The King's enjoyment of this lively brood is best illustrated by the famous audience of the Spanish ambassador who found him on all fours crawling round the presence chamber with some tiny babes on his back; asked, 'Have you children of your own?', the outraged grandee admitted that this was so, whereupon His Most Christian Majesty laughed, 'Then you'll understand' and continued to crawl round the room. It was a far cry from the Escorial of Philip II, indeed from the Versailles of Louis XIV.

The King had need of full-blooded diversions. Like Gargantua, 'Then would he Hunt the Hart, the Roe-buck, the Bear, the Fallow Deer, the Wild Boar, the Hare, the Phesant, the Partridge and the Bustard.' And no doubt the peasant girl too. Péréfixe who had spoken with those who remembered him well says:

> That in Feasts and Merriments he would appear as good a Companion and as Jovial as another: That he was of a merry humour when he had the glass in his hand, though very sober: That his Mirth and Good Discourses were the delicatest part of the good Chear: That he witnessed no less Agility and Strength in Combats at the Barriers, Courses at the Ring, and all sorts of Gallantries, than the youngest Lords: That he took delight in Balls, and Danced sometimes; but to speak the truth with more spirit than good grace. Some carped that so great a Prince should abase himself to such follies, and that a Greybeard should please to act the young man. It may be said for his excuse, that the great toiles of his spirit had need of these divertisements. But I know not what to answer to those who reproach him with too great a love to playing Cards and Dice, little befitting a great King and that withal he was no fair Gamester, but greedy of Coin, fearful at great Stakes and humorous [bad tempered] upon a loss.[37]

Dallington also heard tales how Henri was a bad loser: 'If you remember when we saw him play at dice, here in Orléans, with his Noblesse, he would euer tell his money very precisely, before he gaue it backe again'.[38] And Carew noticed this weakness 'in his play, where he sheweth extreme passion in small losses, and is content to gain by all kinds of shifts and devices'.[39] Sometimes he played billiards or pall mall (a sort of croquet) but as he grew older and stiffer he gave up tennis. He liked strolling in his gardens just as Charles II loved to saunter, he swam in the Seine, he hawked, and he hunted more than ever; on at least one occasion he was nearly killed by an enraged stag. The Bourbon lusts for lechery, gluttony, violent exercise and the chase, excesses which so awed the courtiers of Louis XIV and Louis XV, were already evident in their ancestor.

Henri could not bear to be alone. Bellegarde reminisced about old campaigns while Zamet continued to give amusing dinners, and if the Constable de Montmorency was brutish and illiterate he shared the King's taste for hunting and horses. Another companion was Charles, fourth Duke of Guise, the young son of the murdered Henri le Balafré but unlike his father in being small, snub-nosed and of mediocre intellect; he was famed as a liar yet nonetheless amiable and generous. The King regarded him with mixed feelings; at one time it was rumoured that he had secretly married Henriette. Then there was a wild young protégé of Henri, François de Bassompierre from Lorraine, a future Colonel of the Swiss Guard and Marshal of France, who had fought in Savoy, and also in Hungary against the Turk; this needy, impudent, philandering, duelling adventurer, twenty-five years younger than himself, with irrepressible high spirits and excessively bawdy humour, may well have reminded the King of his own youth. Above all Henri enjoyed visiting Sully at the Arsenal where he delighted in the craggy eccentricity of that strange minister. On one occasion the latter was told by the King: 'I went to the kitchen while waiting for you where I saw the finest fish possible and spiced stews in the way I like them and, because you were so long in coming, I ate eight of your little "huntsman's oysters", the finest one can eat, and drank some of your Arbois wine, the best I've ever drunk.'[40] Perhaps the man who quipped, '*Les Anglais s'amusent tristement selon leur façon*' was not such bad company. Henri wrote to old cronies far away from court, like Crillon who was living on his estate in Provence, to ask how they were. A new and rather surprising friend was his confessor, Fr Pierre Coton. This suave yet saintly Jesuit belonged to a spiritual coterie which included Mme de Bérulle and her son (the Cardinal, who established the French Oratory) together with Mme Acarie, a disciple of Teresa of Avila, who introduced the Carmelite reform into France. Fr Coton, something of a theologian, Italian trained, and a protégé of St Charles Borromeo, was first sent by his Order to plead that it might be allowed to return to France. Henri took such a fancy to Coton that he made him Preacher to the Court in 1603, and his own Confessor in 1608 with responsibility for the Dauphin's education; he wished to make him Archbishop of Arles and a Cardinal but the Jesuit refused. Though Henri was irritated by this Counter-Reformation champion's advocacy of a Spanish alliance he liked him so well that it was said that the King 'had Cotton in his ears'. For all his politics Père Coton seems to have genuinely understood and sympathized with the emotional, physical and spiritual vagaries of his Royal patient—one can hardly say 'penitent'.

In 1605 a very old friend indeed returned to Paris, Henri's former wife. Margot in middle age was a spectacle neither graceful nor dignified. She had grown monstrously fat from gluttony and her rouged face with its pendulous cheeks was crowned by a bushy golden wig; blond footmen were kept specially for this purpose, their heads being shaved whenever she needed a new coiffure. In addition she retained the clothes of the Valois court which now seemed ludicrously old-fashioned, with clumsy farthingales, great puffed sleeves and scandalous décolletages: her vast skirts and huge figure could block an entire doorway. Eventually she built a magnificent hôtel opposite the Louvre where she took up residence with her various lovers (whom she was rumoured to beat) among which was a musician known as 'le Roy Margot'. Queen Marguerite—Henri had allowed her to retain the title—overspent wildly, giving splendid banquets and balls, dispensing extravagant charity, marching in religious processions with showy piety, and became one of the sights of Paris, whose inhabitants delighted in circulating obscene tales about 'Queen Venus'. She had preserved her strangely conflicting tastes; learning, vice and religion in equal proportion—St Vincent de Paul was one of her chaplains while savants frequented her house no less than gigolos. Oddly enough Marie de Medici, who perhaps felt a certain inferiority, made firm friends with her predecessor, who soon grew devoted to Henri's children, loading them with presents, and they learnt to call this extraordinary but amiable apparition 'Aunt'.

The court enjoyed the play, the Queen importing the very best companies from Italy who presented many comedies at the Louvre besides displays by acrobats and jugglers. The court also visited the theatre at the Hôtel de Bourgogne though here the acting, by a French troupe, was so bad that Henri often fell asleep. Sometimes there were concerts by the Royal orchestra. At balls lively country dances were danced besides more formal galliards in which the gentlemen had to wear hats and swords; when partnering the Queen they were only allowed to touch the hem of her long sleeve. However, Marie took most enjoyment in elaborate court ballets played by exotically attired lords and ladies against a background of rich and wonderful tableaux and transformation scenes in the hall of the Louvre or some other great palace and illuminated by a thousand candles in silver brackets. Even on the most ordinary occasions the courtiers' magnificent clothes glittered and flashed in torch or candle light which also shone upon the fine cabinets, statuary, silken tapestries, hangings of cloth of gold and silver, and crimson velvet furniture with which the King had furnished his palaces. Fynes Moryson explained: 'In France as well men as women, vse richly to bee adorned with jewels. The men weare rings of Diamonds and broad Iewels in their hats, placed vpon the roote of their feathers. The Ladies weare their Iewels commonly at the brest or vpon the left arme, and many other waies, for who can containe the mutable French in one and the same fashion?'[41] Carew likewise commented on 'the multitude of their pearls, stones, broderies and such like', corroborating Moryson: 'In the court the riches partly appeareth in the sumptuousness of the attire and furniture for the houses and persons of the lords and ladies of the same.'[42] If the court of Henri IV was without the over refined grace of that of Henri III it did not lack for splendour.

It is well to remember that in many ways the tastes of the early Seventeenth century were little removed from those of the Middle Ages. Jousting was not yet extinct. On Sunday, 25 February 1605, François de Bassompierre and Charles de Guise, who disputed the favours of Henriette's sister Marie, tilted at the barrier in the courtyard of the Louvre before the King and Queen, Bassompierre in silver armour with pink and white plumes, Guise in an armour of black and gold. The Duke broke his lance against Bassompierre's helmet but then lowered the butt instead of raising it, so that a splinter as long as a man's arm pierced his adversary's stomach. Bassompierre nonetheless bravely rode forward to break his own lance correctly against Guise's helmet before collapsing from his horse, his entrails falling through a gaping wound. Miraculously he survived and was on his feet again within a fortnight.[43]

The wealth of Henri's court was beginning to impress all Europe. Sully remembered how by 1605 'the government had already an appearance of opulence and strength, which banished all remembrance of its former indigence', while that calculating observer, George Carew, was genuinely awed and most of all by 'the great reserve, which (all charges defrayed) he puts up every year in his Bastille. So as though he came to a broken state, and much indebted, yet in few years he hath gathered more treasure than perchance any other king of Europe possesseth at this day'.[44] Henri's new army demonstrated this wealth even more formidably than did his court.

As Péréfixe said, Henri 'was by constraint a Man of War and of the Field' and it was obvious to all who met him that here was a soldier as well as a sovereign. 'The king ... hath in the course of his life run through the most hazards of any great personage that now liveth, or of whom mention is to be found in almost any histories,'[45] wrote Carew, noting that Henri had been in 125 battles and 200 sieges. When the Papal Nuncio tactfully asked Henri how many times he had made war the King replied, with Gascon licence: 'All my life—and my armies never had any general other then myself.' Many of his personal habits were the result of a lifetime's campaigning, such as his irregular sleeping and eating; his meals were either snacks or Gargantuan gorging while like Napoleon most of his sleep consisted of occasional catnaps—he rarely took a full night's rest. It was therefore hardly surprising that he did not neglect his army; the King's majesty must manifest itself in both fighting power and martial pomp.

George Carew marvelled at 'the number of his guards and men of war, which attend him (wherein he exceedeth all the other courts in Christendom)'.[46] Until now the kingdom's cavalry had consisted mainly of noblemen who paid their own way—or lived on plunder even in time of peace—while its infantry were hired mercenaries. Henri was determined to replace this ill-ordered mob of feudal volunteers and foreign hirelings by a professional force, properly disciplined, forbidden to live off the country and paid on a regular footing. As Carew realized this was no easy task: '... most of the French busying themselves now in handling the pen, and then the sword. So as their kings may more easily levy at this day 200,000 penmen and chicaneurs than 30,000 men of war.[47] However, Henri had achieved his aim by the end of 1609 when in an army of thirty-seven thousand only one thousand were mounted nobles serving at their own expense (in the *cornette blanche du Roy*); four thousand were regular cavalry (i.e. serving on a paid basis), twenty thousand were French regular infantry and no more than twelve thousand were Swiss or German mercenaries. During the reign's peaceful years a much smaller establishment had been maintained, but with a vast arsenal of arms and munitions and a steadily growing war chest. Sir George was fully aware of the military potential of Henri's treasure 'whereof also he ceaseth not to vaunt, when he walketh in his garden between the Arsenal and the Bastille, saying that none other hath such an alley to walk in, having at the one end thereof armour for 40,000 men ready prepared; and at the other end money to pay them, even to the end of a long war'.[48] The artillery was given its own commissariat under Sully—still Grand Master of the Ordnance—to organize the manufacture of powder and shot and the founding of cannon. A corps of engineers was formed, sappers trained in the latest techniques of siege warfare. The new army continued to be officered by noblemen, who now served on a professional instead of a feudal basis. Two military academies were instituted for cadets largely recruited from penniless noble families. An earlier 'Invalides' was founded, the 'House of Christian Charity' in the rue d'Oursine, for veterans or those incapacitated by wounds (who hitherto had to beg in the streets), pensions were given at the King's discretion to aged officers and funds made available for the widows and orphans of soldiers who fell in action. The career of arms had become a true profession, not just an excuse for brigandage. Henri was always anxious to recruit good men; on one occasion he recognized the Leaguer who had wounded him at Aumâle and promptly enlisted the nervous ex-trooper in his own Guards. At the end of his reign he could muster one hundred thousand men and France had become a first-class military power.

If this new might was not apparent until Henri's last years, through-out the reign his splendidly uniformed and accoutred household brigade impressed all who saw it. Coryate was full of admiration despite his envy as an Englishman:

> The French guard consisteth partly of French, partly of Scots, and partly of Switzers. Of the French Guarde there are three rankes: the first is the Regiment of the Gard which consisteth of sixteene hundred foote, Musketeers, Harquebushers and Pikemen, which waite always by turns, two hundred at a time before the Lou(v)re Gate in Paris or before the Kings house wheresoeuer he lieth. The second bee the Archers, which are vnder the Captaine of the Gate, and waite in the very Gate, whereof there be about fiftie. The third sort bee the Gard of the body, whereof there are foure hundred, but one hundred of them be Scots. These are Archers and Harquebushers on horsebacke. Of the Switzers, there is a Regiment of fiue hundred, which waite before the Gate by turnes with the French Regiment, and one hundred more who carie onely Halberts and weare swords, who waite in the Hall of the Kings house wheresoeuer he lyeth. The Archers of the Garde of the body weare long-skirted halfe-sleeued Coates made of white Cloth, but their skirts mingled with Red and Greene, and the bodies of the Cotes trimmed before and behind with

Mayles of plaine Siluer, but not so thick as the rich Coates of the English Garde.

However, he found the Swiss Guard a little ridiculous, with their 'motley' uniforms—rather like those of the present Papal Guard—and ostentatious virility:

The Switzers weare no Coates, but doublets and hose of panes, intermingled with Red and Yellow, and some with Blew, trimmed with long Puffes of Yellow and Blewe Sarcenet rising vp betwixt the Panes, besides Codpieces of the like colours, which Codpiece because it is by that merrie French vvriter Rablais stiled the first and principal piece of Armour, the Switzers do vveare it as a significant Symbole of the assured seruice they are to doe to the French King in his Warres ... I obserued that all these Switzers doe vveare Veluet Cappes vvith Feathers in them, and I noted many of them to be very cluster-fisted lubbers. As for their attire, it is made so phantastically that a nouice newly come to the Court, who neuer saw any one of them before, would halfe imagine, if hee should see one of them alone vvithout his vveapon, hee vvere the Kings foole.[49]

'Some there are who would insinuate that he did not love Men of Learning but they are much deceived.'[50] Though a soldier in his tastes Henri was directly involved in the cultural life of his time if only as a lavish patron. The penniless Malherbe was made a Gentleman of the Bedchamber with a pension of one thousand livres and became court poet, Pierre Matthieu was appointed Historiographer Royal while another historian, Jacques Auguste de Thou (author of a Latin *History of My Own Time*) was made Grand Master of the King's Library. Then there was the Huguenot theologian and classical scholar Isaac Casaubon whom Coryate so admired, 'that rare ornament of learning Isaac Casaubonus ... the very glory of the French Protestants'.[51] who was created a Librarian to the King in 1606; it is significant that Casaubon found the court so hostile after Henri's death that he emigrated to England. Unlike Napoleon's the Henrician reconstruction was not a cultural desert. The poets of the Pléiade were still singing; Desportes only died in 1606. Meanwhile Agrippa d'Aubigné, the Huguenot Don Quixote who has been called an Ezekiel on horseback, was composing his masterpiece *Les Tragiques*, 'seven songs of blood and fury', an epic of French Protestantism which rivals Isaiah and Jeremiah in its defiance and whose sombre music has sometimes an almost Shakespearian grandeur. Others were preparing the ground for the great period of classical French literature which, unlike the Romantic flowering of the early nineteenth century, was not a reaction against sterility. Malherbe, that destroyer of the Renaissance and harbinger of the Baroque, defined the versification and vocabulary to be used by Corneille and Racine, while Alexandre Hardy, a French Lope de Vega, composed a spate of comedies and tragicomedies which if somewhat mediocre nevertheless stimulated interest in the theatre. Lamartine and Victor Hugo had no such heralds.

Henri also introduced reforms in education and religion. The Jesuits, pioneers of new teaching methods, were allowed to return and set up schools; soon the education of the French nobility was in their hands. At the University of Paris, where the Order was given a college, measures were taken to improve discipline and studies. Though he retained the pernicious practice of appointing absentee bishops the King was anxious for the Church to renew itself. Such spiritual giants as the Oratorian Pierre de Bérulle, Jean Pierre de Camus and St Vincent de Paul began their ministries in his reign while St François de Sales, whose *Introduction to the Devout Life* influenced a number of courtiers, preached before him; characteristically Henri commented, 'A saint! And, more surprising, a gentleman too.' The King tried without success to persuade the Savoyard to leave his mountain diocese for an opulent French see. In almost all religious orders a movement for reform was springing up while flocks of zealous preachers evangelized the peasantry; it was this latter work which marked the real turn of the tide against Calvinism. Admittedly there remained many black spots. A particularly lurid instance came to light later in 1618, when Angèle d'Estrées, Gabrielle's sister and abbess of the ancient Cistercian abbey of Maubuisson, was discovered to have borne twelve children by twelve different men; her nuns were hardly less sinful than their Mother Superior who was sent to the Convent for Fallen Women. At the end of Henri's reign Carew sneered: 'I have heard some, who have come papists out of England, say that to see the manner of the papists living here hath almost perswaded them to abandon that religion.'[52] Nevertheless the Counter-Reformation was reaping a rich harvest.

By now, though politically still formidable, the Huguenots had not merely lost the battle for the soul of France but were in rapid decline. Intellectually Catholicism had regained the advantage, mustering a great army of expert theologians. This polemical revolution was symbolized by a public disputation in May 1600 at Fontainebleau, in the King's presence, between du Plessis Mornay, the intellectual leader of the French Protestants—he was known as the Huguenot Pope—who had recently published a treatise attacking the eucharistic doctrine of the Real Presence and identifying the Papacy with Anti-Christ, and that same Cardinal du Perron who had reconciled the King to Rome; the former was cunningly deprived of books and papers and given insufficient time to prepare so that the silver-tongued Cardinal, the Bossuet of the age, had an easy triumph—the debate is said to have finally removed any doubts from Henri's mind about Catholic dogma. Though du Plessis Mornay's academy at Saumur continued with distinction for many years, attracting students from Scotland in particular, more and more French Calvinist divines were turning Papist; significantly du Perron was himself a convert, the son of a minister. It was clear that the Reform was very much on the defensive. Fynes Moryson gave a typically English explanation: '… the reformed are very strict in the Censure of manners, forbidding daunces and restrayning the peoples liberty in sports and conversation. To conclude, great and wise men of that Reformed Church haue freely sayd, that this striktnes in manners, the taking away of all Ceremonyes, and the disallowing of Bishopps, haue greatly hindred the increase of the Reformed Church, which was like ere this tyme to haue prevayled throughout all Fraunce, if in these thinges they had followed in some good measure the Reformation established in England.'[53] Carew surmised grimly that Henri 'seeketh gently to supplant them'. It was indeed a different era from the days of Beza and Coligny.

By 1609 the King suffered from gout, appalling indigestion, catarrh, influenza, and occasionally the nervous prostration to be expected from such a misspent life, but nothing worse; he was lucky not to have contracted syphilis, having escaped with merely a mild dose of gonorrhoea in his youth (which he had caught from his groom's doxy after surprising her in the stable). In fact he was astonishingly well and vigorous for his fifty-six years. Sir George observed: 'His health and strength he hath in a great proportion, his body being not only able for all exercises, but even for excesses and distempers, both in intemperance and incontinency. And though he be sometimes bitten by the gout yet ever he findeth means suddenly to shake it off. And in the four years, that I served in that court, I found him little decayed in his countenance, or other disposition of his body, but he rather grew to look younger every day than other.'[54]

Henri's worst affliction was the melancholy to which he had always been subject and which now plagued him increasingly. He could astound courtiers by blurting out 'I wish I were dead', suffered from bouts of sleeplessness, evil dreams and restless nerves, knowing too well both the fear at night-time and the noonday devil. Yet he also experienced such wild moods of gaiety as to be heard dancing and whistling by himself in his private cabinet. The miseries were intensified when he fell in love or quarrelled with a mistress or the Queen, but usually, though not always, his judgement in matters of state remained unaffected. While much of his jesting came from a genuine sense of fun together with an unfeigned zest for life, like so many men who joke incessantly he did so partly to keep the demon of depression at bay. This was why he dreaded solitude and was so pathetically dependent on the company of such cronies as Bassompierre.

To some extent he could be soothed by religion, for he had become a convinced if sinning Catholic; when he abstained from adultery to receive the Sacraments it was from genuine piety. Near the Louvre one day he met a priest carrying the Host and immediately dismounted to kneel in the gutter with a devotion which was obviously unfeigned. Sully, who was with him, asked, 'Sir, is it possible that you can believe in this after the things which I have seen?' The King answered, 'Yes, by the Living God, I believe, and he must be a Madman who believes not. I would willingly lose a Finger, that you also believed as I do.'[55] Undoubtedly he regretted his vices and even consulted theologians for some condoning doctrine, to no avail. For him sex was a consuming, dreaded need, mental and physical, and his skilled confessor, Père Coton, no sycophant but a true spiritual director, realized that Henri was less guilty than the majority of adulterers. Indeed it was rumoured most cruelly by Calvinists that Coton had told the King that he was 'in the assured way to Salvation; in respect of his merits for those being balanced with his crimes are in the proportion of 8 to 4'.[56] The modern historian who has shown most understanding of Henri IV, Raymond Ritter, writes: 'So, if Henri had once been able to be a Protestant in all honesty, his entire mental make-up and all his instincts led him towards that poets' garden which lies within Catholicism where, apart from paths reserved for ascetics, there seem to be so many refuges and props for the weaknesses of men as well as havens for their dreams.'[57]

A portrait painted by Pourbus towards the close of the reign shows Henri after he had 'arrived', formally dressed in a suit of rich black, with the period's ungainly breeches, shoes with great clocks, and the jewelled cross of the St Esprit hanging from his neck by a broad ribbon. Yet above the starched ruff his face remains tanned, his hair—almost white now—is cropped *en brosse*, and his beard still bristles. The impression, though unmistakably regal, is that of a royal general in court dress rather than that of a First Gentleman, the hand on the hip expressing martial swagger rather than gracious hauteur. Here, if not a self-made man, is one who has known what it is to face heavy odds before succeeding. But, far from being worn out and despite already legendary achievements, the 'Restorer of the French State' who was by general consent the richest and most admired ruler in Europe, wished in his late middle age to attempt one last, Herculean labour.

8. THE GRAND DESIGN

'... *le grand dessein, se contentant le Roi de reduire*
l'Espagne aux frontieres des Pirénées et de la mer.'
Agrippa d'Aubigné[1]

'He desired perfectly to unite all Christendom, so that it should be one body, which had been and should be called the Christian Commonwealth.'
Péréfixe[2]

So far little has been said of Henri's foreign policy and in fact it was not until almost the very last year of his reign that he revealed his intention of destroying the Habsburg imperium by force of arms. As late as the end of July 1609 the informed English view was that the French King 'studiously avoideth all occasions of war, especially where he doubteth find any strong opposition'[3] even if the French were clearly aware that 'their most potent borderer, and with whom for the present they are in most opposition and greatest struggling, is the king of Spain. The contention between them resembleth those fights, of which the writers of romance talk, between a well proportioned knight and a huge unwieldy giant'. But though Sir George Carew understood that where France and Spain were concerned 'there appeareth a mutual settled disdain and hatred between the two nations' he did not realize that Henri was now ready to take the field.[4]

Hitherto his policy had been one of defence and discreet cold war. As has been seen, he had reorganized his army and amassed an impressive war chest while, as he carefully told Carew, fortifying twenty-eight frontier strongholds. He had also improved his strategic position by the conquests in Savoy, by the control of 'the Spanish Passage', and by the acquisition of Sedan. In Italy new alliances had weakened Habsburg dominance, notably a growing rapprochement with Charles Emmanuel of Savoy and the continuing friendship of Tuscany. French prestige soared in 1607 when Henri's mediation averted war between Venice and the Papacy after Paul V had laid the Serene Republic under an interdict for asserting its authority over Venetian clergy. In October 1604 the commercial Treaty of Paris with England improved relations between the two kingdoms; it was unfortunate that James I should ultimately decide in favour of an alliance with Philip III despite Henri's claim that the Gunpowder Treason had been devised by Spain. The touchy Scot must have been considerably irritated by Henri's part in the 'Flight of the Earls' from Ulster in 1607, an early instance of French kindness to the Irish; when Tyrone and Tyrconnell and their families fled to Normandy in a French ship Carew demanded that they be held until James' pleasure was known but Henri insisted on giving them a safe passage to Brussels, adding with some truth that 'it appears not, for any thing that he knew, but that they were retired out of their country for matter of religion, and private discontentment'.[5] Henri also fished in the war between Spain and the United Provinces, committing himself to neither side. At all costs he wished to avoid any serious confrontation until France had been restored to full health. But now in 1609, as d'Aubigné put it: 'After the cruel travail of war slumber is sweet and grateful; this long sleep renewed the strength of the King and that of his kingdom which had enjoyed ten years of his rule.'[6]

The Habsburgs appeared as formidable as ever. Despite the failure to crush the Dutch after so many years of costly war, despite Spain's growing economic miseries, and despite the small but hurtful diplomatic triumphs of Henri Philip III commanded daunting might. His Most Catholic Majesty ruled the Five Spains (including Portugal), the entire South American continent (with a large part of North America), the Two Sicilies and Milan, and the Burgundian lands of Franche Comté and Flanders. His armies retained an unchallenged superiority; Spanish pikemen were still accounted the best infantry in the world. His cousins possessed Austria, Bohemia and much of Hungary besides, as Holy Roman Emperors, controlling if not ruling much of Germany. Finally the Habsburgs, both Spanish and German, could claim to be the chief secular champions of the Counter-Reformation. Indeed in France herself there were many exponents of an *entente cordiale* with Spain, especially Jesuits and ex-Leaguers; among these were the Secretary of State, Villeroy, and Père Coton who was always whispering in the King's ear about the virtue and glory of a Spanish alliance. Their case was strengthened in 1607 when Spain and the United Provinces negotiated a truce. Next year the former proposed an alliance to Henri by the terms of which France was to declare war on the Dutch and which was to be sealed by marriages between the two dynasties. However, nothing came of it and in October 1608 Spain at last recognized Dutch independence. Then in April 1609 a twelve years' truce was concluded between France and Spain.

Such a truce meant little to Henri who never wavered in his determination to break the Habsburgs' encirclement of France. He might make empty diplomatic gestures to gain time yet secretly he never ceased to wage an unrelenting cold war on Spain. This is dramatically apparent from his negotiations of 1602–5 with the Moriscos, the persecuted Muslims of southern and western Spain, who offered him Navarre in return for arms and advisers. This was not just fanciful thinking on Henri's part for the Moriscos numbered two million, were desperate and might possibly obtain help from Turkey or North Africa. Unrest was rife in Portugal and Catalonia, while there were grandees who nursed separatist ambitions; the whole rickety edifice of Habsburg rule could well have come crashing down (as it very nearly did in 1640), but the negotiations were betrayed in 1605 by Villeroy's secretary who was a spy in Spanish pay. Philip III was so frightened that in 1609 he ordered the expulsion of all Moriscos from Spain. France was more successful in economic warfare. Like Carew, Henri 'must have heard it reported by some of our Spanish merchants, that after the arrival of the Indian (i.e. American) fleets, the treasure they bring in is suddenly dispersed, and most of it carried into

France in lieu of the corn which hath been brought thence'.[7] A good Mercantilist like the King must have been smugly aware of the damage inflicted by this trade.

It was in German affairs that Henri showed himself most perceptive, foreseeing the Thirty Years War which would end with French primacy in Europe. In Germany as in France, Protestantism, both Lutheran and Calvinist, was on the defensive against the Counter-Reformation. The Protestant princes and their *Landes-kirchen* feared that a strong Habsburg might reimpose imperial authority and Catholicism by force (as in fact would happen in Bohemia after the battle of the White Mountain). But the present Emperor was the half-crazy Rudolf II, obsessed with astrology and the occult, and at odds with his brother Matthias who had wrested the larger part of his domains from him. The crisis came a month before the signing of the twelve years' truce with Spain, when in March 1609 Duke Johann-Wilhelm of Cleves-Julich-Berg died; the succession was disputed, and the Emperor, pending a decision, occupied the duchies, to the horrified alarm of the princes. This was the opportunity for which Henri had been waiting as the duchies, being on the Rhine frontier of the Netherlands, constituted a key military position. Now was the time for him, a proven champion of religious co-existence, to free the princes of the Reich from Habsburg tyranny; if it was hardly likely that he would become the first French Emperor since the Carolingians, he still had great hopes of dealing the Habsburgs a cruel blow. He had recourse to a fiery old friend whom he had shabbily treated and who was living in obscure retirement, Agrippa d'Aubigné; the King commissioned him to be his ambassador extraordinary in Germany and visit each tiny court to enlist Protestant princes. By August 1609 Henri was arming for war.

In talking to his intimates the King seems to have referred to his ultimate objectives as his *grand dessein*, and in the past many historians credited him with a great plan for European peace, a Grand Design which anticipated the United Nations. The earliest account occurs in the memoirs of Sully who appears, ostensibly, to have reconstructed it from conversations with his master. In Louis XIV's reign Péréfixe seized upon it to credit his idol with the intention of founding 'a Christian

Commonwealth', while in the eighteenth century the alleged project took more definite shape in the revised version of Sully's memoirs. The scheme was aimed at guaranteeing nations and creeds by the collective agreement of all European states upon a general reorganization; 'those who speak Spanish should remain under the rule of the King of Spain, those who speak English under the rule of the King of England, but I ought to rule those who speak French'. Europe was to have six hereditary monarchies: France, England, Spain, Denmark, Sweden and Lombardy (under the house of Savoy); five elective states, Poland, Bohemia, Hungary, the Empire (Germany only) and the Papacy (which would rule the greater part of Italy); four republics, Switzerland (to include the Tyrol), the Netherlands, Venice and Genoa-Florence. This new Europe would constitute an overall republic with a supreme council to arbitrate and prevent wars. 'There was onely the house of Austria which would suffer any loss, and which was to be despoiled to accomodate others.'[8] Anticipating their role in the later seventeenth and subsequent centuries, the deprived Habsburgs were to be compensated by strengthening their kingdom of Hungary to fight the Turks more effectively. Modern historians agree that the Grand Design was in large part invented by Sully in the vain hope of gaining influence with Richelieu when he published his memoirs in 1636; possibly a few ideas may be ascribed to Henri—plainly his determination that French-speaking lands should be ruled by France is among these. D'Aubigné, who was first to use the expression *grand dessein* (in 1620, in the final volume of his *Histoire Universelle*), limited it to confining Spain within the bounds of the Pyrenees and the sea. Yet Henri hoped for more than this. Probably his true foreign policy was identical with that of Richelieu—to make France the greatest power in Europe by breaking the Habsburg hegemony.

It has been seen that Henri was a gambler. He was now preparing to put his entire life's work to the hazard. Though well preserved he was not young and he was impatient for action. Ironically, as his thirst for battle waxed so did his lust. D'Aubigné noticed the coincidence: 'But then there appeared a remarkable change in his old age, warmed (as people say) by a violent love whose fire made his desire burst into flame, blowing away timidity and its attendant melancholy.'[9] Agrippa was referring to Henri's shameful passion for the pretty little daughter of the Constable de Montmorency whom he met in early 1609 when she was only fifteen. According to Tallemant he first laid eyes on Charlotte de Montmorency by unexpectedly attending a ballet rehearsal at the Louvre. All the ladies including Mlle Charlotte were clad as nymphs, carrying javelins. Finding herself face to face with the King the pert young jade raised her spear as if to stab him at which Henri immediately became infatuated; in his own words he 'almost swooned away'. He was determined to secure possession of this exquisite vision though at first he deluded himself into believing that his affection was platonic. She was engaged to François de Bassompierre who thought that 'under heaven there was nothing so beautiful as Mlle de Montmorency, nothing more graceful or more perfect'.[10] Bassompierre saw at once that the King was deeply smitten; in his memoirs he remembered dryly how Henri 'hardly slept, because love and gout affect the rejuvenated in this way when they smite them'.[11] Henri began to make himself a laughing stock; he who had once said he liked his nobles plainly dressed but well mounted was sporting scented neckwear and 'sleeves of Chinese satin' besides vying with his young gentlemen in the court game of 'running the ring'.[12] Soon he took Charlotte's betrothed aside and, heaving a deep sigh, said

Bassompierre, I want to talk to you as a friend. I have not just fallen in love, I am bewitched and worse by Mlle de Montmorency. If you marry her and she loves you I will hate you; if she loves me you will hate me. It is better this business should not end by destroying the good understanding between us because I am naturally disposed to like you. I have decided to marry her to my nephew, the Prince de Condé, and keep her near my family. She will be a consolation and a support in the old age which I am about to enter. I shall give my nephew, who is young and vastly prefers hunting to ladies, 100,000 francs a year to amuse himself, and shall want no other thanks from her than affection, asking nothing more.[13]

Bassompierre, 'always a servant of those who rule', replied smoothly that he was only too glad to break off the engagement because it gave him an opportunity of showing how fond he was of the King, whereupon Henri, bursting into tears, embraced him and cried that he would make his fortune 'as though you were one of my own bastards'.[14] The desolate fiancé consoled himself by pretending that as it was an arranged marriage he did not mind too much and by making fierce love to Henriette's sister, Marie, whom he got with child.

It was now that Henri at last ceased to sleep with Henriette who had shared his bed so tumultuously for nearly eleven years. The little hell cat who had first captivated him began to grow into a fat, malevolent old puss wholly given up to the grossest kind of gluttony. Nothing had come of her fine ambitions; she had failed to find even a husband, let alone marry the King of France.

Condé, the first Prince of the Blood who had been heir to the throne until the birth of the Dauphin, seemed an excellent choice for a complaisant husband, a reserved, awkward youth of twenty. Carew, who had plainly received an unfortunate personal impression, commented that though the Prince had 'a comely countenance and able body' he possessed 'many imperfections natural, as want of hearing, together with weakness of speech and understanding, and withal being without hope of issue.... His education hath been so disordered and ignoble, as he is noted for one of the most dissolute young men of France, both for lasciviousness in women's matters and the disease accompanying the same; and besides for delighting in drinking of wine, and frequenting taverns to that end among base company'.[15] Condé and the Montmorency were betrothed in March and married on 17 May 1609. But Henri had underestimated his nephew whose pride would not allow him to be cuckolded though it was some time before the King discovered this odd prejudice.

He had become obsessed by 'Madame la Princesse' with the insane passion of green old age for golden youth. 'Monsieur le Prince seeing that the King's love was so violent took his family off to Muret near Soissons. The King could not stay long without seeing her. Wearing a false beard he went to a hunt in which she was to take part; Monsieur le Prince learnt of this and postponed the meet to another occasion. Some days after that, the King ordered M. de Traigny, a local squire, to invite Monsieur le Prince and Madame la Princesse to dinner so he could hide behind a tapestry where he watched them through a hole at his pleasure.'[16] Charlotte, no more than a spoilt and giddy child, was exhilarated rather than alarmed by these attentions and was persuaded to sign a petition that her marriage be annulled. 'The King had obliged her parents to draw up this petition and the Constable was a knave who hoped that this love of the King would shower him with money and dignities. The household of Madame la Princesse, who was very young, made her think she would be queen. Once must realize what that meant! It would have been necessary to poison Queen Marie de Medici because she had children. [i.e. the Papacy would therefore refuse an annulment.] Monsieur le Prince could never bring himself to forgive his wife for having signed the petition.'[17] When the King reprimanded Condé for not bringing his wife to court, the Prince called him a tyrant, at which Henri reacted violently. Carew was probably referring to this occasion when he commented 'his birth hath many exceptions against it, the King having reproached it bitterly to his teeth, that he was in doubt, whether he was his kinsman or not; and that by his means, and favour only, he came to be declared a prince of the blood. And the count Soissons still affirming among his familiars, that he is not his brother's son, but bastard of that page, who was called in question for poisoning of Henry the late prince of Condé'.[18] It was no doubt after the same incident that the King wrote to Sully, in June 1609, asking him to stop Condé's quarterly allowance and grumbling that 'Monseiur le Prince is here and playing the devil. You would have been angry and ashamed at the things he said about me'.[19] But Condé could not be brought to heel. Sir George thought there were 'such jealousies, scandals and indignities as it is doubtful whether that matter will end in a tragedy or a comedy'.[20]

For a time relations between Henri and the young couple kept some veneer of propriety, at least in public. Condé attended the wedding of Mlle de Mercoeur, the greatest heiress in France, to the Duc de Vendôme in July. Carew described the latter as 'in shape the most handsome, in age the most mature and in affection the best beloved of this king's natural children. His fashion and manner of entertainment is discreet and agreeable'.[21] The ceremony was very splendid, the bride wearing a cloak of crimson velvet, fastened at the shoulders by jewelled clasps and lined with ermine, over a dress of cloth of silver. 'These nuptials were both triumphant and magnificent, where people did nothing but laugh and dance. His Majesty seemed as much above the other guests as the sun is above the stars, glittering in pearls and precious stones of incalculable value, with a suit of the utmost richness and dressed (so people say) as a lover …'. Henri and the Queen attended the happy pair's *coucher*. As L'Estoile gleefully recounts, the King had forgotten nothing which might impede their wedded bliss. Fearing that Vendôme because of his extreme youth—he was only sixteen—'might be taken short and make a fool of himself', Henri had arranged for him to be tried out a week before by an expert professional lady 'on whom he might sharpen his knife'. Proudly he told the bride's astounded mother of his thoughtful precaution, adding, 'And you, Madame, who have known for a long time how to perform this business, I leave you to guide your daughter and show her the place best suited for the execution and accomplishment of such work.'[22]

In the end Condé fled with his wife to Brussels where they arrived in December 1609. The King's gentleman-in-waiting, that prim poet Malherbe who must have made a somewhat bizarre procurer, took part in a tardy and unsuccessful pursuit, reporting untruthfully that Madame la Princesse had been reluctant to accompany her husband. In Brussels French agents actually tried to kidnap the Princess; one abortive scheme entailed lowering Charlotte out of her window by ropes. The King raved and stormed, even threatening war. Eventually the Prince found refuge with this wife in Milan. Henri never saw her again. Throughout this shabby business, crazed by unseemly desire and losing all sense of honour or dignity, he had shown unsuspected depths of spite and pettiness. There were undertones of self-destruction; it was as though all Henri's past lusts and lecheries had at the end of his life culminated in one final gross act of egotism when total sensuality at last consumed what had been a great man, leaving nothing more than a doting old satyr. Yet, like David after his sin with the wife of Uriah the Hittite, Henri was still a great King. His subjects found his frailty endearing rather than otherwise; it may have been now that they named him *le Vert Galant*—the Evergreen Gallant. Though he consoled himself with other mistresses the Princesse de Condé was the last of his loves.

His threats of war were genuine enough, for he was setting in motion his great plan against the Habsburgs, which until that August he had skilfully concealed. George Carew had left France in July 1609 after four strenuous years. Henri's ministers were glad to see the ambassador go, regarding him as a friend of Spain and an intriguer. But, keen observer though he was, Sir George had not managed to discover the King's design on the Empire, even at this late date. Next month Henri at last showed his hand and throughout the winter of 1609–10 France was arming, the great war machine so carefully prepared operating at full throttle; troops were mobilized and grouped, garrisons relieved, fortresses revictualled, munitions and supplies brought up to depots. By the spring of 1610 Henri had massed forty thousand men with powerful artillery in Champagne near the frontier while ensuring the Pyrenees and his eastern flank were adequately guarded by other forces; these latter also watched the Spanish Passage, the strategic link between the Habsburg domains. In May he intended to invade the Empire and drive the Imperial troops out of Cleves-Julich when, he confidently hoped, the Protestant princes of Germany would join him for the ensuing conflict. The soldier king who had not ridden out to battle for almost a decade longed to be back in the saddle. The coming struggle would be very different from those of the 1590s when he had had to fight not only Spaniards but his fellow countrymen with a handful of unreliable troops, without money or adequate supplies. Now the war lord of a rich and united kingdom was going to crush his enemies with a mighty steamroller of an army. So he must have dreamed, in his sanguine moods.

Yet Henri was not a happy man.

Every hour of delay seemed to him a year, as if he had presaged some misfortune to himself, and certainly both Heaven and Earth had given but too many Prognosticks of what arrived. A very great Eclipse of the whole body of the Sun which happened in the year 1608: A terrible Comet which appeared the year preceding: Earthquakes in several places: Monsters born in divers Countries of France: Rains of blood which fell in several places: a great Plague which afflicted Paris in the year 1606: Apparitions of Fantosms and many other Prodigies kept men in fear of some horrible event.[23]

The Queen's astrologers foretold death and ruin with gloomy regularity. 'Himself, who was not over-credulous, gave some faith to these Prognosticks, and seemed as one condemned to death. So sad and cast down he was, though naturally he was neither melancholy nor fearful.'[24]

Everyone was uneasy, and sensed some impending evil. It would have been odd if they had not. To many this war was thoroughly disquieting. Politiques feared with justice that Henri was jeopardizing his entire reconstruction in a reckless gamble, while Catholics were horrified by his championship of heretics; the loyal wondered whether he was endangering the Counter-Reformation—the ill-affected thought that the ally of Turks and Moriscos meant to attack Catholicism itself. Religious faith, still a warmer tie than nationality, induced covert opposition in almost every quarter. Even members of his Council had Habsburg sympathies and Père Coton who understood Henri so well must have intimated disapproval gently but tellingly. Probably he himself doubted his own judgement, in certain moods. Meanwhile 'by furbishing his weapons the King had aroused fear where friendship no longer existed',[25] at home as well as abroad. It was chillingly clear that there was danger in France, above all in Paris, danger from knife or pistol. The capital seethed with enemies, not merely the spies and secret agents of Spain and Austria, but vengeful irreconcilables from Leaguer days who claimed they had at last been vindicated in refusing to believe in Henri's conversion and who now began to make fresh recruits. Nearly every year of the reign there had been a plot on his life; it was said that nineteen attempts had been unsuccessful, that the twentieth would be fatal. Less than five years before, England's Gunpowder Treason had shocked France, and no one had forgotten how the King's predecessor had been assassinated by a Papist zealot; no one—friend or foe. There was some hope of anticipating feudal conspiracies like that of Biron but none of unearthing the grub like scheming of obscure bigots deep in the murky tumult of the Paris mob. Most dangerous of all, because least detectable, was the solitary, crazed fanatic.

Such a man was living in Paris, a lawyer's hack lodging at cheap hostelries such as 'Les Rats' or Les Trois Pigeons'. François Ravaillac was what would nowadays be called a victim of society, and probably a schizophrenic. Thirty-two years old, tall, bulky, 'red haired, down looked and melancholy',[26] he was a bankrupt schoolmaster from Angoulême where his parents lived on alms and where he had been in prison for debt. He had recently tried to join the Feuillant Franciscans but the friars hastily turned him out when they learnt about his 'visions'. Miserably poor, religious to the point of mania and dreaming strange dreams, he roamed the underworld of Paris. Just after Christmas 1609 he attempted to give Henri, jolting through the streets in his coach, a petition for the expulsion or forcible conversion of Huguenots, but the King brushed him aside with his stick. Then one day he had a terrifying revelation, that King Henri was an evil tyrant whom he must kill. Frightened and bewildered the unhappy madman decided to return home but the visions continued and halfway to Angoulême he turned back to Paris where, alone in his garret, half starved, a figure at once sinister and pathetic, Ravaillac brooded in a state of exaltation and indecision, nursing a bag in which he kept a broken table knife.

By the spring of 1610 Henri himself was in a strange, morbid mood. The business of Madame la Princesse had hurt him badly, damaging his mental equilibrium and command of self no less than it struck at his self-respect. Prone to gloomy reflection, no longer soothed by hunting, gambling or whoring, kinder to the Queen, always worried and pensive save for odd fits of feverish gaiety, the hero of so many battlefields lived in constant apprehension. A premonition of violent, unexpected death haunted him, sapping the energy and vitality of this least cowardly of men. Public ceremonies became occasions of dread, like the Queen's coronation on 13 May. Marie herself was fearful; some months before she had dreamt of the King's murder, that he had been stabbed twice, and it was her own wish that she should be crowned, as though feeling it would enhance her stature in an imminent widowhood. 'By God! I'm going to die in this city, I'll never get out of it,' he told Sully, nervously tapping his spectacle case. '*They* will kill me because the only remedy for their peril is my death. Ah! This cursed coronation is going to be my death'![27] However, according to Bassompierre, when the Queen was crowned at St Denis with great splendour 'the King was extraordinarily gay'.[28] Comic relief was provided by Margot in fantastic robes and wearing a crown. And the royal armies would march within the week; as Sully reminded him, once outside Paris he would be safe.

But next day Henri's gloom returned. He burst out to Guise and Bassompierre in the morning: 'You don't understand me now, you people, but I'm going to die one of these days and when you've lost me you'll realize just how much I was worth, what a difference there was between me and other men.'[29] That day, 14 May, was 'A daye which many Astrologians have iudged fatall to his Maiesty, whereof he was aduertised both by the Queene, and by Monsr. de Vendosme, with request not to goe abroad that day. But hee (not belieuing Predictions) sayd, that it was an offence to God to giue credit vnto them, and that hauing God for his guarde hee feared no man ...'.[30] Sully was ill. The King decided to visit him at the Arsenal, then muttered several times, 'I do not know what is amiss with me but I cannot leave this place'.[31] Three times he said goodbye to the Queen, coming back each time with a worried look. Marie grew even more frightened, begging her husband to postpone his visit till the following day. Henri insisted he could not rest easy until he had spoken to Sully. Finally, one of his guards said the air would do the King good whereupon Henri donned his breastplate, though leaving it unfastened because the weather was hot, and called for his carriage. This was a huge, lumbering waggon with open windows, covered in velvet, suspended by leather straps on enormous wooden wheels and drawn by eight horses, as much like the royal coaches of modern England as a brewer's dray. Seven courtiers sat inside with him while for escort he only had a few outriders and walking footmen.

The clumsy vehicle rumbled and lurched over the cobbles of the rue St Honoré till it was held up by a jam of carriages at the corner of the rue de la Ferronerie. Ravaillac had followed the royal coach from the Louvre. When it halted he jumped on to a small pillar at the side of the road, leant through the window—whose leather curtains were undrawn—and stabbed the King. Henri whispered, 'I am wounded,' raising his arm, at which Ravaillac stabbed him again, thrusting the knife into his ribs, cutting the aorta and piercing a lung. The King coughed, spat out some blood, then fell back dead. The murderer did not try to escape—those who arrested him only saved him with difficulty from a howling mob.

As the great coach trundled home to the Louvre the dismal news ran through Paris: 'For the poore people were so confused with sorrowe, that a man could see them doe nothing else but goe wayling up and downe the streetes, lamenting the losse of their King.'[32] Sully, informed that Henri was mortally wounded, cried, 'This is what he always feared: God have pity and mercy upon us and upon the state. For he would not have died had not God let so strange a thing befall to make known his anger and to punish France, France which must now pass into strange hands.' Barricading himself in the Bastille, he sent to his son-in-law, the Duc de Rohan, to hurry from Champagne with his six thousand Swiss. However, Sully's fears were unfounded; the capital was so stunned that Marie was quickly established as Regent.

Ravaillac, bewildered, rambling and haltingly penitent was tried by the *Parlement* of Paris; despite strong suspicions he maintained, even in the torture chamber, that he had no accomplices. To the crowd's joy, his execution was unusually protracted. Having burnt off his hand with flaming brimstone and torn flesh with glowing pincers from his chest and limbs, the executioners then poured boiling oil on the wounds and molten lead into his navel after which four strong horses were set to rend him in four, without success; throughout he prayed and 'yelled out with such horrible cryes euen as it had beene a Diuell or some tormented soule in hel'[33] but he also screamed that he alone was guilty. After a long hour he died whereupon the mob paid Henri their own special tribute in their own bestial way; rushing on the poor, broken quarters with knives and sticks they tore them in pieces which they then burnt in the streets. Popular opinion refused to accept that there had not been a plot. Wild rumours circulated; the Spaniards were accused, Henrietta, Coton and the entire Society of Jesus, even the Queen. Perhaps there had been some scheming, in Leaguer circles, but it was never more than talk and had no link with Ravaillac.

For a final assessment of Henri IV and his achievement one must realize he was a product of the later Renaissance inheriting a ruined kingdom whose needs precluded long term measures; his reign over an undivided France lasted little more than a decade. To complain that instead of giving France a new, sounder system of government he simply restored the traditional structure and built the *Ancien Régime* which perished in 1789, is to ask that he should have been a man before his time. No contemporary ruler achieved more than Henri, who made a bankrupt and discredited crown the most powerful in Europe, bequeathing a government which would endure for the better part of two centuries; whereas in England, by contrast, the monarchy came to grief within fifty years of Elizabeth's death. He allowed France to exploit her natural wealth, laying foundations for Louis XIV. Once in control of his kingdom he exorcized the Spanish menace, making valuable additions to French territory. Though the Cleves-Julich business never reached fruition it shows that, anticipating Richelieu, he would have begun the Thirty Years War a decade earlier; no ruler of what was starting to feel itself the most powerful state in the world could have done otherwise. That Sully even imputed to him such a scheme as the Grand Design illustrates how imaginative was his approach to foreign affairs. During his early career as a prisoner of the Valois and then as war lord of Guyenne, whether in court intrigue, faction fighting or civil war, he proved himself a master of politics, escaping liquidation as Huguenot champion and the ruling dynasty's most dangerous rival, enlisting every possible ally at home and abroad. He made mistakes, like the Lovers' War, but they were few. In his struggle for the throne he never deviated from an inspired advocacy of fundamental law while running Calvinist zealot, Papist bigot and godless adventurer in harness together. Nor was he less successful in winning over rebel magnates and then, when peace arrived, in governing both them and the Huguenot state within the state. The Edict of Nantes was not the masterpiece of toleration which has been claimed yet it was essentially realistic. Nonetheless, if he seldom put a foot wrong in matters of state or politics it was not so in war where he showed himself a bonny fighter but a poor strategist whose victories were largely due to luck or to inferior opponents. For Henri, war was a passion, and where his passions were concerned he was always at his worst. Indeed it is as a man that he is most open to criticism.

He soon became a legend, a figure from another age. France was ceasing to be the land of religious war and robber barons, and entering the Grand Siècle. As Pascal says: 'Time heals griefs and quarrels, for we change and are no longer the same persons. Neither the offender nor the offended are any more themselves. It is like a nation which we have provoked, but meet again after two generations. They are still Frenchmen, but not the same.'[34] It was Henri IV's glory to be the eternal Frenchman. In 1661 Bishop Péréfixe published a eulogistic yet highly readable *Histoire du Roy Henry le Grand* in tribute to his totally dissimilar grandson, Louis XIV. This was speedily translated into English by 'John Dauncey, Gent., Souldier in His Majesties Regiment of Guards' for a public anxious to know more of their new sovereign, Charles II; selections from Péréfixe were being published in England during the reign of another grandson, James II. In 1728 Voltaire brought out, first in London and then in Paris, his *Henriade* (which owed much to Péréfixe), a turgid epic surprisingly popular in its own day. By now the Bourbons had canonized their progenitor who even in official documents was referred to as 'Henry the Great'. In 1790 Edmund Burke, addressing 'a gentleman in Paris', wrote, 'I have observed the affectation, which for many years past, has prevailed in Paris even to a degree perfectly childish, of idolizing the memory of your "Henry the Fourth".'[35] Under the Empire the one monarch of the Ancien Régime whose statue Napoleon retained at the Tuileries was Henri who had been his precursor in so many things. He was the solace of the émigrés, the symbol of the Restoration and, within living memory, the inspiration of French royalists. In the France of La Belle Epoque, of Charles le Coq, of Proust, the gay, stirring old tune of *Vive Henri Quatre* still had power to rouse ancient loyalties.

Even today Henri IV is the epitome of France. Sir John Neale has said, 'He was a great and charming man,'[36] and what is so remarkable about his legend, what makes it so different from that of any other hero king, is that it preserves the memory of his failings as well as of his virtues. It is the most human of all royal legends.

$\mathcal{N}$OTE ON SOURCES

The list which is given here has been made as comprehensive as possible, partly because no adequate bibliography is given in any of the modern studies of Henri IV, either French or English. However, it is far from exhaustive.

All the following works have been consulted, but principally the 'Recueil des Lettres Missives de Henri IV', the memoirs and the 'Histoire Universelle' of Agrippa d'Aubigné, Sully's 'Oeconomies Royales' and the near contemporary biography by Péréfixe (mainly derived from the histories by Matthieu, de Thou and Legrain who actually knew the King). D'Aubigné has too often been dismissed as a bigot, but he tried to be fair and was, it must be remembered, the first historian as opposed to a mere writer of memoirs to have known his sovereign intimately since Commynes under Louis XI. In any case I have, I hope, allowed sufficiently for personal prejudice, whether d'Aubigné's Protestant bias, Sully's self-glorification or the sycophancy of Péréfixe as court historian to Louis XIV. Quotations from Charlotte Lennox's translation of the eighteenth-century adaptation of Sully's memoirs have been checked against the 1638–63 edition of the 'Oeconomies Royales'; they rarely conflict with the sense of the original and their prose is generally preferable to that of any modern rendering. Similarly, John Dauncey's elegant translation of Péréfixes' 'Histoire du Roy le Grand' has only been used after comparing it with the first French edition of 1660 and the revised edition of 1664.

In addition I have leant heavily on the neglected English sources of the period, notably Unton's dispatches, the travelogues of Coryate, Fynes Moryson and Dallington, and above all Sir George Carew's secret report on 'the State of France' of 1609.

Among secondary works Poirson's 'Histoire du Règne de Henri IV' is helpful as a rough guide to the period 1594–1610 even if old-fashioned and sometimes inaccurate and if its author was much too uncritical of Sully. Of modern studies Pierre de Vaissière's 'Henri IV', written forty years ago, remains the best biography while, though he has little time for d'Aubigné, Raymond Ritter's 'Henry IV lui-même; l'Homme' which employs an ingenious psychological approach shows remarkable insight into the King's character.

ℳORKS CONSULTED

I

Collections of Sources:

'Archives curieuses de l'histoire de France depuis Luis XI jusqu'à Louis XVIII', ed. L. Cimber and F. Danjou, Paris 1834 etc.

'Calendar of State Papers, Foreign Series, of the reign of Elizabeth', 1569–71, 1572–74, London 1876.

'Calendar of State Papers, Domestic Series, of the reigns of Edward VI, Mary and Elizabeth, 1547–1580', London 1856.

'Collection Complète des Mémoires relatifs à l'histoire de France,' Paris 1819 etc.

'A Collection of State Papers, From Letters and Memorials left by William Cecil, Lord Burghley', ed. S. Haynes and W. Murdin, London 1740–59 (2 vols.).

'The Compleat Ambassador', ed. Sir D. Digges, London 1655.

'The Complete Works of Montaigne', transl. D. Frame, Hamish Hamilton 1958.

'Los Fors et Costumas de Béarn', Pau 1716.

'Full View of Public Transactions in the Reign of Elizabeth', ed. P. Forbes, London 1740 (2 vols.).

'Henri IV raconté par lui-même', ed. J. Nouaillac, Paris 1913.

'An Historical View of the Negotiations between the Courts of England, France and Brussels from the Year 1592 to 1617', ed. T. Birch, London 1749.

'The Letters and the Life of Francis Bacon', ed. J. Spedding, R. L. Ellis and D. D. Heath, London 1857–74 (14 vols.).

'The Letters of Queen Elizabeth', ed. G. B. Harrison, Cassell 1968.

'Lettres d'Antoine de Bourbon et de Jehanne d'Albret', ed. A. de Ruble, Paris 1877.

'Lettres inédites de Henry IV', ed. A. Galitzin, Paris 1860.

'Lettres intimes de Henri IV', ed. L. E. Dussieux, Paris 1878.

'Ordonnances feites per Henric II rey de Navarre, Signour souviran de Béarn sus la direction de Justicy', Pau 1717.

'Recueil de diverses pièces servans à l'histoire de Henri III', The Hague 1666.

'Recueil des Lettres Missives de Henri IV', ed. J. Berger de Xivrey, Paris 1843–76 (9 vols.).

'Relation des Ambassadeurs Vénitiens, sur les affaires de France au XIVe siècle', ed. M. N. Tommaseo, Paris 1832 (2 vols.).

'Stil de la Justicy deu Pais de Bearn … publicat en l'an cinq cens sixante quouaie, Regente Johanne Dame Souvirane de Bearn', Pau 1716.

'Les Testaments des derniers rois de Navarre', ed. R. Anthony and H. Courteault, Paris 1940.

II

Contemporary works and works written within 50 years of Henry IV's death:

J. d'Albret: 'Mémoires et Poésies de Jeanne d'Albret', ed. A. de Ruble, Paris 1893.

Anon: 'Discours merveilleuse de la vie, actions et déportemens de la Reyne Catherine de Medicis' in 'Archives curieuses', series 4, vol. 9, Paris 1836.

Anon: 'Divorce Satyrique ou les amours de la Reyne Marguerite' in 'Recueil de diverses pièces …'.

Anon: 'The Order of Ceremonies obserued in the annointing and Coronation of the most Christian French King & of Navarre [sic], Henry the IIII of that name, celebrated in our Lady Church, in the Cittie of Chartres vpon Sonday the 27. of February 1594', (transl.), London 1594.

Anon: 'The sighes of Fraunce for the death of their late King, Henry the Fourth', London (John Budge) 1610.

Anon: 'A True Report of the most execrable Murder committed upon the late French King Henrie the 4', London (John Budge) 1610.

T. A. d'Aubigné: 'L'Histoire Universelle', Maillé 1616–20 (3 vols.).

———— Mémoires de la Vie de Theodore-Agrippa d'Aubigné', Amsterdam 1731.

Sir F. Bacon: 'Essays', London 1625.

F. de Bassompierre: 'Mémoires du Mareschal de Bassompierre', Cologne 1665 (2 vols.).

H. de Beaumont de Péréfixe: 'Histoire du Roy Henry le Grand', Amsterdam (Elzevir) 1664 (Eng. transl. by J. Dauncey as 'the History of Henry IV', London 1663).

—— 'Recueil de quelques Belles Actions et paroles memorables du Roy Henry le Grand', Amsterdam 1664 (Eng. transl. as 'A Collection of some Brave Actions and Memorable Sayings of King Henry the Great', London (Abel Roper) 1688).

'La Bible' (the first Huguenot Bible, with the Psalms translated by Clement Marot and Beza), Geneva 1567.

P. de Bourdeille de Brantôme: 'Les Vies des Dames Illustres de France de son temps', Amsterdam 1665.

—— 'Les Vies de Hommes Illustres & grands Capitaines estrangers de son temps', Amsterdam 1665.

—— 'Les Vies des Hommes Illustres & grands Capitaines François de son temps', Amsterdam 1666 (4 vols.).

—— 'Mémoires de Mre. Pierre de Bourdeille de Brantôme, contenans les Anecdotes de la Cour de France sous les Rois Henry II, François II, Henry III & IV touchant les Duels', Leyden 1722.

—— 'Les Vies des Dames Galantes', Paris 1891.

Sir G. Carew: 'A Relation of the State of France, with the characters of Henry IV, and the principal persons of that Court' in 'An Historical View ...'.

G. de Chappuys: 'L'Histoire du Royaume de Navarre', Paris 1596.

Sir T. Coningsby: 'Journal of the Siege of Rouen, 1591', ed. J. G. Nichols, Camden Society, London 1847.

Louise, Princesse de Conti: 'Histoire des Amours du grand Alcandre' in 'Recueil de diverses pièces ...'.

T. Coryate: Coryat's Crudities: Hastily gobled up in Five Moneths Travells', London 1611

Sir R. Dallington: 'The View of Fraunce', London 1604.

S. Dupleix: 'Histoire de Henry le grand IV du nom, Roy de France et de Navarre', Paris 1635.

—— 'Histoire de Henry III, Roy de France et de Pologne', Paris 1636.

P. de L'Estoile: 'Mémoires pour servir à l'histoire de France', Cologne 1719 (2 vols.—transl. by N. L. Roelker: 'The Paris of Henry of Navarre' Cambridge, U.S.A. 1958).

—— 'Journal de L'Estoile', ed. L. R. Lefèvre, Paris 1948–60 (3 vols.).

A Favyn: 'Histoire de Navarre', Paris 1612.

T. Fuller: 'The Worthies of England', London 1662.

J. B. Legrain: 'Décade contenant La Vie et Gestes de Henry le Grand Roy de France et de Navarre, IIII du Nom', Paris 1614.

C. Groulard: 'Mémoires de Messire Claude Groulard' in 'Collection Complète …' series 1, vol. 49, Paris 1826.

M. de la Huguerye: 'Mémoires inédits de Michel de la Huguerye', Paris 1877.

M. de Marolles: 'Les Mémoires de Michel de Marolles, abbé de Villeloin', Paris 1656–57 (2 vols.).

P. Matthieu: 'Histoire de France sous les règnes de François I, Henry II, François II, Henry III, Henry IV, Louis XIII, Paris 1631 (2 vols.).

M. Eyquem de Montaigne: 'The Essays on Morall, Politike, and Millitarie Discourses of Lo. Michaell de Montaigne', transl. John Florio, London 1603.

B. de Lasseran-Massencome de Montluc: 'Commentaires de Messire de Monluc', Lyons 1593 (2 vols.—Eng. transl. by C. Cotton as 'The Commentaries of Messire Blaize de Montluc', London 1674).

F. Moryson: 'An Itinerary … written by Fynes Moryson, Gent.', London 1617.

—— 'Shakespeare's Europe: unpublished chapters of Fynes Moryson's Itinerary', ed. C. Hughes, London 1903.

B. de Salignac de la Mothe Fénélon: 'Correspondence diplomatique …' in 'Recueil des dépêches, rapports, instructions et mémoires des

Ambassadeurs de France en Angleterre et en Ecosse pendant le XVIe siècle', Paris 1838 (7 vols.).

Louis, Duc de Nevers: 'Les Mémoires de Monsieur le Duc de Nevers', 1665 (2 vols.).

F. de La Noue: 'Mémoires du sieur François de La Noue' (in vol. 34 in series 1 of 'Collection Complète ...', Paris 1823).

P. Olhagaray: 'Histoire de Foix, Béarn et Navarre', Paris 1609.

T. Owen, S. J.: 'A letter of a Catholike man beyond the seas, written to his friend in England; including another of Peter Coton, Priest of the Society of Iesus, to the Queene Regent of France. Translated out of French into English. Tovching the imputation of the death of Henry the IIII, late K. of France, to Priests, Iesuites, or Catholicke doctrine', St Omer 1610.

P. V. Palma Cayet: 'Chronologie Novenaire', Paris 1608 (4 vols.).

Sir W. Raleigh: 'History of the World', London 1614.

J. F. Ravaillac: 'Procez, Exament, confessions et negations du meschant & execrable parricide François Rauaillac sur la mort de Henry Le Grand, & ce qui l'a faict entreprendre le malheureux acte', Paris 1611.

—— 'The Trial of F. Ravaillac' in vol. V. of Sully's Memoirs (Eng. transl., edn. of 1819).

—— 'The terrible and deserued death of Francis Rauilliack, shewing the manner of his strange torments at his Execution, vpon Fryday the 25. of May last past for the murther of the late French King, Henry the fourth' (transl.), London, William Barley & John Baylie 1610.

G. du Sable: 'La Muse chasseresse', Paris 1884.

M. de Béthune, Duc de Sully: 'Mémoires des sages et royales oeconomies d'estat, domestiques, politiques, et militaires de Henry le Grand ...', Amsterdam and Paris 1638–63 (4 vols.).

—— rearranged by the abbé de L'Ecluse, London 1747 (11 vols.—Eng. transl. by Charlotte Lennox as 'Memoirs of Maximilian de Béthune, Duc of Sully', Edinburgh 1819–5 vols.).

G. Tallemant des Réaux: 'Les Historiettes de Tallemant des Réaux', Paris 1854–60 (8 vols.).

G. de Saulx de Tavannes: 'Mémoires ...', Paris 1829.

J. A. de Thou: 'Historiarum sui temporis,' London 1733 (7 vols.)

—— 'Histoire Universelle', La Haye 1740 (11 vols.).

—— 'Mémoires de Jacques-Auguste de Thou' in 'Collection Complète …', series 1, vol. 37, Paris 1823.

Sir H. Unton: 'Correspondence of Sir Henry Unton', ed. T. Stevenson, Roxburghe Club, London 1847.

Marguerite de Valois: 'Les Mémoires de la roine Marguerite', Paris 1628.

R. Verstegan (R. Rowlands): 'Theatrum Crudelitatum Haereticorum nostri temporis', Antwerp 1604 (transl. 'Théatre des Cruautez des Hereticques de nostre temps', Antwerp 1607).

F. Racine de Villegomblain: 'Mémoires des troubles arrivés en France sous les règnes des rois Charles IX, Henri III et Henri IV', Paris 1667–68 (2 vols.).

III

Later works

Lord Acton: 'History of Freedom and other essays', London 1907.

G. Allard: 'Les Vies de François de Beaumont, Baron des Adrets, de Charles Dupuy, Seigneur du Montbrun, et de Soffrey de Calignon, Chancellier de Navarre', Grenoble 1676.

Henri, Duc d'Aumâle: 'Historoire des Princes de Condé pendant les XVIe & XVIIe, siècles,' Paris 1863–96 (8 vols.).

M. Andrieux: 'Henri IV dans ses années pacifiques', Paris 1954.

H. Barthety: 'Le Berceau de Henri IV', Pau 1893.

L. Batiffol: 'La vie intime d'une reine de France (Marie de Médicis) au XVIIe siècle,' Paris 1906.

J. B. Black: 'Elizabeth and Henry IV', O.U.P. 1914.

J. B. Black: 'The Reign of Elizabeth, 1558–1603', O.U.P. 1959 (2nd ed.).

M. Bloch: 'Les Rois Thaumaturges', Strasburg 1924.

F. P. Braudel: 'Prices in Europe from 1450–1750' in 'The Cambridge Economic History of Europe', vol. IV, C.U.P. 1967.

D. Buisseret: 'Sully and the growth of centralised government in France, 1598–1610', Eyre & Spottiswoode 1968.

E. Burke: 'Reflections on the Revolution in France', London 1790.

R. de Bury: 'Histoire de la vie de Henri IV, roi de France et de Navarre', Paris 1765 (4 vols.).

A. J. Butler: 'The Wars of Religion in France' in the 'Cambridge Modern History', vol. III, C.U.P. 1902.

P. Erlanger: 'The Age of Courts and Kings', Weidenfeld & Nicolson 1967.

P. Erlanger: 'Henri III', Paris 1935.

P. Erlanger: 'La Jeunesse d'Henri III', Paris 1933.

P. Erlanger: 'Le Massacre de la Saint-Barthelemy', Paris 1960 (transl. by P. O'Brian as 'The Massacre of St Bartholomew', Weidenfeld & Nicolson 1962).

P. Erlanger: 'L'Étrange mort de Henri IV', Paris 1967.

G. Fagniez: 'L'Economie sociale de la France sous Henri IV', Paris 1897.

J. Heritier: 'Catherine de Médicis', Paris 1959 (transl. by C. Haldane as 'Catherine de Medici', George Allen & Unwin 1963).

Q. Hurst: 'Henry of Navarre', London 1937.

J. Hurstfield: 'Social Structure, Office-holding and Politics, chiefly in Western Europe' in 'The New Cambridge Modern History', vol. III, C.U.P. 1968.

Charlotte, Lady Jackson: 'The Last of the Valois', London 1888 (2 vols.).

G. P. R. James: 'The Life of Henry the Fourth, King of France and Navarre', London 1847 (3 vols.).

E. Jung: 'Henri IV Ecrivain', Paris 1855.

H. G. Koenigsberger: 'Western Europe and the Rise of Spain' in 'The New Cambridge Modern History', vol. III, C.U.P. 1968.

Sir S. Leathes: 'Henry IV of France' in 'The Cambridge Modern History', vol. III, C.U.P. 1902.

J. Leclerc: 'Toleration and the Reformation', transl. by J. Westow, Longmans, Green & Co., 1960 (2 vols.).

Le Petit Homme Rouge: 'The Favourites of Henry of Navarre', London 1910.

J. H. Mariéjol: 'La Réforme et la Ligue. L'Edit de Nantes. 1559–98' in 'Histoire de France depuis les origines jusqu'à la Révolution', ed. E. Lavisse, vol. VI pt. 1, Paris 1904.

—— 'Henri IV et Louis XIII. 1598–1643' in ibid. pt. 2, Paris 1905.

G. B. Masefield: 'Crops and Livestock' in 'The Cambridge Economic History of Europe', vol. IV, C.U.P. 1967.

J. Michelet: 'Henri Quatre', Paris 1881.

Sir J. Neale: 'The Age of Catherine de Medici', Jonathan Cape 1957 (new ed.).

Sir J. Neale: 'Queen Elizabeth I', Jonathan Cape 1952 (new ed.).

D. Ogg: 'Europe in the Seventeenth Century', London 1952 (6th ed.).

Sir C. Oman: 'A History of the Art of War in the Sixteenth Century', Methuen 1937.

H. Pearson: 'Henry of Navarre', Heinemann 1963.

A. Poirson: 'Histoire du Règne de Henri IV', Paris 1862–67 (4 vols.).

L. Prault: 'L'Esprit de Henri IV ou Anecdotes de ce Prince', Paris 1775 (transl. 'Interesting Anecdotes of Henry IV of France', Dublin 1792).

C. Read: 'Mr. Secretary Walsingham and the Policy of Queen Elizabeth', Oxford 1925 (3 vols.).

M. Reinhard: 'La Légende de Henry IV', Paris 1936.

R. Ritter: 'Henri IV lui-même; l'Homme', Paris 1944.

—— 'Cette Grande Corisande', Paris 1936.

—— 'Charmante Gabrielle', Paris 1937.

S. Rocheblave: 'Agrippa d'Aubigné', Paris 1910.

C. A. Sainte-Beuve: 'Galerie de portraits historiques—souverains—hommes d'état—militaires—tirée des causeries de lundi et des portraits Litteraires', Paris 1883.

H. D. Sedgwick: 'Henry of Navarre', Indianapolis 1930.

—— 'The House of Guise', Indianapolis 1938.

G. Slocombe: 'Henry of Navarre', London 1931.

F. C. Spooner: 'The Economy of Europe 1559–1610' in 'The New Cambridge Modern History', vol. III, C.U.P. 1968.

P. de Vaissière: 'Henri IV', Paris 1928.

Voltaire: 'Essay sur l'Histoire générale et sur les moeurs et l'esprit des nations, depuis Charlemagne jusqu'à nos jours', Geneva 1756 (7 vols.).

M. Wilkinson: 'A History of the League or Sainte Union, 1576–1595', Glasgow 1929.

C. H. Wilson: 'Trade, Society and the State' in 'The Cambridge Economic History of Europe', vol. IV, C.U.P. 1967.

J. M. Yanguas y Miranda: 'Historia compendiada del reino de Navarra', San Sebastian 1832.

IV

Plays, Verse and Novels:

Anon: 'Poesies en diuerses langues sur la naissance de Henry de Bourbon Prince tres hevrevs', Toulouse 1554.

T. A. d'Aubigné: 'Les Tragiques', 1616.

G. Chapman: 'The conspiracie and Tragedie of Charles Duke of Byron, Marshall of France. Acted lately in two playes', London 1608.

C. Collé: 'La Partie de Chasse de Henri IV', Paris 1766.

A. Dumas: 'La Reine Margot', Paris 1962 (1st ed. 1845).

—— 'La Dame de Monsoreau', Paris 1962 (1st ed. 1846).

—— 'Les Quarante-cinq', Paris 1962 (1st ed. 1847–48).

Lord Macaulay: 'Ivry'.

H. Mann: 'Die Jugend des Koenigs Henri Quatre', Amsterdam 1935. (transl. E. Sutton as 'King Wren: the Youth of Henri IV', Secker & Warburg 1937).

P. Merimée: 'Chronique du règne de Charles IX', Paris 1949 (ed. of 1853).

F. Rabelais: 'The Whole Works of F. Rabelais M.D.... or the Lives, Heroic Deeds and Sayings of Gargantua and Pantagruel' (transl. by Sir T. Urquhart and P. Motteux), London 1708 (2 vols.).

Voltaire: 'La Henriade', London 1728.

F. Walder: 'Saint-Germain ou la Négotiation', Paris 1958 (transl. by D. Folliot as 'The Negotiators', Heinemann 1960).

NOTES

INTRODUCTION

1. The tune may be found in Collé's 'La Partie de Chasse de Henri IV'.
2. Péréfixe, 'Recueil de Quelques Belles Actions et paroles memorables du Roy Henry le Grand', p. 538.

1 THE WARS OF RELIGION

1. d'Aubigné, 'Les Tragiques'—Misères, liv. I, p. 4.
2. Voltaire, 'La Henriade'—Second Chant, p. 30.
3. L'Estoile, 'Mémoires pour servir à l'histoire de France', vol. II, p. 2.
4. Favyn, 'Histoire de Navarre', p. 809.
5. Péréfixe, 'Histoire du Roy Henry le Grand', pp. 14–19.
6. See Barthety, 'Le Berceau de Henri IV'.
7. 'Poesies en diuerses langues sur la naissance de Henry de Bourbon Prince tres hevrevs'—the languages include the Béarnais form of Provençal.
8. As in his Royal proclamations—see 'Los Fors et Costumas de Béarn'.
9. Favyn, p. 504.
10. ibid, pp. 809–810; d'Aubigné, 'Histoire Universelle', vol. I, p. 13.
11. Favyn, p. 819.
12. ibid., p. 831.
13. Paul Tillich.
14. Groulard, 'Mémoires', p. 383.
15. Quoted by Butler, 'The Wars of Religion in France', C.M.H., vol. 3, p. 8.
16. Favyn, p. 838.
17. 'Mémoires', pp. 3–4.
18. Péréfixe, 'Histoire du Roy Henry le Grand', p. 22.
19. Montluc, 'Commentaries (transl. Cotton), p. 38.
20. ibid., p. 246.
21. D.N.B.

22. d'Aubigné, 'Histoire Universelle', vol. I, p. 158.
23. Aumâle, 'Histoire des Princes de Condé', vol. 1, p. 245.
24. Favyn, p. 842.
25. Nevers, 'Mémoires', vol. II, p. 585—letter of 1567.
26. ibid., p. 586—another letter of 1567.
27. Péréfixe, 'Histoire du Roy Henry le Grand', p. 23.
28. Nouaillac, p. 28.
29. So called because he replaced a lost arm with one of iron.
30. Favyn, pp. 858–859; Matthieu, pp. 314–317.
31. This was Laynez, Loyola's successor.
32. See Acton, 'The History of Freedom and other essays', p. 141.
33. François Walder's remarkable novel, 'Saint-Germain ou le Négotiation', which won the Prix Goncourt in 1957, is based on the negotiations for this peace.
34. Which is set in Navarre.
35. Berger de Xivrey, vol. VIII, p. 78—letter of 13th June 1572 to Monsieur d'Arros, governor of Béarn.
36. To judge from a contemporary portrait.
37. d'Aubigné, op. cit., vol. II, p. 8. See also Sully's 'Oeconomics Royales', vol. I, p. 11 and L'Estoile, vol. I, p. 20.
38. Marguerite de Valois, 'Mémoires', p. 47.

2 THE PRISONER

1. d'Aubigné, 'Histoire Universelle', vol. II, p. 187.
2. Berger de Xivrey, vol. I, pp. 81–82—letter of late 1575 to Jean d'Albret.
3. d'Aubigné, op. cit., vol. II, p. 129.
4. Brantôme, 'Les Vies des Dames Illustres', p. 202.
5. 'Divorce Satyrique', pp. 236–237.
6. ibid., p. 237.
7. La Huguerye, 'Mémoires', vol. I, p. 40.
8. La Mothe Fénélon, 'Recueil des dépêches …', vol. III, p. 359.
9. Ruble, 'Lettres d'Antoine de Bourbon et de Jehanne d'Albret', p. 342—letter of 21 February 1572.
10. Sully, 'Oeconomies Royales', 1638 edn., vol. I, p. 6.

11. Marguerite de Valois, 'Mémoires', p. 48.

12. Letter to Charles IX shortly after the massacre—quoted by Lord Acton in 'The History of Freedom and other essays', p. 107, n. 2.

13. Marguerite de Valois, 'Mémoires', p. 62.

14. See Acton, op. cit., p. 141.

15. Marguerite de Valois, 'Mémoires', p. 63.

16. Sully, 'Oeconomies Royales', 1638 edn., vol. I, p. 15.

17. Péréfixe, 'Histoire du Roy Henry le Grand', p. 31.

18. Sully, 'Oeconomies Royales', 1638 edn., vol. I, p. 16.

19. 'La Reine Margot'.

20. Villegomblain, 'Mémoires', vol. I, p. 263.

21. d'Aubigné, 'Mémoires', p. 49.

22. Brantôme, 'Les Vies des Dames Illustres', p. 244.

23. 'The Compleat Ambassador', p. 343.

24. 'Discours merveilleuse ...', p. 108.

25. ibid., p. 102.

26. Neale, p. 87.

27. d'Aubigné, 'Mémoires', p. 45.

28. Brantôme, 'Les Vies des Hommes Illustres ... & grands Capitaines François', vol. IV, p. 21.

29. 'Divorce Satyrique', p. 238.

30. Sully, 'Oeconomies Royales', 1638 edn., vol. I, p. 16.

31. L'Estoile, 'Mémoires pour servir à l'histoire de France', vol. I, p. 32.

32. Sully, 'Oeconomies Royales', 1638 edn., vol. I, p. 11.

33. d'Aubigné, 'Histoire Universelle', vol. II, p. 129.

34. Péréfixe, op. cit., p. 37.

35. Scipion Dupleix, 'Histoire de Henry III ...', p. 8.

36. ibid., p. 13.

37. ibid., p. 24.

38. L'Estoile, op, cit., vol. I, p. 51.

39. Berger de Xivrey, vol. I, pp. 81–82, dates this letter as January 1576, but Mariéjol, op. cit., p. 168, considers it was written before 15 September 1575.

40. L'Estoile, op. cit., vol. I, p. 62.

41. 'Relations des Ambassadeurs Vénitiens ...', vol. II, p. 252.

42. ibid.
43. L'Estoile, op. cit., vol. I, p. 50.
44. d'Aubigné, 'Histoire Universelle', vol. II, p. 185.
45. L'Estoile, op. cit., vol. I, p. 63.
46. d'Aubigné, op. cit., vol. II, p. 187.
47. ibid.
48. ibid., p. 188.
49. d'Aubigné, 'Mémoires', p. 52.
50. L'Estoile, op. cit., vol. I, p. 63.

3 THE LORD OF GASCONY

1. Marguerite de Valois, 'Mémoires', p. 322.
2. Berger de Xivrey, vol. I, p. 121—letter to M. de Batz of early 1577.
3. Michelet, 'Henri IV', p. 16.
4. Marguerite de Valois, op. cit., p. 329.
5. d'Aubigné, 'Histoire Universelle', vol. II, p. 230.
6. L'Estoile, 'Mémoires pour servir à l'histoire de France', vol. I, p. 77.
7. Mariéjol, 'La Réforme et la Ligue', p. 197.
8. Sully, 'Oeconomies Royales', 1638 edn., vol. I, p. 35.
9. 'The Letters and Life of Francis Bacon', vol. I, pp. 26–27—'Notes on the Present State of Christendom'.
10. Marguerite de Valois, op. cit., p. 40.
11. Brantôme, 'Les Vies des Dames Illustres', p. 213.
12. Sully, 'Oeconomies Royales', 1638 edn., vol. I, p. 37.
13. ibid., vol. I, p. 38.
14. 'Love's Labour Lost', Act I.
15. 'Divorce Satyrique', p. 241.
16. d'Aubigné, 'Histoire Universelle', vol. II, p. 344.
17. ibid.
18. Vaissière, p. 159.
19. d'Aubigné, 'Histoire Universelle', vol. II, p. 345.
20. ibid.
21. ibid.

22. Montaigne, 'Essays', Bk. 2, ch. VIII—'Of the Recompenses or Rewards of Honour'.

23. Berger de Xivrey, vol. I, p. 302—letter to Mme de Batz of 31 May 1580.

24. Marguerite de Valois, op. cit., p. 329.

25. d'Aubigné, 'Mémoires', p. 84.

26. Mariéjol, op. cit., p. 237.

27. Marguerite de Valois, op. cit., p. 350.

28. André Maurois' comment.

29. Proust credited the Duchesse de Guermantes with the gift of writing 'Le français exquis de Henri IV'—'Le Côté de Guermantes', p. 503.

30. Berger de Xivrey, vol. II, pp. 224–225—letter of 17 June 1586.

31. ibid., p. 318—letter of 8 December 1587.

32. ibid., p. 400—letter of 30 November 1588.

33. ibid., p. 224—letter of 17 June 1586.

34. ibid., p. 216—letter of 25 May 1586.

35. ibid., vol. III, p. 216—letter of 15 July 1590.

36. ibid., vol. II, pp. 343–344—letter of 10 March 1588.

37. ibid., p. 224—letter of 17 June 1586.

38. Montaigne, Essays, Bk. I, ch. XXVIII.

39. Montaigne, 'Complete Works', p. 1077—letter to Marshal de Matignon of 18 January 1585.

40. Montaigne, 'Essays', Bk. 3, ch. IX—'Of Vanitie', p. 235.

41. de Thou, 'Historiarum sui temporis', vol. VII, p. 88—conversation with Montaigne.

42. d'Aubigné, 'Mémoires', p. 102.

43. Nevers, 'Mémoires', vol. I, p. 91.

44. ibid., p. 163.

45. d'Aubigné, 'Histoire Universelle', vol. II, p. 423.

46. Tallemant des Réaux, 'Historiettes', vol. I—'Henry Quatriesme', p. 19.

47. Berger de Xivrey, vol. II, p. 199—letter to M. de Batz of 12 March 1586.

48. Bacon, Essay XXIII—'Of Wisdom for a Man's Self'.

49. Berger de Xivrey, vol. II, pp. 343–344—letter of 10 March 1588.

50. ibid., p. 342—letter of 8 March 1588.

51. ibid., p. 487—letter of 18 May 1589.

52. Péréfixe, 'Histoire du Roy Henry le Grand', p. 63.

53. Berger de Xivrey, vol. II, pp. 168–171—letters to the clergy and to the nobility, 1 January 1586.

54. d'Aubigné, 'Histoire Universelle', vol. II, p. 336.

55. Péréfixe, op. cit., p. 85.

56. Matthieu, 'Histoire de France', vol. I, p. 533.

57. Berger de Xivrey, vol. II, p. 309—letter to Marshal de Matignon of 23 Oct. 1587.

58. d'Aubigné, 'Histoire Universelle', vol. III, p. 58.

59. d'Aubigné, 'Mémoires', p. 128.

60. Berger de Xivrey, vol. II, p. 342—letter of 8 March 1582.

61. Sully, 'Oeconomies Royales', 1638 edn., vol. I, p. 79.

62. L'Estoile, op. cit., vol. I, p. 241.

63. ibid., p. 258.

64. 'The Letters and Life of Francis Bacon', vol. I, p. 95—letter to Lord Shrewsbury of 27 May 1589.

65. L'Estoile, op. cit., vol. I, p. 285.

66. d'Aubigné, 'Histoire Universelle', vol. III, p. 183.

67. Raleigh, 'History of the World'—preface.

68. d'Aubigné, op. cit., p. 184.

4 A THEATRE OF MISERY

1. From the original Huguenot Bible of 1567.

2. 'Les Tragiques', La Chambre Dorée, liv. III, p. 3.

3. 'The Letters and Life of Francis Bacon', vol. I, pp. 160–161—'Certain Observations made upon a libel published this present year 1592'.

4. ibid., vol. I, p. 134—'Mr. Bacon's Discourse in Praise of his Sovereign'.

5. La Noue, 'Mémoires', p. 289.

6. d'Aubigné, 'Histoire Universelle', vol. III, p. 187.

7. Péréfixe, 'Histoire du Roy Henry le Grand', p. 122.

8. 'Les Illusions Perdues' (transl. Kathleen Raine).

9. Péréfixe, op. cit., p. 138.

10. ibid., op. cit., p. 139.

11. Essays, Bk. 3, ch. IX—'Of Vanitie.'
12. L'Estoile, 'Mémoires pour servir à l'histoire de France', vol. II, p. 6 (transl. Roelker, p. 184).
13. Cit. Black, p. 17.
14. Péréfixe, op. cit., p. 148; d'Aubigné, op. cit., vol. III, p. 231.
15. Berger de Xivrey, vol. III, p. 171—letter of 14 March 1590.
16. L'Estoile, op. cit., vol. II, p. 11.
17. Tallemant des Réaux, 'Historiettes'. vol.I—'Henry Quatriesme', p. 17.
18. Péréfixe, op, cit., p. 166.
19. Sully, 'Oeconomies Royales', 1638 edn., vol. I, p. 128; L'Ecluse version, transl. Lennox, vol. I, p. 241.
20. Péréfixe, op. cit., p. 160.
21. ibid., p. 167.
22. ibid., p. 167.
23. Berger de Xivley, vol. III, p. 244—letter of 31 August 1590.
24. Péréfixe, op. cit., p. 194.
25. Tallemant des Réaux, op. cit., vol. I—'Henry Quatriesme', p. 5.
26. Berger de Xivrey, vol. III, p. 754—letter of 15 April 1593.
27. ibid., vol. III, p. 755—letter of 16 April 1593.
28. ibid., vol. III, p. 756—letter of 19 April 1593.
29. ibid., vol. III, p. 758—letter of 20 April 1593.
30. ibid., vol. III, p. 760—letter of 21 April 1593.
31. ibid., vol. IV, p. 998—Berger gives 1598 as date but Ritter argues, convincingly, that May 1593 is more likely.
32. ibid., vol. III, p. 804—letter of 15 June 1593.
33. D.N.B.
34. Palma-Cayet, 'Chronologie Novenaire', vol. II, pp. 502–503.
35. Harrison, 'The Letters of Queen Elizabeth' p. 219–23 December 1591.
36. D.N.B.; Fuller, 'Worthies of England'—'Worthies of Wales,' p. 52.
37. Unton, 'Correspondence', p. 129.
38. Sully, 'Oeconomies Royales …', 1638 edn., vol. I, p. 136.
39. Unton, 'Correspondence', p. 308—dispatch of 8 February 1592.
40. Dallington, n.p.
41. ibid., n.p.

42. Unton, 'Correspondence', p. 291—letter of 29 January 1592.

43. Unton, 'Correspondence', pp. 296–297—letter of 1st February 1592.

44. Dallington, n.p.

45. Berger de Xivrey, vol. III, p. 362—letter of March 1591.

46. ibid., p. 588—letter of 25 March 1592.

47. Sully, 'Oeconomies Royales', 1638 edn., vol. I, p. 176.

48. d'Aubigné, 'Histoire Universelle', vol. III, p. 289.

49. Berger de Xivrey, vol. III, p. 821—letter of 23 July 1593.

50. L'Estoile, op. cit., vol. II, p. 140.

51. d'Aubigné, op. cit., vol. III, p. 294.

52. I am grateful to Maître J. Mandon-Joly of Limoges for a particularly valuable account of French legal history.

53. See 'The Order of Ceremonies …', Matthieu, vol. II, pp. 170–173; Favyn p. 1013 et seq.

5 THE HEALING HANDS OF A KING

1. Fynes Moryson, 'Unpublished Chapters', p. 173.

2. 'The View of Fraunce', n.p.

3. See Bloch, 'Les Rois Thaumaturges'.

4. Péréfixe, 'Histoire du Roy Henry le Grand', p. 223; Dauncey, p. 172.

5. ibid., p. 224; Dauncey, p. 174.

6. ibid., p. 236.

7. 'The View of Fraunce', n.p.

8. Berger de Xivrey, vol. IV, p. 364—letter of 7 June 1595.

9. Dallington, n.p.

10. Legrain, 'Décade', p. 367.

11. d'Aubigné, 'L'Histoire Universelle', vol. III, p. 462.

12. Sully, 'Oeconomies Royales', 1638 edn., vol. I, p. 345—letter of 15 April 1596.

13. Legrain, op. cit., p. 402.

14. 'The View of Fraunce', n.p.

15. Péréfixe, op. cit., p. 244.

16. Unton, 'A Collection of State Papers', p. 703.

17. Péréfixe, op. cit., p. 252; Dauncey, p. 195.

18. 'The View of Fraunce', n.p.

19. ibid., n.p.

20. Péréfixe, op. cit., p. 285; Dauncey, p. 219.

21. 'Journal de L'Estoile' (ed. Lefèvre), vol. I, p. 495.

22. d'Aubigné, 'Histoire Universelle', vol. III, p. 462.

23. L'Estoile, op. cit., vol. I, p. 455.

24. Unton, 'A Collection of State Papers', p. 718—letter to Queen Elizabeth of 3 February 1595/6.

25. D.N.B.

26. Cecil, 'An Historical View', p. 113—letter of 23 March 1598.

27. Unton, ibid.

28. Berger de Xivrey, vol. V, p. 50—letter of 14 October 1598.

29. ibid., vol. V, p. 110—letter of 15th April 1599.

30. Carew, 'A Relation of the State of France', p. 499.

31. Brantôme, 'Les Vies des Hommes Illustres & grands Capitaines François', vol. III, p. 326.

32. Péréfixe, op. cit., p. 317, Dauncey, p. 243.

33. Berger de Xivrey, vol. V, p. 321—letter of 11 October 1601.

34. ibid., vol. V, p. 373—letter to M. de St. Julien of end of January 1601.

35. 'The View of Fraunce', n.p.

6 LA BELLE ET DOUCE FRANCE

1. Péréfixe, 'Recueil', p. 555.

2. Sir Thomas Urquhart's translation, vol. II, p. 167.

3. 'The View of Fraunce', n.p.

4. Spooner, 'The Economy of Europe 1559–1610' in N.C.M.H., vol. III, p. 33.

5. 'The View of Fraunce', n.p.

6. Carew, 'A Relation of the State of France', p. 491.

7. ibid., p. 481.

8. ibid., p. 489.

9. 'The Alchemist', Act IV, Scene IV.

10. Tallemant des Réaux, 'Historiettes', vol. I—'M. de Sully', p. 115.

11. Sir S. Leathes, C.M.H., vol. III, p. 678.

12. 'The View of Fraunce', n.p.
13. Carew, op. cit., p. 478.
14. 'The View of Fraunce', n.p.
15. ibid.
16. Mariéjol, 'Henri IV et Louis XIII', p. 10.
17. Berger de Xivrey, vol. VI, p. 432—letter of 21 May 1605.
18. Cecil, 'An Historical View', p. 113—letter of 23 March 1598.
19. Péréfixe, 'Histoire du Roy Henry le Grand', p. 290; Dauncy, p. 223.
20. ibid., p. 291; Dauncey, p. 224.
21. Carew, op. cit., p. 453.
22. Péréfixe, 'Histoire du Roy Henry le Grand', p. 305; Dauncey, p. 235.
23. The document is printed in Dussieux, p. 311.
24. Péréfixe, 'Histoire du Roy Henry le Grand', p. 343; Dauncey, p. 264.
25. ibid.; Dauncey, p. 263.
26. 'The View of France', n.p.
27. Dauncey, p. 266.
28. Carew, op. cit., p. 486.
29. ibid., p. 462.
30. Péréfixe, 'Recueil', p. 555.
31. ibid., p. 556.
32. 'The View of Fraunce', n.p.
33. Carew, opt. cit., p. 474.
34. ibid., p. 485.
35. ibid.
36. ibid., p. 480.
37. 'The View of Fraunce', n.p.
38. ibid., n.p.
39. Péréfixe, 'Histoire du Roy Henry le Grand', p. 341.
40. Péréfixe, op. cit., p. 374.
41. Chapman, 'The Conspiracie and Tragedie of Charles, Duke of Byron'.
42. Carew, op. cit., p. 430.
43. Wilson, 'Trade, Society and the State', Cambridge Economic History of Europe', vol. IV, p. 525.
44. Péréfixe, 'Histoire du Roy Henry le Grand', p. 276; Dauncey, p. 213.

45. Tallemant des Réaux, op. cit., vol. I—'M. de Sully', p. 114.
46. Carew, op. cit., p. 441.
47. 'Mémoires de l'abbé de Marolles', vol. I, p. 11.

7 HENRICIAN MAJESTY

1. Sully, 'Oeconomies Royales', 1638 edn., vol. II—foreword, n.p.
2. Péréfixe, 'Histoire du Roy Henry le Grand', p. 461.
3. Erlanger, 'The Age of Courts and Kings', p. 36.
4. Tallemant des Réaux, 'Historiettes', vol. I—'Henry Quatriesme', p. 19.
5. 'The View of Fraunce', n.p.
6. 'Journal de l'Estoile' (ed. Lefèvre), vol. II, p. 82.
7. Tallemant des Réaux, op. cit., vol. I—'Henry Quatriesme', p. 9.
8. Carew, 'A Relation of the State of France', p. 479.
9. Tallemant des Réaux, op. cit., vol. I—'Henry Quatriesme', p. 12.
10. 'Journal de L'Estoile' (ed. Lefèvre), vol. II, p. 223.
11. Fynes Moryson, 'An Itinerary …', Pt. I, p. 195.
12. 'Coryat's Crudities', pp. 38–41.
13. 'The View of Fraunce', n.p.
14. 'Coryat's Crudities', pp. 24–25.
15. ibid., p. 26.
16. ibid., p. 21.
17. Poirson, 'Histoire du Règne de Henri IV', vol. III, p. 701.
18. Dauncey, 'The History of Henry IV', p. 391.
19. ibid., p. 305.
20. Sully, 'Oeconomies Royales', L'Ecluse version transl. Lennox, vol. III, p. 330.
21. ibid., p. 320.
22. Carew, op. cit., pp. 450–451.
23. Sully, ibid.
24. Sully, 'Oeconomies Royales', 1638 edn., vol. II, p. 329.
25. ibid.
26. Péréfixe, 'Histoire du Roy Henry le Grand', pp. 398–399; Dauncey, pp. 305–306.
27. Berger de Xivrey, vol. VII, p. 508—letter of beginning of April 1608.

28. Sully, 'Oeconomies Royales', 1638 edn., vol. III, p. 4.
29. Carew, op. cit., pp. 491–492.
30. Dauncey, op. cit., p. 391.
31. Péréfixe, op. cit., p. 399; Dauncey, p. 306.
32. Tallemant des Réaux, op. cit., vol. I—'Madame de Moret—M. de Césy', p. 158.
33. ibid., p. 155.
34. Péréfixe, op. cit., p. 462; Dauncey, p. 354.
35. Carew, op. cit., p. 493.
36. 'Coryat's Crudities', p. 46.
37. Péréfixe, op. cit., pp. 460–461; Dauncey, pp. 352–353.
38. 'The View of Fraunce', n.p.
39. Carew, op. cit., p. 478.
40. Sully, 'Oeconomies Royales', 1663 edn., vol. III, p. 8.
41. Fynes Moryson, 'An Itinerary ...', Pt. III, p. 177.
42. Carew, op. cit., p. 435.
43. Bassompierre, vol. I, p. 140.
44. Carew, op. cit., p. 436.
45. ibid., p. 476.
46. ibid., p. 435.
47. ibid., p. 427.
48. ibid., p. 436.
49. 'Coryat's Crudities', pp. 42–44.
50. Péréfixe, 'Recueil', p. 548.
51. 'Coryat's Crudities', p. 32.
52. Carew, op. cit., p. 472.
53. Fynes Moryson, 'Unpublished Chapters', p. 284.
54. Carew, op. cit., p. 481.
55. Péréfixe, 'Recueil', p. 538; 'A Collection', p. 29.
56. Carew, op. cit., p. 480.
57. Ritter, 'Henry IV lui-même: l'Homme', p. 392.

8 THE GRAND DESIGN

1. d'Aubigné, 'Histoire Universelle', vol. III, p. 543.
2. Péréfixe, 'Histoire du Roy Henry le Grand', p. 467; Dauncey, p. 357.

3.   Carew, 'A Relation of the State of France', p. 477.

4.   ibid., pp. 504–507.

5.   'An Historical View', p. 276.

6.   d'Aubigné, op. cit., vol. III, p. 542.

7.   Carew, op. cit., p. 430.

8.   Péréfixe, op. cit., p. 472 et seq.; Dauncey, p. 357 et seq.

9.   d'Aubigné, op. cit., vol. III, p. 542.

10. Bassompierre, 'Mémoires', vol. I, p. 191.

11. ibid., vol. I, p. 187.

12. Tallemant des Réaux, 'Historiettes', vol. I—'Madames la Princesse', p. 172.

13. Bassompierre, op. cit., vol. I, pp. 189–190.

14. ibid., p. 191.

15. Carew, op. cit., pp. 447–448.

16. Tallemant des Réaux, op. cit., vol. I—'Madame la Princesse', p. 172.

17. ibid., pp. 172–173.

18. Carew, op. cit., p. 448.

19. Berger de Xivrey, vol. VII, p. 722—letter of 12 June 1609.

20. Carew, op. cit., p. 449.

21. ibid., p. 493.

22. 'Journal de L'Estoile' (ed. Lefèvre), vol. II, p. 488.

23. Péréfixe, op. cit., p. 491; Dauncey, p. 376.

24. ibid.

25. d'Aubigné, op. cit., vol. III, p. 543.

26. Péréfixe, op. cit., p. 493; Dauncey, p. 377.

27. Sully, 'Oeconomies Royales', 1663 edn., vol. IV, p. 476.

28. Bassompierre, op. cit., vol. I, p. 245.

29. ibid., p. 246.

30. 'A True Report of the most execrable Murder committed upon the late French King Henrie the 4', p. 2.

31. ibid., p. 6.

32. Sully, 'Oeconomies Royales', 1663 edn., vol. IV, p. 1.

33. 'The terrible and deserued death of Francis Rauilliack'.

34. Pascal, 'Pensées', 122.

35. Burke, 'Reflections on the Revolution in France', p. 132.

36. Neale, 'The Age of Catherine de Medici', p. 100.

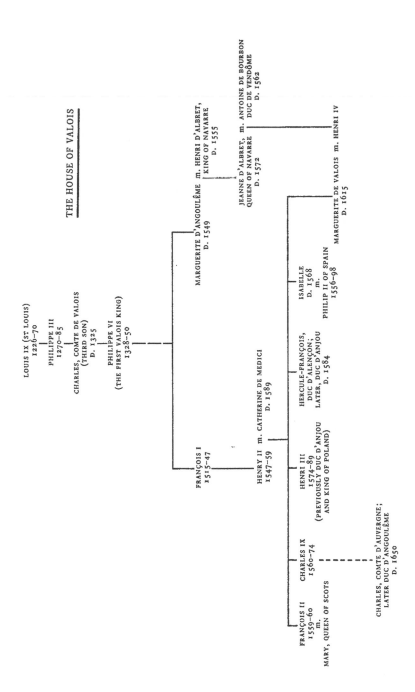

THE HOUSE OF VALOIS

LOUIS IX (ST LOUIS)
1226–70

PHILIPPE III
1270–85

CHARLES, COMTE DE VALOIS
(THIRD SON)
D. 1325

PHILIPPE VI
(THE FIRST VALOIS KING)
1328–50

MARGUERITE D'ANGOULÊME   m. HENRI D'ALBRET,
D. 1549   KING OF NAVARRE
                               D. 1555

JEANNE D'ALBRET,   m. ANTOINE DE BOURBON
QUEEN OF NAVARRE   DUC DE VENDÔME
D. 1572   D. 1562

FRANÇOIS I
1515–47

HENRY II   m. CATHERINE DE MEDICI
1547–59   D. 1589

HERCULE-FRANÇOIS,
DUC D'ALENÇON,
LATER, DUC D'ANJOU
D. 1584

ISABELLE
D. 1568
m.
PHILIP II OF SPAIN
1556–98

MARGUERITE DE VALOIS   m. HENRI IV
D. 1615

HENRI III
1574–89
(PREVIOUSLY DUC D'ANJOU
AND KING OF POLAND)

FRANÇOIS II   CHARLES IX
1559–60   1560–74
m.
MARY, QUEEN OF SCOTS

CHARLES, COMTE D'AUVERGNE;
LATER DUC D'ANGOULÊME
D. 1650

231

THE HOUSE OF BOURBON

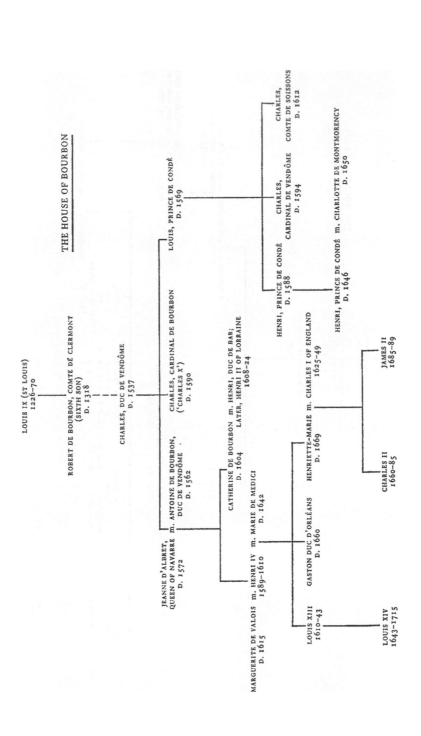

ABOUT THE AUTHOR

Desmond Seward was born in Paris and educated at Ampleforth and St Catharine's College, Cambridge. He is the author of many books including The Monks of War: The Military Religious Orders, The Hundred Years War, The Wars of the Roses, Eleanor of Aquitaine and Henry V as Warlord, Josephus, Masada and the Fall of Judaea (da Capo, US, April 2009), Wings over the Desert: in action with an RFC pilot in Palestine 1916–18 (Haynes Military, July 2009) and Old Puglia: A Portrait of South Eastern Italy (Haus August 2009).

Lightning Source UK Ltd.
Milton Keynes UK
UKOW06f1935140616

276320UK00008B/188/P